Making and Manipulating Marionettes

Making and Manipulating Marionettes

David Currell

The Crowood Press

First published in 2004 by
The Crowood Press Ltd
Ramsbury, Marlborough
Wiltshire SN8 2HR

www.crowood.com

British Library Cataloguing-in-Publication Data
A catalogue record for this book is available from the British Library.

ISBN 1 86126 663 4

Frontispiece: 'Bubbles' by Paul Doran, Shadowstring Theatre

To the memory of my father, Leonard Currell, whose encouragement and support in my childhood fostered my interest in crafts and design. We worked together on my first marionette before his early death.

Designed and edited by Focus Publishing,
11a St Botolph's Road,
Sevenoaks
Kent TN13 3AJ

Printed and bound in Malaysia by Times Offset (M) Sdn Bhd

Contents

Acknowledgements

Puppeteers are renowned for their willingness to share techniques and the secrets of their creations, none more so than those who have contributed to this book and to whom I am particularly grateful. Gordon Staight introduced me to the magic of marionettes, spent countless hours over many years teaching me his techniques, and shared the clever, but often simple, ways in which he surprised and amazed his audiences. Paul Doran welcomed me to his theatre and allowed me to delve into all aspects of his marionettes' construction and performance. Gren Middleton and John Roberts have supplied photographs of their beautiful marionettes and freely shared technical information. Lyndie Wright has allowed me use of photos of the work of the late John Wright, OBE, whose work I always admired. The Puppet Centre has also allowed me to photograph items in its splendid and important collection. Further details about these contributors are included in the Appendices.

Over the years I have also been involved closely with major puppet theatre organisations, especially the Puppet Centre in London, the British Section of UNIMA (Union Internationale de la Marionnette), and the British Puppet and Model Theatre Guild, through which I have been entertained, learned a host of techniques, and made many friends, too numerous to mention here.

I am extremely grateful also to Ian Howes for photographs of some of my work in progress, and to my friends and colleagues at Roehampton University, David Rose and Robert Watts, David for photographs of figures in my troupe and the Puppet Centre Collection, and Robert for assistance with the numerous illustrations.

Specialized puppetry techniques, like conjuring tricks, generally come down to a set of a few basic principles. Methods and materials might develop but the principles themselves are timeless. So the reader will find in this book many techniques that I learned with Gordon Staight, both of us depending heavily on a few classics of puppet lierature, all published by Wells Gardner, Darton & Co Ltd. In particular, we found inspiration in *Everybody's Marionette Book* (1948), *Animal Puppetry* (1948), *A Bench Book of Puppetry* (1957) and *A Second Bench Book of Puppetry* (1957), all by H.W. Whanslaw, and *Specialised Puppetry* (1948) by H.W. Whanslaw and Victor Hotchkiss. Later I also found useful ideas in *Puppet Circus* (1971) by Peter Fraser (B.T. Batsford Ltd). Those familiar with these works will recognise that a few of my illustrations, sketched for my own puppets, are based upon drawings in these books. I gratefully acknowledge these sources of information and inspiration.

Last but not least, my thanks are extended to the team at The Crowood Press for their support, patience and helpful suggestions, shaping this into a clear, colourful and attractive book that I trust the reader will enjoy as much I as I have writing it.

Photo Credits

All photos of Movingstage Marionettes: Gren Middleton.

Photos of PuppetCraft: John Roberts, except pages 20 (left), 68; these are courtesy of John Roberts and Graham Hodgson.

Photos of Shadowstring Theatre/Paul Doran: David Currell, courtesy Paul Doran, except: page 13 (right), courtesy Paul Doran; page 101, Steve Guscott, courtesy Paul Doran.

Photos of Gordon Staight's marionettes: David Currell (author's collection).

Photos from Puppet Centre Collection, pages 9, 19 (left), 26, 97, 98: David Rose, courtesy Puppet Centre Ltd.

Photos from Puppet Centre Collection, pages 11, 18, 34 (left), 48, 65, 78, 160: David Currell, courtesy Puppet Centre Ltd.

Image page 17 (left): courtesy Puppet Centre Ltd (Crafts Council Collection).

Image page 19 (right): courtesy John Blundall.

Image pages 55 and 69: courtesy Lyndie Wright.

Image page 57: courtesy Albrecht Roser, Stuttgart, Germany.

Photos of author at work, pages 24, 25, 40: Ian Howes.

All other photos (author's collection): David Currell, except pages 33, 47, 93: David Rose; 89, 92: Emre Currell; 180, 183: Emily Currell.

1 The Marionette Tradition

The term 'marionette' is used in English specifically for string puppets, to be distinguished from the French *marionnette*, which is a generic term for all types of puppet. While it is widely agreed that 'puppet' is derived from *pupa*, the Italian for doll, the origin of 'marionette' is uncertain. Some writers suggest that it derives from 'little Mary', referring to the use of puppets in churches.

Marionettes have a long, sometimes distinguished, history. It is quite possible that early types of marionette included figures used in fertility rites; others, operated remotely by strings, were used in ancient temples to inspire the congregation with wonder. In some cultures, marionettes were in use before human actors because of religious taboos on impersonation. In Indian Sanskrit plays, for example, the leading player is called *sutradhara* or 'the holder of strings' because he was originally a marionette operator. Early marionette performances in India took their themes from the *Mahabharata* and the *Ramayana*, the great Sanskrit epics, the contents of which are well suited to puppet theatre.

We know that marionettes were in use in China by the eighth century but the Greeks might have used puppets as early as 800BC. References to marionettes appear in Roman literature by 400BC, by which time it was certainly a common form of entertainment in Greece.

There appears to be no documentary evidence of the puppet show between the fall of Rome and the seventh century but it seems reasonable to assume that vestiges of this dramatic tradition survived, for between the seventh and ninth centuries we find puppets being used for religious purposes.

We can trace the use of puppets in Britain back to the fourteenth century, possibly introduced by French entertainers in the previous century, and we know also that marionettes were in use in Elizabethan England.

The puppet theatre was patronized by Charles II and his court and, on his return to Britain in 1660,

***OPPOSITE:* Orlando Furioso, a Sicilian rod-marionette, carved in wood with beaten armour.**

A traditional Burmese marionette in the Puppet Centre collection.

puppeteers among his entourage introduced Polichinelle to Britain. Formerly Pulcinella, a puppet version of one of the *zanni*, or buffoons, in the Italian *Commedia dell' Arte*, the French version in Britain soon became Punchinello, subsequently shortened to Punch. When Samuel Pepys noted this character's first recorded appearance in

England, in Covent Garden in 1662, the puppet is believed to have been a marionette.

Although we have no specific details of the puppets themselves, George Speaight[1], cites convincing evidence in support of the view that these were indeed marionettes. The size of the booth erected for a performance before Charles II at Whitehall Palace was of such dimensions that it is inconceivable that it was intended for glove puppets. There are references to puppets that 'fly through clouds' and perform other feats that are most naturally accomplished by marionettes, and allusions to political 'wire-pulling' also associated with marionettes. According to Speaight, the popularity of glove puppets in the first half of the seventeenth century was surpassed in the second half by the attractions of the marionette performances and the widespread popularity of Punch among all levels of society – John Milton, for example, certainly frequented the puppet theatre: he attributed the inspiration for *Paradise Lost*, which first appeared in 1667, to a puppet version of the story of Adam and Eve.

In early eighteenth-century England, puppetry was a fashionable entertainment, the puppet show being one of the places at which to be 'seen', and many of the continental aristocracy had their own private puppet theatres. In France, the live actors felt so threatened by the popularity of the marionette operas that in 1720 a special parliament was called to consider demands to have the puppet performances restricted, but it found in favour of the puppeteers.

In 1738 we find the first record in the USA of an English-style marionette show, *The Adventures of Harlequin and Scaramouche* by a puppeteer named Holt. The USA also provides evidence that, in some cultures, the marionette might have developed from the mask. Among the north-west coast Native Americans, for example, there was the use of masks which then acquired articulated jaws. Next they were held in the hands rather than worn on the head and later were suspended on strings.

As *Kapellmeister* at the Eisenstadt palace of Prince Esterhazy between 1761 and 1790, Haydn composed the music for five marionette operettas, and *Philemon and Baucis* was composed for a marionette performance for the Empress Maria Theresa. Gluck, too, composed marionette operas to entertain patrons such as Queen Marie Antoinette and later as *Kapellmeister* to Maria Theresa. Haydn and Goethe both acknowledged the influence of puppet theatre in their formative years. Goethe was presented with a puppet theatre at six years of age, for which he subsequently wrote many plays; this is said to have given him inspiration many years later for Faust, which also became a significant work for puppet theatre.

In the second half of the eighteenth century, Mozart composed works such as *Don Giovanni, Die Fledermaus, Il Seraglio* and *Die Zauberflote* which, though not written for puppet theatre, have become classics of puppet theatre, especially at the renowned Salzburg Marionette Theatre.

In Britain, interest in puppetry was flagging in the later part of the eighteenth century. Fortunately, the Italian *fantoccini* marionettes arrived on the scene and raised the popularity of puppets with performances full of tricks and transformations, a marionette tradition that survives to this day.

By 1820 the puppeteers in England were catering for children and the popularity of the marionettes had given way to Mr Punch, now presented as a glove puppet. The permanent puppet theatres closed and the marionettes, like the glove puppets, took first to the streets and then to the pleasure gardens. The travelling marionette companies now took up the melodramas of the live theatre as well as presenting the old tricks and transformations in pantomime-style shows. Towards the end of the nineteenth century, England's marionette troupes were considered to be the best in the world. These companies toured the globe with wagons carrying large theatres for elaborate productions.

Despite the impact of the arrival of the cinema and then television, throughout the past century there has been a revival of puppet theatre in general and even today there remain examples of the influence of the marionette on the human dance-drama.

Marionette productions, created and developed by U Thaw, a minister of royal entertainment in the eighteenth century, have had such an influence on the live dance-drama that in Burma the dancer's skill is measured by the ability to re-create convincingly the movements of the marionette.

In a performance I saw by the Burmese National Dancers and Puppets, two stages were in view with two sets of marionettes of different sizes at rest. The puppeteers first operated the puppets on the smaller stage, and then moved on to the large stage. The larger

1. Speaight, G., *Punch & Judy, A History* (Studio Vista, 1970).

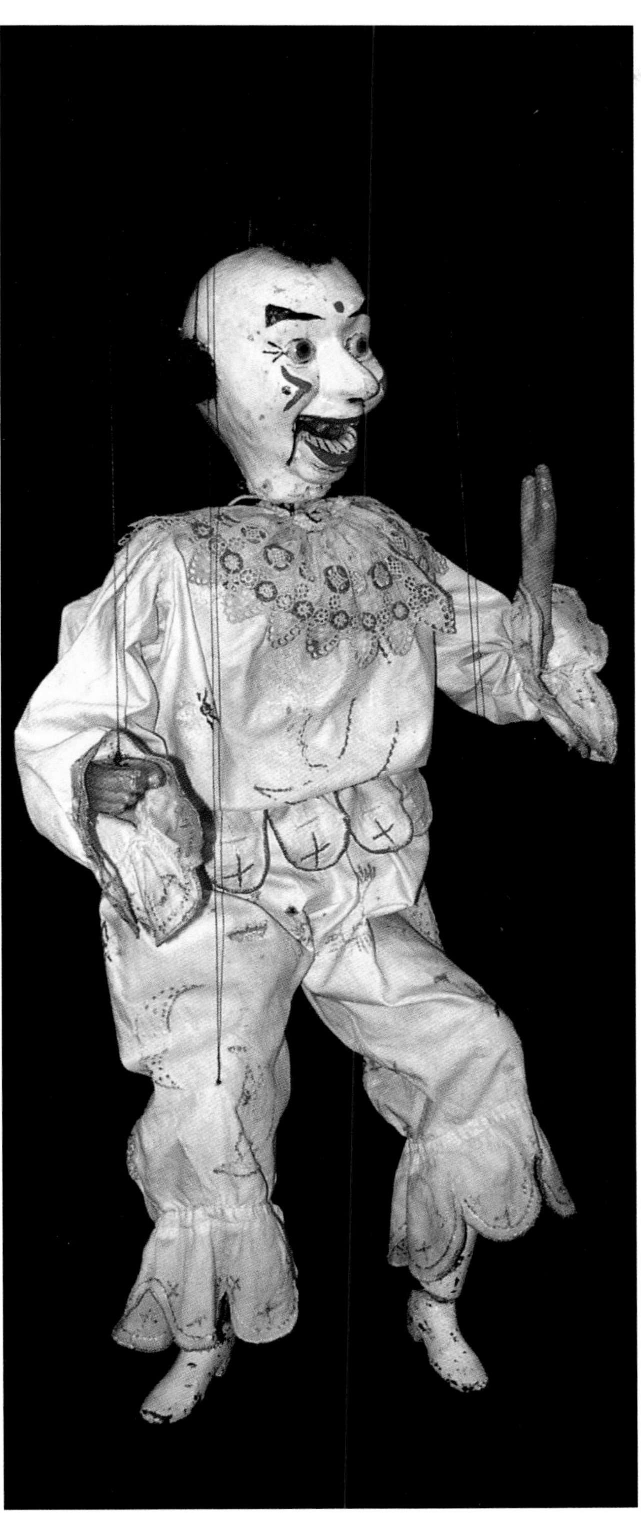

marionettes came to life and gradually it became clear that these were dancers, not puppets.

The comparative complexity of construction, manipulation and staging of marionettes has contributed to a greater take up of other types of puppet but marionettes retain a significant position in puppet theatre. They are regarded with a mixture of respect and affection, a long-standing tradition in popular culture with a special attraction for performers and their audiences.

A fantoccini-*style Victorian marionette, believed to be Joey the Clown, based on the famous Joey Grimaldi. In the Hogarth Collection at the Puppet Centre.*

2 MARIONETTE DESIGN

Characters from Aesop's Fables (*left*) *and* The Tempest (*above*), *carved by Gren Middleton, costumes by Juliet Rogers, Movingstage Marionettes. The heads, hands and feet are carved in limewood and the bodies and limbs of the larger characters are carved from jelutong. Smaller figures are limewood throughout. The wood is finished with stains or left plain, rather than painted.*

PRINCIPLES OF MARIONETTE DESIGN

In order to understand and design marionettes, one should appreciate something of the nature of puppet theatre in general and marionettes in particular. They are not actors in miniature and generally they fail as puppets if they are made too lifelike for that is to misunderstand what it is about puppets that has captivated human audiences for thousands of years.

An actor acts but a puppet is. The marionette is sometimes referred to as the complete mask, the mask from which the human actor has withdrawn. It was this that appealed to Edward Gordon Craig when he proposed

Fiery Jack by Paul Doran, Shadowstring Theatre.

the Uber-marionette and George Bernard Shaw argued the case for a puppet theatre to be attached to every drama school to teach the quality of 'not acting'.

All puppets, including marionettes, need to be an essence and an emphasis of whatever they represent, whether human, animal, or an abstract concept. They hint at or suggest qualities, movements or emotions and they are most effective when they interpret rather than copy the human form. The power of the puppet resides in large part in the fact that it is a simplification of form; it invites the audience to participate in a rather special way – to supplement those dimensions of character and movement that are merely suggested by the puppet through its design and by skilful manipulation.

Prospero and Ariel*: carved by Gren Middleton, costume by Juliet Rogers, Movingstage Marionettes. Ariel was created in glass by a professional glass blower to designs by Gren Middleton; the use of glass was inspired by the stage direction 'Enter Ariel invisible'.*

A marionette built to human proportions tends to look too long and thin, so it is usual to exaggerate the head, hands and feet slightly. Finely detailed modelling or carving will be lost to an audience more than a few feet away, so keep the modelling bold. When designing or creating the head, think of the modelling and painting as akin to stage make-up compared with everyday cosmetics. Despite the ways in which the puppet departs from human proportion, it is useful for characterization to study books on human anatomy for artists, and basic 'how to draw' books of the human form.

With puppets, one is liberated to create characters that can defy natural laws; they can fly through the air, turn inside out and transform in all manner of ways. Their design is not limited by the human form, for one creates not only the costumes of the actors, but also their heads, faces, body shapes, and so on. Of course, the puppet needs to look like, and move as, the intended character and this is conveyed in part by the shape, size and modelling of every part of the puppet. The way in which it moves is influenced by its structure, the method of control and the skill of the manipulator. So it is important to be clear about what the marionette is to be and to do, and to design it accordingly.

Marionettes can be as simple or as complex as you wish but their apparent complexity and remoteness from their operator distinguish them from other forms of puppet. Unlike a hand or rod-puppet, which you position just where you want it, the marionette, which is controlled via strings, has more independence of movement so it has even more of a life of its own. Therefore a marionette with good balance, appropriate distribution of weight and suitable joints will have intrinsic movement that assists the manipulator. When one operates a well-constructed puppet, the puppet does a good deal of the work but it can also resist intended gestures or other movements, so flexibility or restriction of movement is an important consideration.

Materials should be selected with a view to both the joints required and the relative weight of the different parts. If the pelvis is too light in relation to the legs, for example, the puppet will not walk well. In fact, any part that is too light will not facilitate good control and movement. Marionettes that are entirely carved achieve a unity of design and good distribution of weight that promotes a quality of movement other puppets do not always achieve.

It is always a good idea to plan the puppet, drawing it to actual size both from the front and in profile. You may find that drawing on lightly squared paper eases the transition from the plan to the puppet. If so, work with fair-sized squares of around 2.5cm (1in) so that the figure is divided into manageable segments. When drawing your design, have regard for the notes on proportion and structure that follow.

Marionette Proportion

Marionettes can be any size or shape and the variations of proportion can contribute significantly to characterization, so effectively there are no rules. However, some guidance may be useful in order to achieve relative proportions within a puppet.

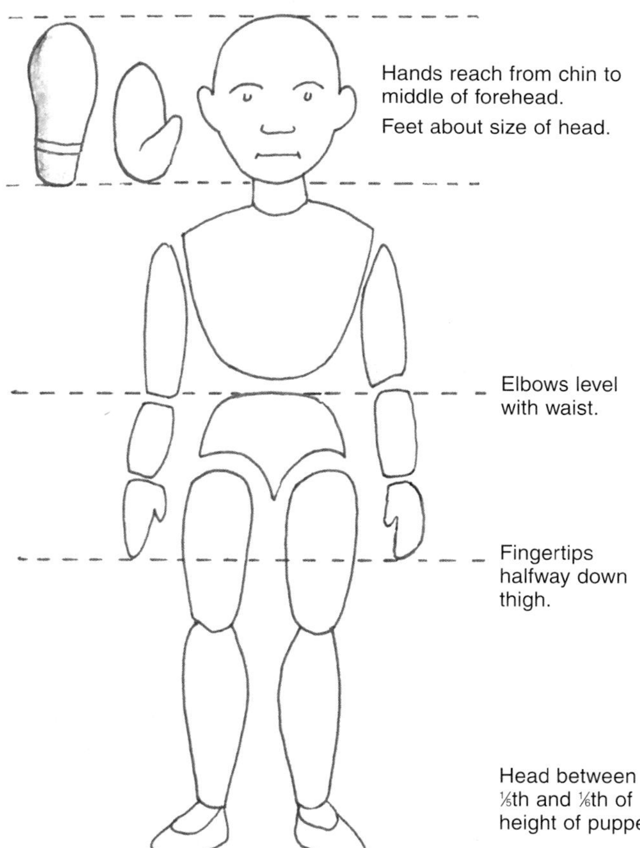

A guide to proportions for a marionette.

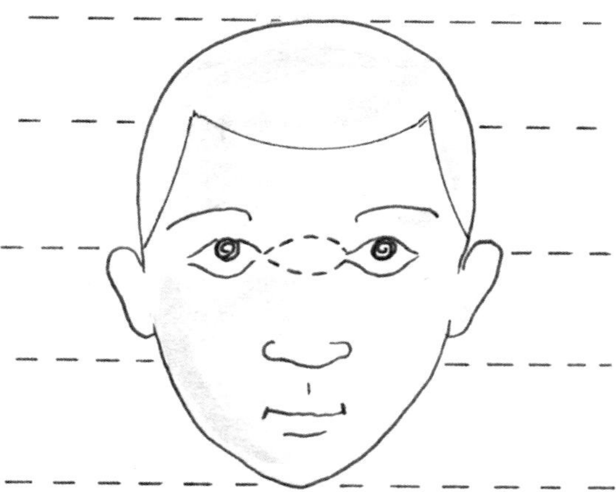

Typical proportions for a head: the ears align with the eyes and nose, and the eyes are approximately one eye's width apart.

A puppet's head is approximately a fifth of its height, or just a little less. As with humans, the hand measures the same as from the chin to the middle of the forehead and covers most of the face. The hand is also about the same length as the forearm and the upper arm. Feet are a little longer, approximately equal to the height of the head. Elbows are level with the waist, the wrist with the bottom of the body, and the fingertips half-way down the thigh. The body is usually a little shorter than the legs.

The way in which the face is framed by the addition of hair can have a strong influence on the puppet's appearance, and the age of a character affects the proportions of the head. As a general guide, the face has three approximately equal divisions: chin to nose; nose to eyebrows; eyebrows to brow-line. The bulk of the hair will often add to the height of the head and can make the proportions appear somewhat different. When designing the head, do not make the profile too flat, particularly the back of the head.

Eyes are a little above the mid-point between the chin and the top of the skull and are usually one eye's width apart, depending on the width of the nose. The top and bottom of the ears normally align with the top and bottom of the nose. The mouth is a little above the mid-point between the chin and the nose, and the corners of the mouth align with the centre of the eyes. The neck is set a little way back from the centre of

The angle at which the head sits in relation to the body contributes significantly to characterization.

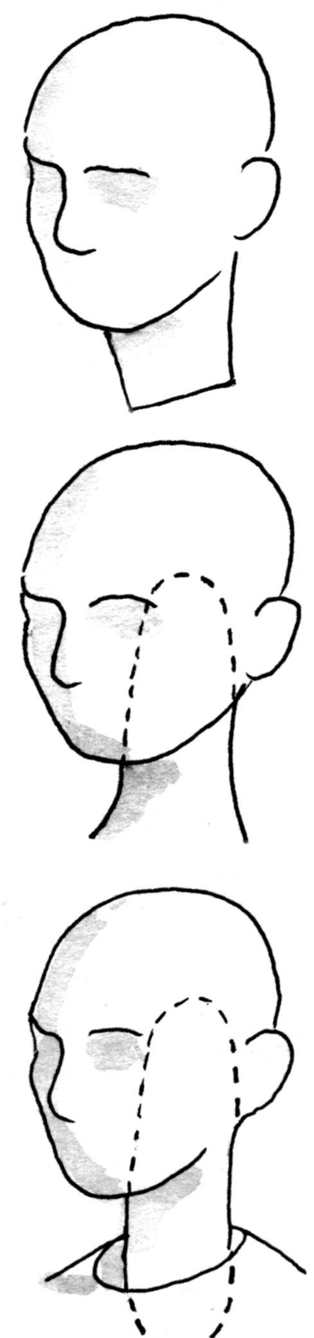

Three types of neck. Top: ***the neck made as part of the head.*** **Middle:** ***the neck made as part of the body and joined inside the head.*** **Bottom:** ***a separate neck joined inside both the head and the body.***

the skull and, for characterization, may be slightly angled by the positioning of joints between the head, neck and body.

Common mistakes are to make the eyes too high or too close together and foreheads too low. Ears are sometimes too high or too small and need to be examined from all angles as they also contribute to characterization.

Consider proportion not only in terms of height but also in terms of the bulk of the body and limbs. Ensure that the neck, arms and legs have sufficient bulk; if they are too thin this will affect the way the costume hangs and moves and the lack of bulk will often become apparent. Check the profile of the entire puppet; if you hold the puppet in a strong beam of light, does it cast a strong, interesting shadow?

Marionette Structure

Generally, a marionette head moves most effectively if the neck is separate from both the head and the body, though the head and neck may be made in one piece. I made most of my early marionettes with head and neck as a single unit and was perfectly satisfied with the result. However,

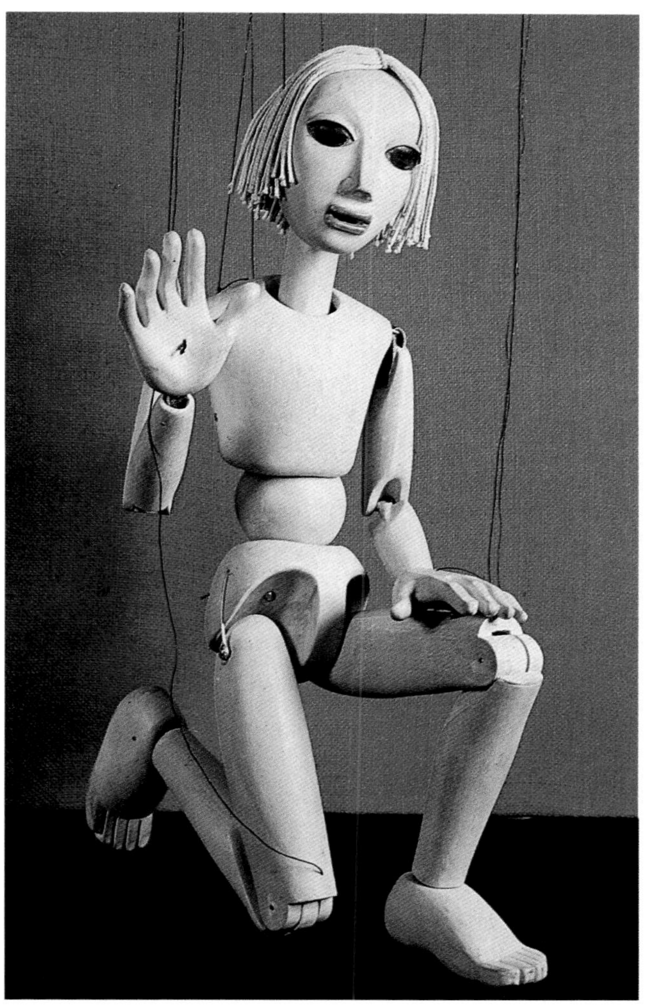

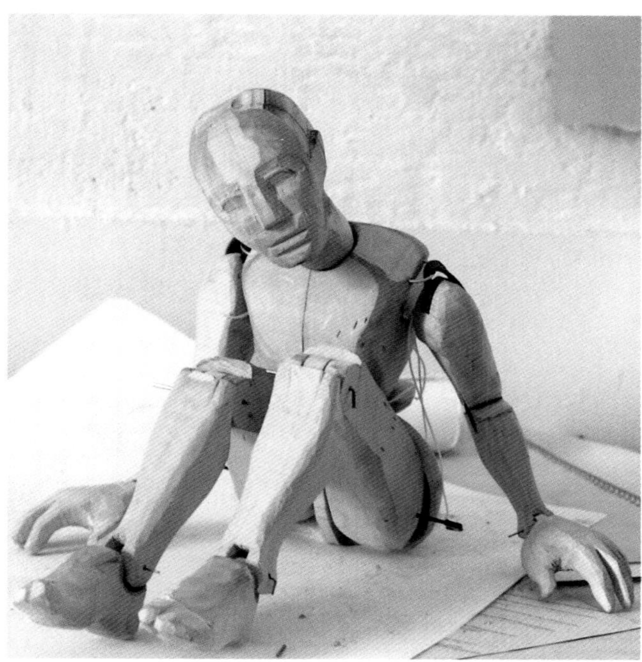

Examples of carved marionettes.
Left: ***a marionette carved by the late John Wright for the Puppet Centre collection. The wooden ball at the waist facilitates smooth movement.***
Above: ***a marionette carved by a student on a course tutored by John Roberts, PuppetCraft. Working from carefully drawn full-size patterns, this large puppet (about 28in tall) has been carved from lime and softer jelutong woods.***

when I later made them separately, I discovered the greater variety of movement that I could achieve. For some purposes the neck may be made as part of the body and joined inside the head.

A marionette body is normally jointed at the waist but movement may be restricted as necessary. Some puppet makers favour a three-part body with the upper body and pelvis separated by a large ball around which they move, which can be most effective. Some applications will require a one-piece body with no waist joint, though this sometimes affects the way the puppet walks.

For unity of design and weight, hands and feet are best constructed in the same material as the head. When different materials are used, ensure that the finished appearance has a coherence of style and texture.

Wrist joints are usually designed to allow a good deal of flexibility but ankle joints tend to be more restricted to ensure a good walking action.

Where necessary, puppet parts may be weighted with sheet lead (available from builders' merchants) or lead curtain weights, glued or nailed on. Puppet parts cast in rubber may be weighted by pouring a little liquid plaster into the hollow part.

Animal Marionettes

Most quadrupeds have the same basic structure (*see* illustration, page 18). The animal parts are made from the same materials described for human puppets but size and weight may be factors in selecting the material and construction method to be used. Legs are usually

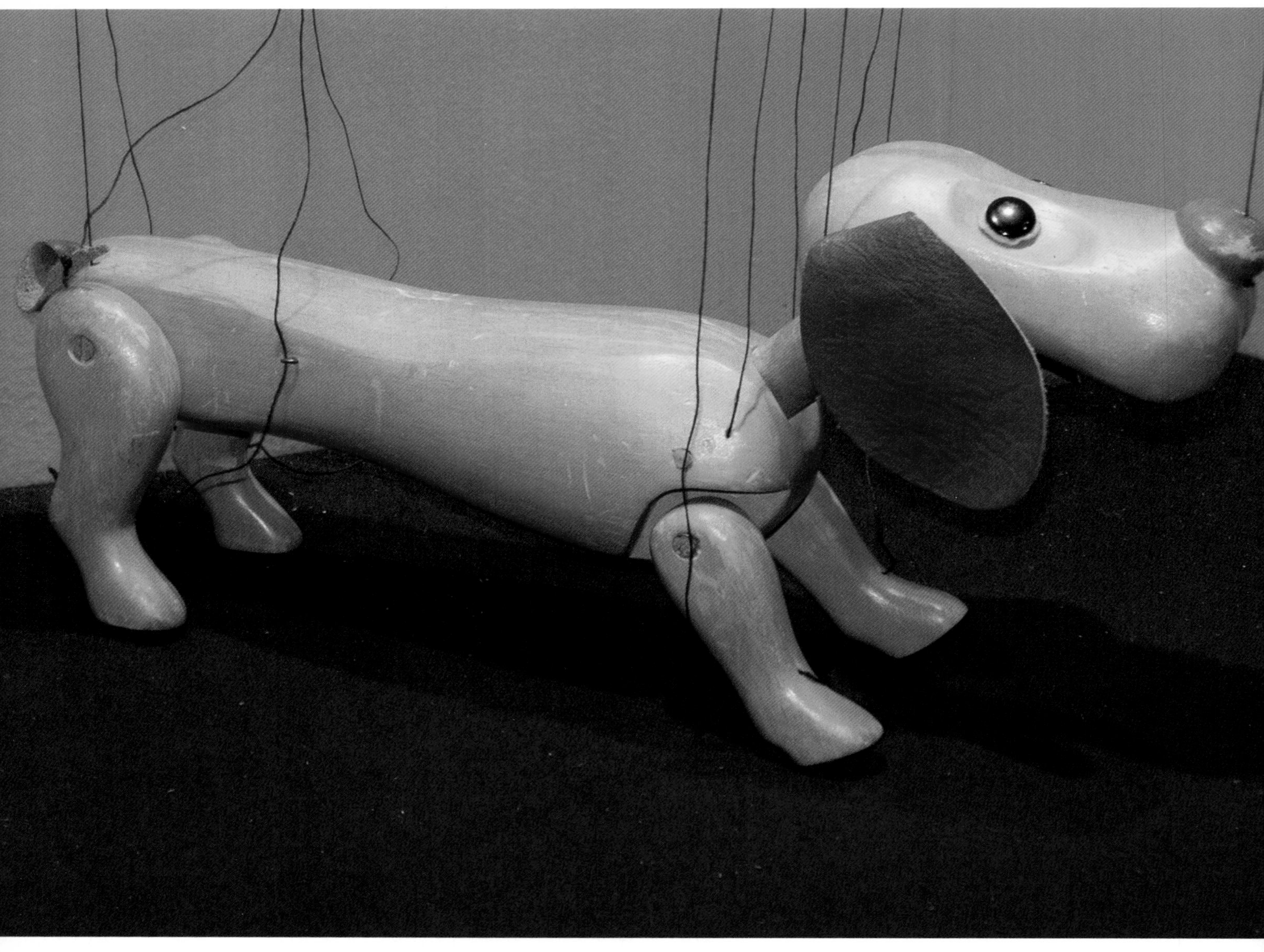

The structure for most quadrupeds follows the same principles as the dog illustrated. Although the legs will normally be jointed, a leg carved as one piece is very effective for this particular puppet, carved by John Thirtle for the Puppet Centre's demonstration collection.

carved or constructed with laminated layers of plywood. If necessary, additional shaping can be achieved with a modelling material, or by padding to shape with foam rubber if the leg is to be covered with fabric. Feet are carved or made from the same material as the head.

Rod-Marionettes

A rod-marionette is a very old style of puppet operated from above, usually by a mixture of rods and strings. The traditional Sicilian puppets, which perform tales of Orlando Furioso, stand some 1m (3ft)

A rod-marionette by the late Barry Smith. The head and body are supported by a single central rod while the hands are controlled by strings.

A rod-marionette or body puppet by John Blundall. This technique, which is common in southern India, has strings from the puppeteer's head and neck to the puppet's head and shoulders, and rods to the hands.

high, are carved throughout in wood, and have brass armour (*see* illustration on page 8). The puppets have the same basic structure as other marionettes but the style of control and method of manipulation are very different.

Another type of rod-marionette, sometimes called a 'body puppet' is found in southern India. This puppet is suspended on strings hung from the puppeteer's head and rods are used to manipulate the puppet's hands. Such a figure might have a flowing robe rather than legs and feet but, if it does have feet, they may be attached to the puppeteer's shoes.

3 Heads – Materials and Methods

Before embarking upon creating a head, refer to the information on marionette design in Chapter 2 and plan the head in relation to the whole puppet. Is the neck to be separate from the head or created with the head as a single unit? At what angle should the head sit in relation to the neck and shoulders? Does the puppet need a moving mouth or moving eyes? How will its personal characteristics and its age influence the design?

The Pied Piper *by John Roberts, PuppetCraft. Head and hands are carved in limewood and finished without paint and with glass-bead eyes.*

A modelled head with moving eyes created by the author.

There are three basic methods for creating heads; these are carving, modelling and casting (or moulding). Traditionally, marionettes were mostly carved in wood and this remains a popular method though it requires more skill than modelling or casting. Older puppetry texts often refer to the use of plastic wood and Celastic for modelling and casting. However, the formulation of plastic wood has been changed and it no longer has suitable properties for modelling, and Celastic, an impregnated woven material used with a solvent, is no longer available. The following pages outline a variety of materials that are suitable for each construction method, including some long-standing methods and the latest materials available.

You will discover a personal preference for particular techniques, so do experiment and always be on the lookout for new materials that appear in craft shops, decorating and DIY outlets, or in theatrical chandlers/suppliers. In theatrical suppliers in particular you will find all manner of materials and hardware of use for puppet construction and finishing, staging and scenery, including many of the modelling and casting materials described in this chapter.

Tools

The beginner could probably manage with the basic tools that one might find in a household toolbox, unless one is to carve puppets in wood. However, a slightly enhanced selection of tools, detailed below, is desirable, and there may be occasions when you add to the collection for a particular purpose – brazing equipment, for example, may be needed for some types of metal work. Keep all tools clean and well maintained, sharp where appropriate, and use them only for their intended purpose.

A vice with wooden jaws is essential for making most types of puppet and their controls. This may be permanently attached to a workbench or the type that can be clamped to any suitable surface.

You will certainly need a few craft knives and a variety of scissors. You will maintain the sharpness of your scissors by keeping each pair for particular materials and not using your fabric scissors for cutting paper or cardboard. A tenon saw, coping saw and a junior hacksaw cover most other cutting, though you will need a hand saw for easier cutting of large blocks of wood.

A power drill is useful, though delicate drilling is best done with a hand drill and occasionally you might need a carpenter's brace. The brace will need augers for drilling larger holes while the other drills need a variety of twist drills, spade drills (or points) up to 5mm (¼in) diameter, and a countersink bit. It is also useful to have an awl, a bradawl and a gimlet.

Shaping and smoothing is facilitated with rasps, files and various grades of glasspaper. Flat and round Surform rasps and a small hand tool are particularly helpful. Chisels with different width blades, mainly flat back and the odd bevelled back, will be needed for general-purpose work, together with a mallet. Carving tools are detailed in the following section.

You also need: screwdrivers, for example ratchet, Phillips and Pozidriv, stub and electrician's; large and small pliers, pincers, wire cutters and tin snips; claw, Warrington and tack hammers; a selection of brushes; measuring implements and a try square.

Carving a Head

Woodcarving Tools

A woodworking vice fixed to a rigid bench is essential to hold the wood firmly and safely while carving. A powered band saw, tenon saw and coping saw are useful for cutting basic shapes. Rasps are also handy. While proper woodcarving rasps are recommended, even a Surform rasp can be helpful for general shaping. Some woods can also be shaped considerably with glasspaper.

From my early days in puppetry I always admired the carving style of (the now late) John Wright from the Little Angel Theatre in London, and followed closely his recommendations, though with nothing like the same degree of skill. He recommended for the beginner a basic set of tools consisting of a 16mm (⅝in) and a 25mm (1in) flat chisel, a 6mm (¼in) fishtail flat, a 6mm (¼in) deep gouge and a 13mm (½in) shallow gouge plus a woodcarving mallet and a pair of callipers for comparing measurements. A sharpening stone and oil are also essential to maintain the tools in good condition and minimize the risk of accidents caused by using blunt tools.

Woods to Use

Well-seasoned limewood, a close-grained hardwood, is recommended for carving a marionette head. It is easily

The main stages in carving a head.

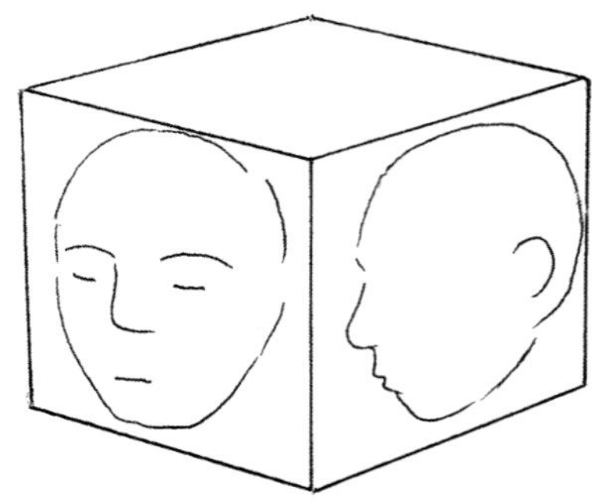

The outline shapes are drawn on the block of wood.

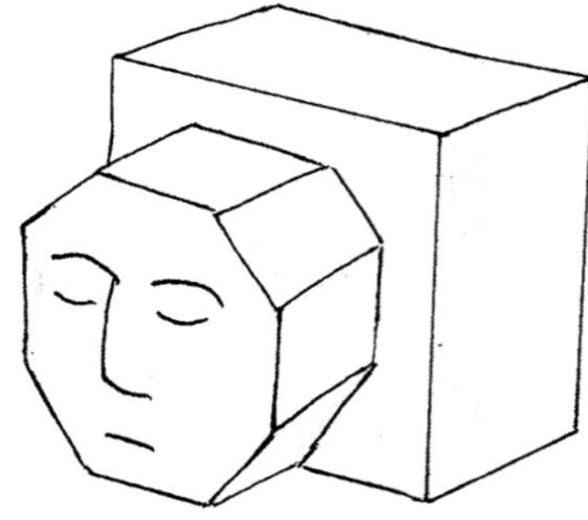

The major waste is removed with a saw and chisel.

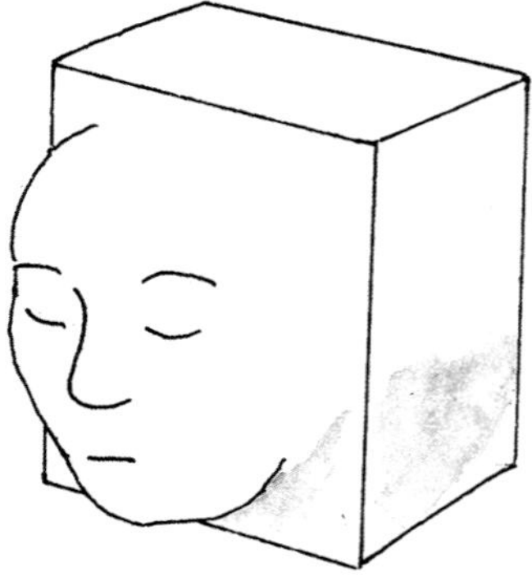

The face is shaped with chisels and sanded before shaping the back of the head.

worked, does not tend to splinter too readily and it is fairly light in weight. However, you might need to find a specialist timber merchant to obtain it. A second choice would be American white wood. Jelutong is suitable for large puppet parts and simple head shapes but it is not recommended for thin or delicate parts.

When selecting the wood, avoid pieces with cracks, stains or knots and look for a straight grain. Remember that the head is much deeper than it is wide, so allow sufficient wood for the front to back dimension, though you can join two pieces with woodworking adhesive if necessary.

Carving Technique

The beginner will find it helpful to practise on spare pieces of the type of wood to be used before attempting to carve the actual puppet. It is also a good idea to carve the simpler parts first, so start with the body, then the limbs, next the feet and hands, and finally carve the head.

Plan to use the wood with the grain running vertically down through the whole puppet, except the feet, which the grain will run along. Draw the outline shapes on to

River Girl and Poet, *carved by Gren Middleton, costumes by Juliet Rogers, Movingstage Marionettes, for a commissioned piece,* River Girl *by Wendy Cope.*

the blocks in thick pencil. As the wood is cut away these outlines will be lost; when this happens, lightly sand the wood to study progress and redraw the outlines as necessary.

Some people screw a block of wood securely to the bottom of the head in order to hold it in the vice for carving and then remove it when the carving is complete. Others carve the ears last, leaving them as blocks for securing in the vice, as described below.

Secure the rear of the block firmly in a vice and carve the face and front half of the head, back almost to the ears. First, cut away any major waste with a saw and a chisel or rasp. Then embark upon the carving proper with chisels. Make the chisel cuts in the same direction as the grain or the wood will split and more than intended will be cut away, ruining the head. For larger cuts, hold the chisel and tap it firmly and sharply, but not too heavily, with the mallet. For fine paring, rest the end of the chisel in the palm of one hand, against the heel, and place the other hand over the shaft and blade, helping to guide it. Always keep both hands behind the direction of the cutting edge. Take care to shape the head fully: a common mistake is to leave the head too angular, reflecting the shape of the block from which it has been carved.

Next, sand the face smooth, first with coarse glasspaper on rough parts, working down in stages to a very fine one. When the face is complete, work towards the back of the head and finally shape the ears, which must be done with care.

If the neck is separate from the head, hollow out the socket for the neck and through this hole cut away as much of the head as possible to reduce its weight.

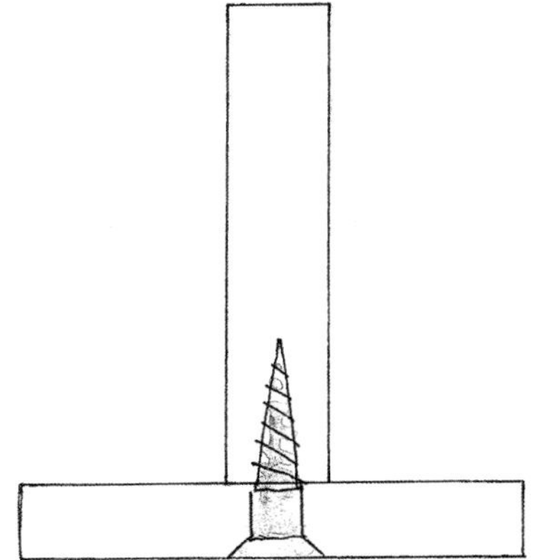

A modelling stand.

Modelling a Head

General Principles

Modelling is a very flexible method for creating heads. Starting with either a base shape or a model in Plasticine (plastilene), you can build the required shape in the chosen material and work on the head until you achieve the desired result. Some materials are fairly flexible, which allows you to cut back or sand the head

Modelling on a Plasticine base.

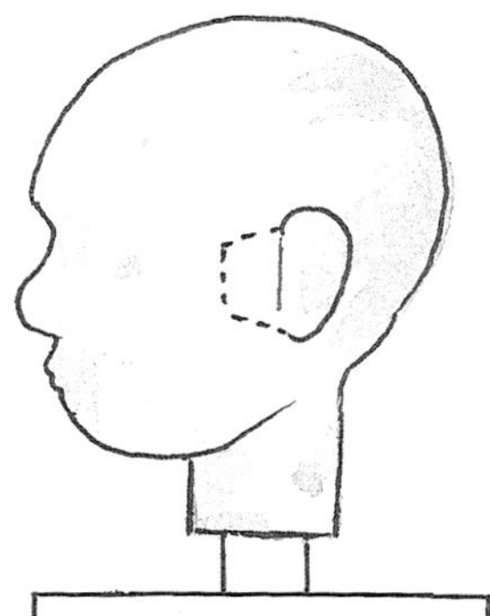

The Plasticine model with cardboard or thin plywood ears.

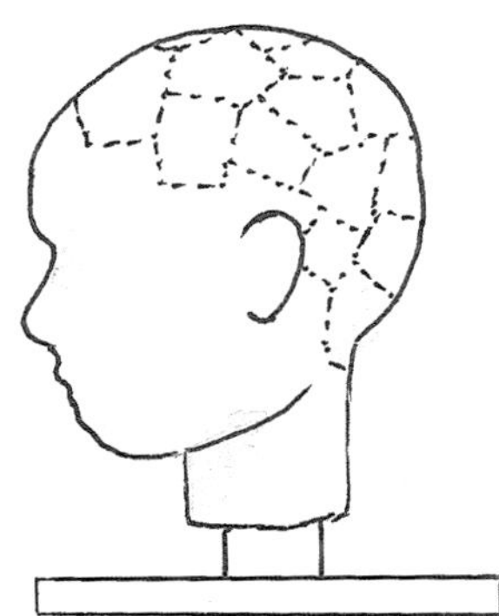

The Plasticine is coated with a release agent and covered with a modelling material.

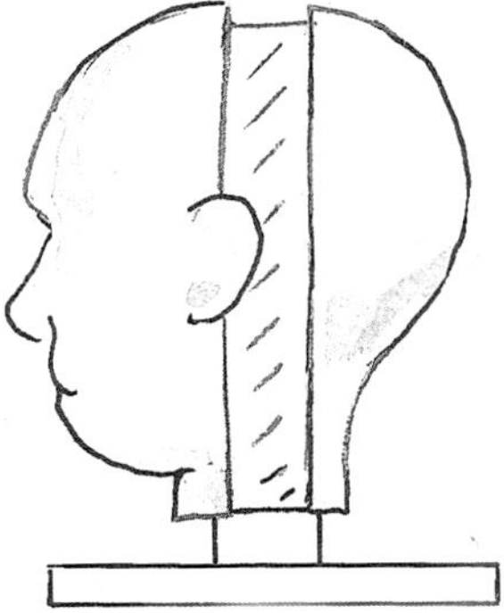

When dry, the head is cut open and the Plasticine removed.

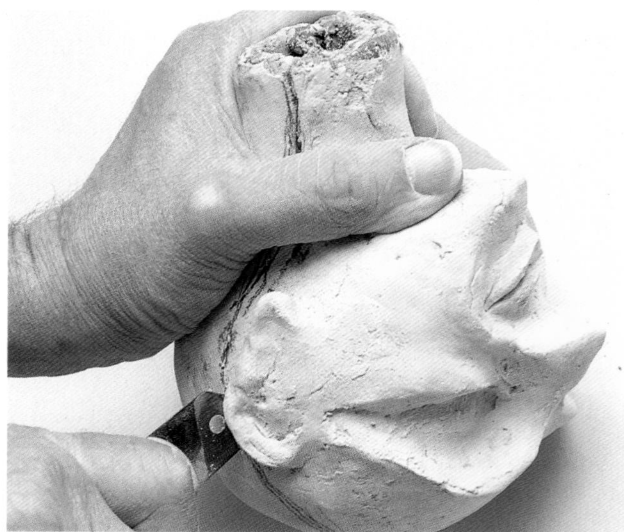

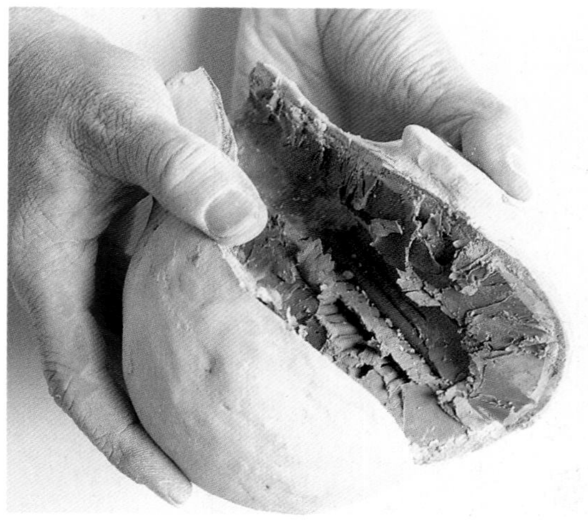

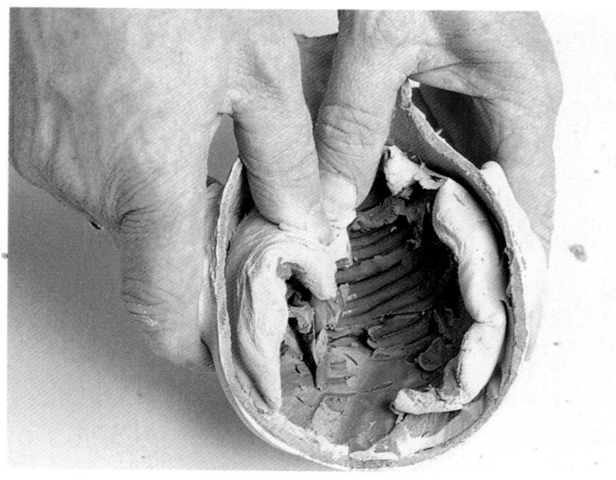

Removing the Plasticine from a modelled head.
Top: ***Cut open the head with a suitable tool: always cut away from the hand holding the head.***
Middle: ***The cut is made with a 'V' shape at the top of the head to assist alignment when rejoining the head shells.***
Bottom: ***The Plasticine in the centre is scooped out and that in contact with the shell is rolled into the space created. Leverage against the shell would cause it to break.***

when dry. Most modelling materials are strong and reasonably lightweight when used in an appropriate thickness.

Modelling on Plasticine

Make a modelling stand by screwing together a substantial dowel and a block of wood. Ensure the base is sufficiently large not to topple over, as the Plasticine model will be quite heavy. Model the basic head shape around the dowel. Alternatives to Plasticine may be used but select one that remains pliable or it may be difficult to remove from the head at a later stage. (If the puppet is to have moving eyes *see* pages 35–6 for details of how to prepare this stage of the model.)

Avoid fine detail at this stage, as this will disappear as the modelling progresses. In fact, with some materials, hollows will become significantly shallower as layers are added, so make the modelling bolder than you wish the final shape to be.

Cut out ear shapes in cardboard or thin plywood. It is important to have a strong base to build on, as the ears will often take much of the weight of the puppet when head strings are attached. Make them a little smaller than the required final size and leave extensions to insert into the Plasticine. Where necessary, apply a coating of release agent or separator to the head (but not the ears), and then cover it with a modelling material that dries to form a hard shell.

Some materials have adhesive properties, but if you are using one that does not, coat the ear shapes in adhesive to ensure the modelling material sticks firmly to them. Pay attention to the thickness of the modelling around the eyes, nose and mouth as beginners often find these areas to be too thin when the base material is removed.

When the head has set hard, cut it open following a line behind the ears and over the top of the head in a 'V' shape to aid alignment when rejoining it. Some modellers make a preliminary cut with a fine blade before the modelling is dry, which is helpful with materials that are difficult to cut when set.

Next, separate the head shells and remove the Plasticine very carefully. If the head does not separate cleanly, slice through the Plasticine with strong, fine thread or wire to separate the front and back sections. Carefully scoop out some of the Plasticine from the centre of the head with a spoon, and roll a little of the surrounding Plasticine into the space created. Scoop it out again and repeat the process until you are able to roll all of the Plasticine away from the shell and remove it. Do not try to remove a large quantity at once and never apply leverage with the spoon against the head shell or the head will break.

Hold the shells up to the light to test for weak points that need strengthening. If you need to strengthen the head shell from the inside, remove any trace of a separator before applying more modelling material. You might scrape the inside of the shell clean with a craft knife or use a cloth soaked in methylated spirit (wood alcohol) or another suitable cleaner.

At this stage, complete any internal mechanisms for moving the mouth or eyes and for attaching the neck, then rejoin the shells. Conceal and strengthen the joint with a little more of the modelling material.

Modelling on a Base Shape

Some puppet makers first create a basic head form, such as an egg shape, in the chosen modelling material as described above. Having removed the Plasticine or other internal material and rejoined the shells, they then add all the detail with more modelling material.

However, you may model upon any suitably shaped object, which may remain inside or be removed from the hardened shell. This is a useful method for any size of puppet, but is particularly helpful for making larger figures. It is a good idea to fix the shape on to a modelling stand, but if you work on it hand-held, ensure that you can either stand it or have some means to hang it up to dry.

An egg-shaped piece of polystyrene is often a good base for modelling human figures, or a block of polystyrene may be shaped with a hacksaw blade and a small Surform rasp. If necessary, the polystyrene may be scooped out of the finished head or dissolved with a few drops of acetone. Rather than model directly on to the polystyrene, some materials are better applied if the polystyrene is first covered with brown wrapping paper or similar applied with PVA (white woodworker's glue).

A cardboard base shape makes a very robust alternative to polystyrene. Draw the profile shape on strong cardboard or a thin sheet of plywood and cut it out. If a strong fixture is required, such as a block of wood or dowelling for securing the neck, glue it in place then build the head around it. Establish the basic head shape by gluing on cardboard 'ribs' a short distance apart. To give strength to the structure, glue further cardboard shapes between the ribs. If the puppet is to have moving

A polystyrene base for modelling.

Left: ***A block of polystyrene is shaped with a rasp.***

Below: ***The polystyrene is coated with brown paper and PVA glue ready for the application of a modelling material.***

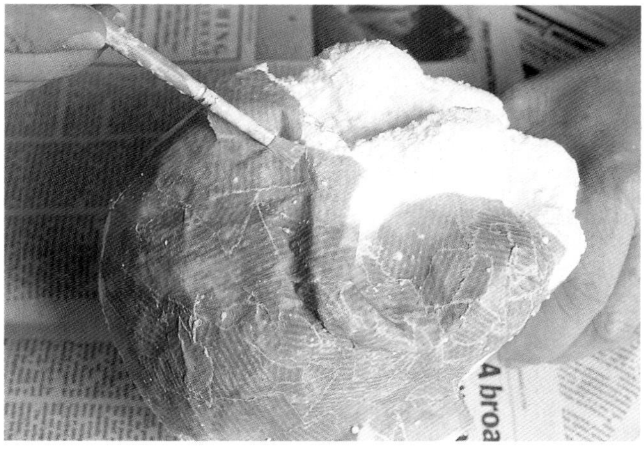

A cardboard base shape for modelling.

A cardboard profile shape with ribs glued on to it.

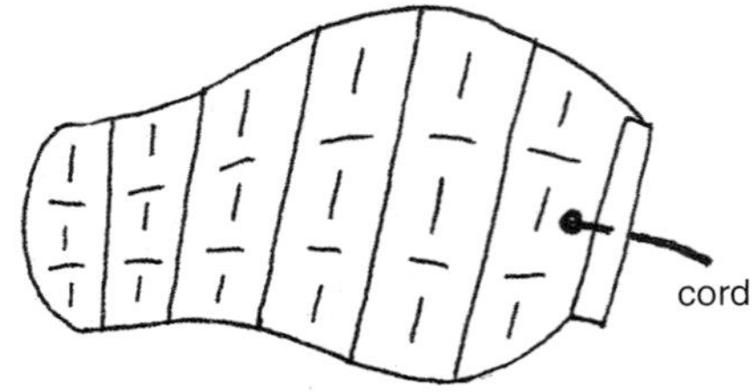

Braces are glued between the ribs.

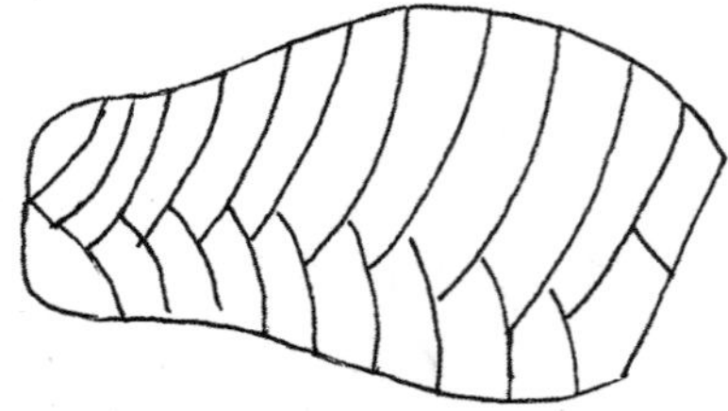

The shape is covered with strips of thin cardboard.

eyes or a moving mouth, cut away the cardboard to accommodate these before proceeding.

Next, cover the structure with layers of thin cardboard. For human characters, cover the cardboard with a thin layer of modelling material, having first smeared it with a suitable adhesive if necessary. Add detail to the modelling as required. Animal heads may be covered in the same way or, instead of a modelling material, the cardboard can be covered with cloth or fur fabric.

Paste and Paper

Create a Plasticine model and insert the cardboard or plywood ear shapes. To prevent the modelled head sticking, cover the Plasticine (but not the ears) with overlapping 2.5cm (1in) squares of damp tissue paper.

Build up the head shell with small squares of newspaper using PVA glue or a cellular paste. For strength, at least four layers of paper are required. It is often difficult to see which areas have been covered and which have not, so it is a good idea to alternate the colour of the newsprint to ensure full coverage. With cellular paste it is necessary to let each layer dry thoroughly before applying the next, whereas with PVA you can proceed immediately. Remember to keep the modelling bold. To highlight features, work in detail with tissue paper, which can be scrunched up or manipulated as necessary, and continue covering it with newspaper.

When the modelled head is thoroughly dry, cut it open and remove the Plasticine, insert any internal structures required and rejoin the shells with paste and paper.

Paper Pulp

Create the pulp by soaking small pieces of newspaper in water. You may use a food processor to speed up the

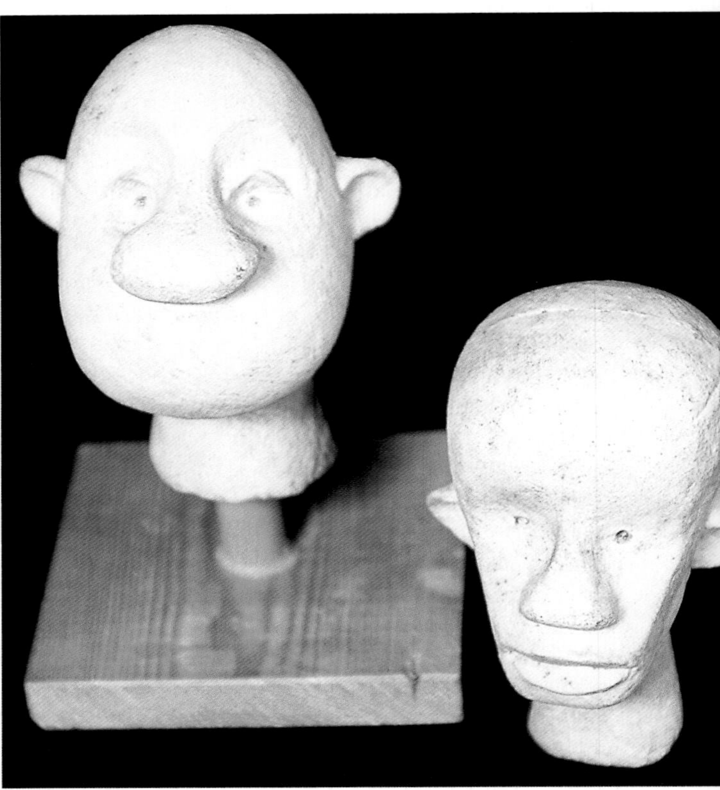

Heads created by the late Barry Smith using paper pulp mixed with fine sawdust.

process. When the paper is thoroughly pulped, drain off excess water. To prepare the pulp for modelling, add powder paste and water to produce a consistency like porridge. The addition of very fine sawdust to the pulp gives a strong and very good finish to the head.

Create the Plasticine base shape on a modelling stand and insert the ear shapes; cover the Plasticine with squares of damp tissue paper as a separator. Model the pulp over the tissue paper. When the head is thoroughly dry, cut it open and remove the Plasticine. Secure any internal fixtures, glue the shells together and strengthen the joint with pulp. Sand the head lightly and add enough pulp to fill any cracks and achieve the finish desired.

Wood-Form

Wood-Form, described by the manufacturer as 'air-drying wood clay', is obtainable from craft shops and educational suppliers. It has the appearance of clay and is similar to clay to manipulate. Once dry, it possesses many characteristics of wood and can be drilled, filed and carved. It dries reasonably quickly when allowed to dry naturally but warming can speed up the process. In fact, under pressure of time, I have held a head on a metal skewer in the heat from a gas hob – but not too closely – and the head has dried very quickly without cracking, though this is not a recommended technique!

Use Wood-Form to model upon Plasticine or on a base shape as described previously. I apply a little clear glue to the basic ear shapes to ensure good adhesion of the material. When modelling upon Plasticine, use petroleum jelly as a release agent, but if you want it to adhere to a base, a polystyrene shape works well. Moisten your fingers to prevent the Wood-Form sticking to them. After applying it to the base, moisten it just a little with your fingers to blend the pieces together and to smooth the surface.

You can model the detail from the outset but generally I prefer with this material to establish the overall shape and to allow it to dry before shaping it further. Additional Wood-Form can be applied without the need for an adhesive but works best if you moisten it, which helps to blend it in. Using small pieces and making it quite wet will enable you to smooth it over the head like a thin paste and achieve an even surface.

When the modelling is dry, cut open the head to remove the base shape, if appropriate, and rejoin the head shells with a clear contact adhesive. Cover the joint with a little more Wood-Form and lightly sand the whole head smooth. The head can then be painted with the usual variety of paints.

A basic shape created in Wood-Form. When dry, it is sanded smooth ready for more detailed modelling of the features.

Plaster and Muslin

Layers of muslin, dipped in plaster filler, are modelled in the same way as paste and paper but, because this material is much thicker, the initial Plasticine modelling must be bolder or the detail will be eroded as successive layers are applied. Ready-mixed filler is too thick and dry for the purpose; use the type that comes in powder form and mix it by adding the powder to the water until it is a creamy consistency. A commercially produced alternative is a cotton bandage impregnated with plaster – all you need to do is dip it into water and it is ready to apply. It sets within five minutes and is hard in half an hour. It can be purchased in rolls as plaster bandage or in pre-cut form as Mod Roc.

Cover the modelled head with damp tissue paper and apply at least three layers of overlapping squares of the muslin and plaster filler. Colour alternate layers with paint to ensure full coverage. Press each layer firmly into the previous one: new layers can be added without waiting for existing ones to dry. To model detail, use finely teased cotton wool saturated in plaster filler. When dry it may be shaped with a craft knife or glasspaper.

When the head is thoroughly dry, cut it open, remove the Plasticine and strengthen the shell if necessary: the nostrils, eyes and mouth are often weak points. Insert any internal fixtures then rejoin and cover the head with another layer of muslin. To achieve a very smooth finish, apply to the surface just enough filler to fill the weave of the muslin; too much plaster will tend to chip if knocked. Smooth it with a wet finger. When it has dried, sand lightly with fine glasspaper if necessary.

Milliput

Milliput is an epoxy putty that sets extremely hard without shrinking and can be cut, drilled, filed and sanded. There are different grades of the substance: Standard Yellow/Grey is satisfactory for puppets but finer grades are available. Each pack contains two sticks of different colour. They are like Plasticine to handle and must be mixed together until a uniform colour with no streaks is achieved. At this point it acquires very adhesive properties and at room temperature sets rock hard in about two or three hours, though setting time can be reduced to a few minutes by heating.

Milliput requires a curing period equivalent to the setting time. After curing it can be worked immediately and detail may be added with modelling tools or other appropriate implements without the use of an adhesive. Keep fingers and tools moist to prevent sticking. Water helps with manipulation and smoothing while the substance is still soft. Either use wet fingers or smooth it under a running tap. Clean the tools immediately after use with a wet rag or paper: once hardened, Milliput is almost impossible to remove.

Milliput may be modelled directly upon a shape such as polystyrene, which may be left in the head or dissolved out. If a Plasticine model is used, a separator is not normally needed; the Plasticine should peel away from the Milliput but it is wise to try a test piece first. If necessary, apply a release agent, which may be Ambersil DP100/2 (a silicone spray) or petroleum jelly, depending on the base shape used.

When the shell is dry, saw it open and remove the Plasticine. Complete any internal mechanisms, rejoin the two shells and cover the joint with more Milliput.

Alternatively, use Milliput to create a basic head shape like a hollow egg or spheroid, as described previously. Then model all the features solidly on to the hollow shell.

Rhenoflex 3000

Rhenoflex comes in sheet form and consists of a core of woven polyester fabric sandwiched between thermoplastic polyester layers with adhesive characteristics. No solvent is needed as modelling or casting requires only heat and pressure. It is available in various thicknesses, the range being RX3120/3140/3170/3202-RX3120 is the thinnest and results in a fairly light finish after processing that resembles a thin cardboard mask while RX3202 results in a very strong finish that could be used on the live stage to replicate armour. Additional layers can be bonded to a previous one if necessary and the shaped material can be sanded, filled and painted with acrylic paints.

To model the material, soften it in hot water or with a hot air blower and model it to shape. You need to work quickly as it remains malleable for less than five minutes and is fully hardened in three hours. If you need to add another layer or more modelling detail, greater heat and more pressure will be required to achieve the necessary bonding.

A release agent should not be needed unless the general shaping has been done at a high temperature but a layer of damp tissue paper could be applied to the base prior to modelling as a precaution.

As soon as the shell has cooled it will be rigid. Cut it open (if the base shape is to be removed), secure any internal fixtures, then glue the shells together and cover the joint with more Rhenoflex. Sand and fill the surface as required to achieve the desired finish.

Varaform

Varaform is a natural cotton mesh impregnated with a thermoplastic resin. There are three types; gauze, light and heavy meshes. The heavy mesh has an open-weave structure and sets the most rigid; the light mesh is open-weave, semi-flexible and suitable for more intricate work; the gauze is a thin fabric, best for details and finishing touches.

Varaform will adhere to itself and can be heated and cooled several times for remodelling. The rigidity of the structure depends on the number of layers: up to three layers at a time can be dipped in hot water then pressed together with a rolling-pin before modelling or moulding. Reinforcing or additional modelling strips can be added but you need to warm the part to which they are to be applied as well as heating the additional material.

Cover the base shape with damp muslin. Immerse the Varaform in hot water for a couple of minutes. As you remove it (always use tongs), let the water drain off and then apply the material over the muslin. Guide it into the shape with your fingers or with a modelling tool. As the working time is less than three minutes, you will need to reheat it to adjust the modelling.

If you have a base shape that is not affected by higher temperatures, you can use a hot air gun for dry modelling. Place the Varaform on to the base shape and then apply the heat. As the material softens it will take the shape of the model but take care not to apply too much heat or the material will take on adhesive properties and attach itself to the base. Retouch or add detail as required.

Cut open the shell and remove the base shape, as required. Attend to any internal fixtures and rejoin the shells with more Varaform. All types of paint can be used on the finished product. Where an adhesive is required for use with this material, a mastic glue without solvent is recommended. If you wish, the shell can be coated with latex, silicone or epoxy products.

Jesmonite

Jesmonite is an acrylic composite, a water-based glass fibre system that is supplied in two-part form, liquid and powder. They are mixed using a high shear mixing blade in an electric drill in the ratio 1 part liquid to 2.5 parts water by weight. Although it is a low-hazard product it is recommended by the manufacturer that you wear eye-protection, a dust mask and rubber gloves. There are different grades but AC300 Multicast should be satisfactory for most puppet construction.

After mixing it is workable for between eight and fifteen minutes at 15–18°C but this period can be extended by the addition of the Jesmonite retarder. There is also a 'Thixotrope' that can be added a drop at a time to achieve the required viscosity so that it does not run or slump if you are applying it vertically. It can be used as a laminate with glass fibre cloth or poured into moulds.

Used in theatre and television for sets and props as well as for architectural details and sculpture, Jesmonite holds fine detail but can be fairly heavy and, like fibreglass, is harder to cut when dry: a rotary disc cutter will facilitate cutting. A coating of petroleum jelly or soft wax should suffice as a release agent but I prefer to apply a layer of damp tissue paper to the base model.

Apply pieces of stitched glass fabric to the model either by dipping it first in the Jesmonite mix or by adding the Jesmonite with a brush, which should be cleaned with water after use. If you are covering a polystyrene base, use 3mm Fibermesh (polypropylene fibre) instead of glass fabric.

Run a sharp blade around the intended dividing line of the shells before the head has fully set. This will facilitate separation when the head has set hard. After removing the base shape, attend to any internal fixtures and rejoin the head using more Jesmonite with the stitched glass fabric. Apply Jesmonite Clear Top Coat to seal the surface for painting.

Fibreglass

Fibreglass heads are created by the application of fibreglass matting saturated in polyester liquid resin to the base model. The matting is available in several grades – select the one most suitable for the task. If the puppet is to have moving eyes or a moving mouth, use 'finishing matt' for the first layer to ensure a smooth internal surface. Build up the head and features in coarse matt, then apply a final layer of fine quality matt. The use of rubber gloves is recommended.

Cover the base model with damp tissue paper before applying the fibreglass. Soak pieces of the matting in the liquid resin, press out all bubbles and then press the matting on to the model with the pieces overlapping. Before the head is completely dry, cut through the shell with a sharp knife so that the Plasticine core can be removed easily when the shells are dry. If this is not done, a saw will be needed to cut it open when the fibreglass has hardened. Rejoin the shells with saturated matting. It may then be filed or sanded.

Casting Methods

General Principles

Casting involves creating a plaster cast of a Plasticine model and using that cast to make copies in the chosen material. The benefits of this method include the opportunity to get the final design exactly right in the initial model, the possibility to renew heads easily or to make identical heads for a character in different costumes. It is also possible to make different finishing touches to the same heads for family members.

Heads can be created using a range of materials, but undercutting is not possible when using materials that dry rigid, unless you are prepared to smash the plaster cast to remove the head. The use of latex rubber does permit undercutting provided it is not allowed to become too thick or used with a hardener.

Some latex mixes and fibreglass can shrink by as much as 10 per cent compared with the original model, so you need to allow for this. It is not at all easy to judge how much to increase the size but one does develop a feel for it. Alternatively, create the basic shape in polystyrene, then finish the modelling with a covering of Plasticine up to 1cm (½in) thick, depending on the size of the head. A little experimentation with the size of the model in relation to the material to be used for the head is worthwhile. If there is any undercutting with a polystyrene model, when the plaster cast is complete, dissolve the polystyrene with acetone, then remove the Plasticine and proceed as usual.

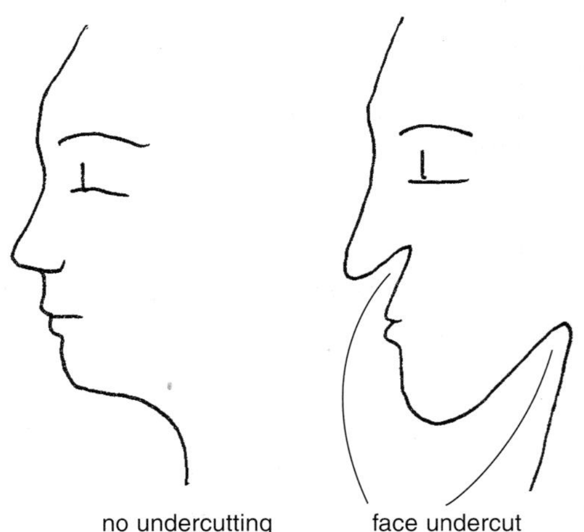

Undercutting: the face on the left has no undercutting but the one on the right is undercut, which would be problematic if casting a head using a material that sets hard.

Making a Plaster Cast

Plaster of Paris may be used for creating the cast but quick-setting 'stonehard' dental plaster is far superior. It sets much faster than plaster of Paris so you must work quickly once it is ready to use. It also dries out ready for moulding in a very short time and is remarkably strong. When mixing the plaster, ensure that you have sufficient for covering the section of head that you are working on, and in a suitable thickness. The finished plaster cast should be about 3–5cm (1½–2in) thick.

Whichever plaster is used, when mixing it add the powder to the water, fairly thinly at first. It will start to thicken and feel warm to the touch when it is ready to use. The two most suitable techniques for making the cast are the hand-held method for moderate-sized heads and the box method for larger heads.

Hand-Held Method

Prepare the Plasticine model for casting by inserting thin strips of tin or a similar metal to divide it into two sections. Overlap the strips by 3–4mm (⅒in) to create a sound division between the front and back of the head. If the head is to be made from a rigid material, make the division over the top of the head and down the sides along the line of the ears.

For a flexible latex head, the same line can be followed. Alternatively, the strips may be placed behind the ears or in a large ring around the back of the head under the hairline. With the latter method, which avoids an unsightly flash down the ears and neck, a flexible head can be manoeuvred out of the cast, but if you allow the latex to become too thick in the cast, it will be impossible to remove it intact.

Prior to casting, smear the Plasticine and the metal strips with petroleum jelly to act as a release agent. Ensure there are no lumps of grease anywhere.

Follow the manufacturer's instructions for mixing the plaster. Holding the back of the head in one hand, work on the front half first. As soon as the plaster starts to thicken, scoop it up with a spoon and carefully fill in all the hollows; avoid trapping air bubbles, as this will spoil the head. Some of the plaster will run off but disregard this and keep applying it. As the consistency of the plaster becomes creamy, pour it all over this half of the

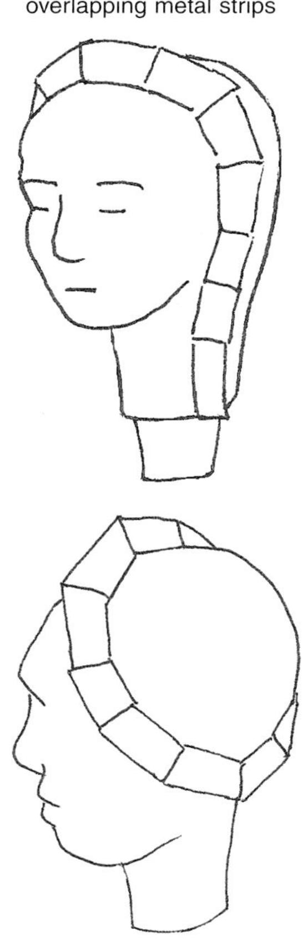

Two ways of placing the metal strips for taking a plaster cast of a Plasticine model.

Metal dividers down the side of the head make the cast suitable for use with all moulding and modelling materials.

Dividing the head within the hairline avoids the possibility of a visible 'flash' at the join but is suitable only for creating fairly flexible heads so that they can be manoeuvred out of the plaster cast.

head. If any plaster falls away, scoop it up and reapply before it sets.

Allow the cast to harden for about thirty minutes then carefully remove the metal strips with tweezers. Smooth any marks made in the Plasticine when removing the strips. Make a few shallow holes in the clean edge left where the metal strips have been and smear the edge of the cast, including the shallow holes, with petroleum jelly. Next, take a cast of the back of the head and, before the plaster sets, carefully scrape away any excess that overlaps the first cast.

When the cast has set, prise the two sections apart and remove the Plasticine. The back section will have knobs around the edge to fit into the holes in the front section, enabling the cast to be aligned accurately for casting a rubber head. When using this casting method for smaller parts, there may not be space for alignment knobs, but smaller casts will align fairly easily if the metal strips follow the undulations of the body parts.

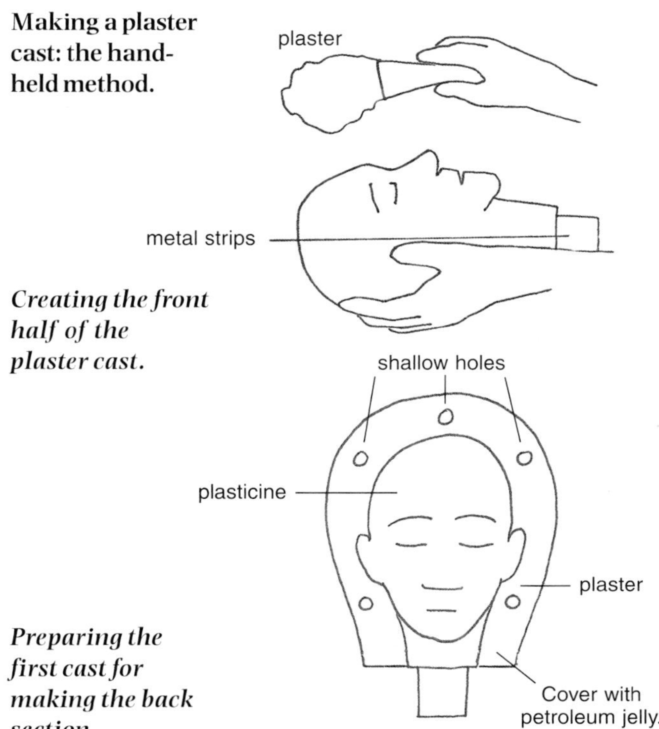

Making a plaster cast: the hand-held method.

Creating the front half of the plaster cast.

Preparing the first cast for making the back section.

Clean the inside of the cast carefully with a rag soaked in methylated spirit. Clean the ears, nose and other awkward cracks with loops of fine wire. If air bubbles have created any tiny holes in the inside surface they will cause small lumps on the puppet, so fill them with a little fresh plaster and smooth carefully.

Leave the cast to dry out until it no longer feels cold and heavy.

Box Method

Create the Plasticine model on a modelling stand with a large base, which will form part of the box for casting. Ensure the head is held securely and does not wobble. Use a rolling-pin to flatten out a long strip of Plasticine, approximately 5cm (2in) wide and 1.2cm (½in) thick. Trim one long side to give a neat, clean edge. Use this strip to divide the head in two. Ensure that it is firmly in place and in contact with the head all the way round but take care not to damage the modelling. Add more Plasticine to the top of the curve to establish corners and trim this divider into a rectangular shape. Smear the back of the head and the divider with petroleum jelly.

Make two folds in a strong piece of cardboard to create

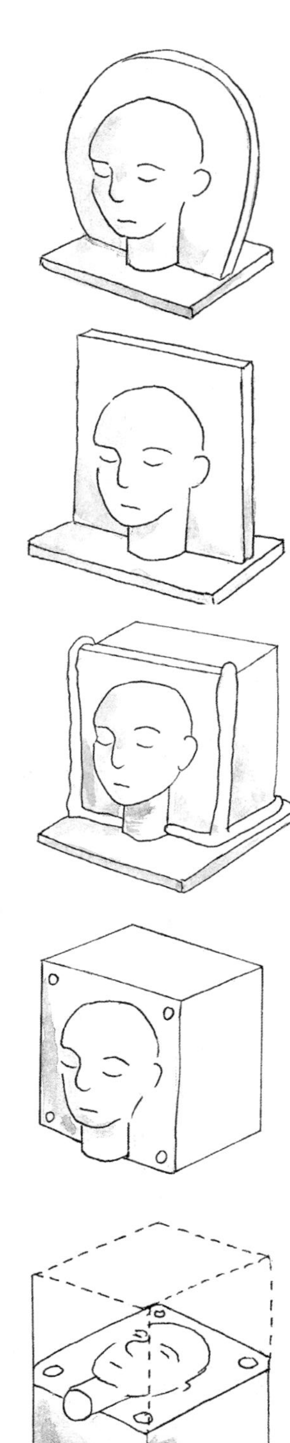

Making a plaster cast: the box method.

Dividing the head with Plasticine.

The divider trimmed to a rectangle.

A box to contain the plaster.

The first half of the cast with holes scooped out to aid later alignment.

Another box created around the plaster block for casting the front of the head.

three sides of a box to enclose the back of the head; the Plasticine divider becomes the fourth side. Where the cardboard meets the baseboard and the divider, seal all the edges with substantial strips of Plasticine so that the plaster cannot leak out, and the box, which is going to retain a significant amount of liquid plaster, does not collapse.

Mix the plaster and, as soon as it starts to thicken, pour it steadily into the box. Shake the baseboard gently with your free hand to release any trapped air bubbles.

When the plaster has set, carefully remove the cardboard and the Plasticine divider, making good any marks left on the head by the divider. Scoop a few shallow holes in the inside edge of the plaster block to facilitate accurate joining of the cast when finished. Smear the front of the head and the inside edge of the block, including the shallow holes, with petroleum jelly. Ensure there are no lumps of grease on any of the surfaces.

Place the block so that the head is face upwards and fold another piece of cardboard around it to box in the front of the head. Secure the cardboard with Plasticine and pour in the plaster, gently shaking the model, as before.

When the second half of the cast is set, remove the cardboard and scrape away any surplus plaster covering the join. Try to do this before the plaster sets rock hard but take care not to remove the cardboard too soon. When both sections of the cast are completely set, prise the two blocks apart very carefully. Remove the Plasticine, clean the cast and allow it to dry.

Casting a Rigid Head

The modelling materials described previously can be used to create heads in plaster casts but remember that if there is any undercutting, you may not be able to release the shell without breaking the cast. With most materials a very thorough coating of release agent is needed to prevent the model sticking to the cast. If petroleum jelly is used, ensure that every trace is removed from the head with methylated spirit before painting and finishing.

Petroleum jelly may be used for paste and paper or paper pulp, but damp tissue paper is recommended. Milliput requires petroleum jelly or a silicone spray such as Ambersil DP100/2. Because Milliput adheres so strongly, as a precaution you should coat the edges as well as the lining of the cast. Clingfilm, pressed firmly into the surface, is useful for lining the cast when muslin and plaster filler are used. Rhenoflex should not adhere to the cast at lower temperatures but always test it on a sample piece of cast material just to be sure there is no reaction with the particular type of cast you are using. Similarly, Varaform should not adhere at lower temperatures but, as a precaution, I would always line the mould with a piece of damp muslin, which must be used at higher temperatures. After casting, the muslin may be peeled gently from the shell or allowed to remain on the head as a base for coating. For casting with Jesmonite, plaster moulds must be sealed with shellac or polyurethane varnish. Fibreglass also needs a commercially produced separator.

Apply the chosen modelling material in accordance with the directions for use given previously. Press it firmly into each section of the cast. When the two shells are dry, remove them from the casts, insert any internal fixtures, and join them in the same way as a modelled head.

Latex rubber can be mixed with a hardener to create a rigid head but may be rather brittle if too thin. How to use it is described below for a flexible latex head.

Casting a Latex-Rubber Head

Liquid latex rubber is available in a variety of colours, qualities and types of mix. Use a fairly strong, soft toy mix or a grade used for hard rubber toys; white provides the best basis for colouring or painting. In order to achieve just the right consistency, you can mix different grades of latex in varying proportions. Some puppet makers report success in using cheaper types of latex from builders' merchants and adding a thickening agent. For some purposes you might colour the latex before use (*see* page 41). My own preference is to paint the head after it has been created.

If the cast has been used previously for making a rigid head, it is essential to clean it thoroughly to remove all traces of any release agent before using it with latex.

Generally, marionette heads are quite small. If you need a larger head, you must either make it much thicker, which will make it significantly heavier, or provide some form of internal support to maintain the shape. To achieve this, either glue a layer of foam rubber to the inside of the head or use the latex head as a mask and attach it to a skull shape created in foam rubber or polystyrene.

To make the head, join the two parts of the cast and secure them with strong rubber bands or cord, then seal the joint with Plasticine. Carefully pour the latex into the cast through the neck, holding the container close to the cast. This will reduce the risk of air bubbles. Tilt the cast as you pour so that the latex runs on to the inside surface, rather than dropping into the centre.

When it is approximately a quarter full, roll the cast in your hand and tap it gently to fill the hollows and remove any air bubbles; continue to roll the cast frequently as it is being filled. When it is full, leave the cast to stand; the level of rubber will drop somewhat so top it up periodically.

The latex forms a skin on the lining of the cast and the longer it is left in the cast the thicker it becomes. Forty-five minutes to an hour will often be sufficient but it depends on the particular rubber mix and the thickness required of the head. Some experimentation may be necessary at first.

When sufficient time has elapsed and the head has thickened, there will be a substantial quantity of liquid latex remaining in the centre of the cast. This is not wasted: pour it back into the container to use for another figure. To allow the rubber to dry, let the cast stand for at least twenty-four hours: again the actual time needed depends on the thickness of the rubber and the mix. The longer you leave the cast full of liquid latex, the longer the head will take to dry out properly. Heating does not seem to make any significant difference to this. If you open the

A head cast in latex rubber by the author: note the shallow holes and matching protrusions on the joining faces of the cast to aid registration.

cast too soon, you will have a squidgy mess rather than a beautiful head so it is better to err on the side of caution.

When you are ready to open the cast, first pour some talcum powder into the head through the neck. Shake the cast and blow the powder around inside, which will prevent the inner surfaces of the rubber sticking together. To ensure full coverage you should use a generous amount of powder and then pour out any surplus for future use.

Prise the plaster cast apart; usually it will come away from the back of the head, leaving the front section still in the cast. Remove the front section carefully, with a little manoeuvring if necessary. If the head has been allowed to become too thick it could lock in the cast as firmly as a rigid head. If there is a 'flash', or ridge, around the head from the join in the cast, trim it off with sharp scissors, a sharp craft knife or a razor blade, taking care not to slice into the head itself.

Leave the head to dry for at least a further twenty-four hours before painting it.

A carved marionette by the late John Wright. The eyeballs are painted entirely in a rich blue colour.

Eyes

Carved and Modelled Eyes

Eyes are often carved, modelled, or cast with the head and then painted at the same time as the head. Alternatives to natural-looking eyes can sometimes be very effective.

- The entire eyeball may be painted a deep colour such as

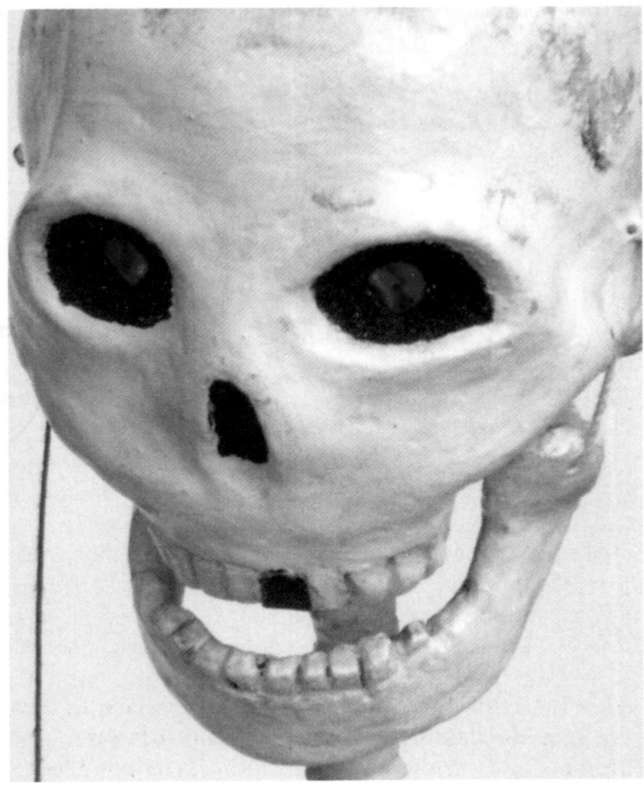

Hollow eye sockets may be painted a dark colour or covered with a reflective material. Skeleton modelled by Gordon Staight.

dark green, purple or blue and possibly varnished.

- Hollow eye sockets may be painted a dark colour, remaining matt or varnished, or they may be covered with a reflective material.
- Deep slits can be made in the eye sockets to produce heavy shadows.
- Painted and varnished wooden balls or beads may be glued into slotted eye sockets.
- Glass dolls' eyes can be used, but are too natural for most puppets.
- Torch bulbs screwed into bulb-holders and wired up to a battery and switch have been used, often behind a small piece of coloured lighting gel so that the eyes glow in a fierce, eerie or comical fashion.

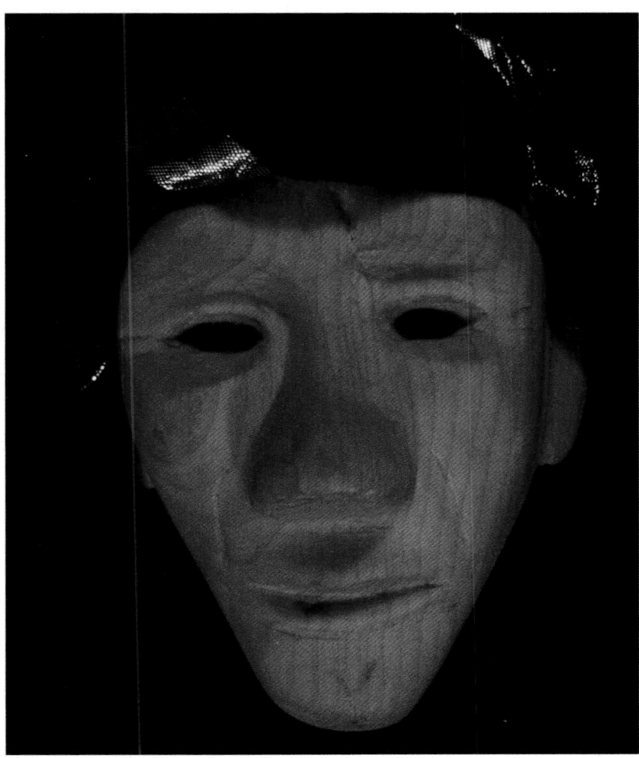

Manfred, carved in limewood, with deep slits for the eyes, by Gren Middleton, Movingstage Marionettes, for Byron's poetic drama of the same name. The gestation period for this production was fourteen years: 'It took this time to have the courage to tackle it, to determine how to do it, to adapt it for puppet theatre, and to construct the characters and the performance,' according to Middleton.

Moving Eyes

Moving eyes can be very expressive but, of course, only if visible to the audience and they tend to be used for circus or variety puppets rather than characters in plays. Ensure that there is sufficient space inside the head for the eye mechanism and note particularly the internal space needed if the puppet is to have moving eyes and a moving mouth.

Sgt Barker, the author's first marionette, has a modelled head with moving eyes and mouth.

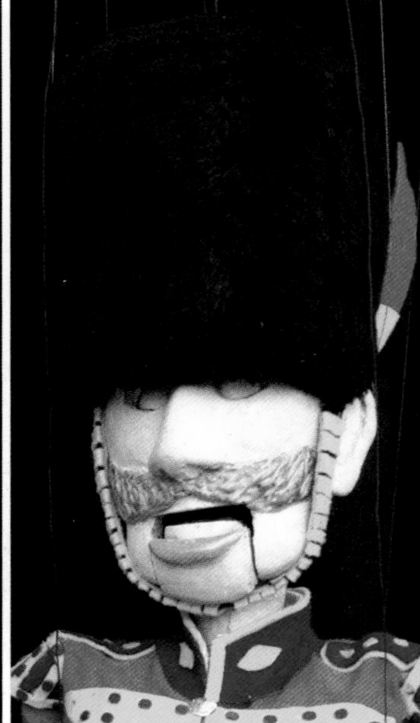

Inside the head: screws in the back of the wooden eyeballs are weighted with lead and a piece of cardboard has been used as a spacer between them. Thin dowels are used to restrict eye movement.

The techniques described below cover the main possibilities, though the straightforward closing eye is by far the most common. However, you may like to invent your own variations, like the performer who mounted the eyes on galvanized wire and designed the mechanism so that they could pop out of the head and then spring back into place!

Closing and Blinking Eyes

Moving eyes are achieved most easily with a modelled head, for which the mechanism is built in at an early stage of the head-making process. Make the eyes from two wooden balls; their size depends on the size of the head. If they are not pre-drilled, carefully drill a hole through the centre of each ball: if the hole is off-centre, it may adversely affect eye movement. Pivot the balls on a piece of 12 or 14 gauge galvanized wire, and use 12mm (½in) diameter dowelling, also drilled through the centre,

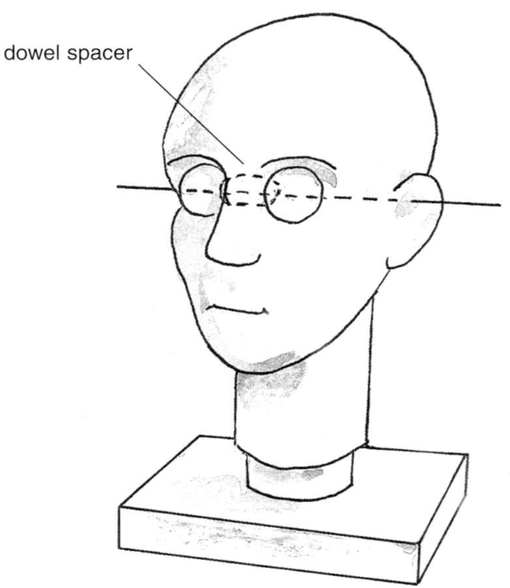

Wooden balls built into a Plasticine base in preparation for modelling.

to give the necessary spacing between the eyes. Sometimes, larger balls in a modest-sized head will need very little spacing and you may need to improvise accordingly.

Place the wooden balls and spacer on the wires, coat them with release agent and build them into the Plasticine model. Model the head as described previously, leaving a suitable amount of eyeball uncovered. Let the ends of the wire project through the sides of the head. When the head is dry, cut it open and take out the Plasticine, then remove and thoroughly clean the balls.

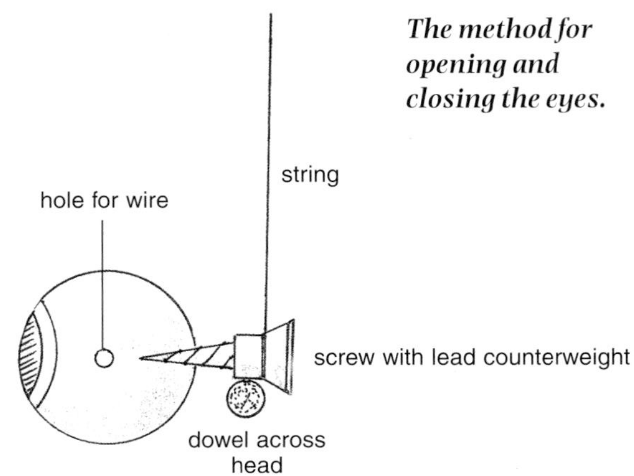

The method for opening and closing the eyes.

In the back of each ball fix a screw weighted with lead to keep the eyes open. Some puppet makers use a spring instead of a weight but the weighted screw works perfectly well for most purposes. Replace the balls in the head, cut the wire to the required length and fasten it in the head by covering the ends with the modelling material. You might add a little more material to the inside of the head around the wire for extra security.

To stop the eyes opening too far, fix a thin dowel rod across the head for the screws to rest on. Ensure that the eyes can be fully closed from this position. If the dowel is set too high, some of the eyeball might remain visible when the screw is fully raised by the control string. Attach a string to the end of each screw. Raising the string closes the eyes; they will resume the open position when the string is released.

The eye strings pass through two holes drilled in the top of the head. To prevent fraying, wax the strings thoroughly with beeswax. Some puppet makers also glue a small piece of rubber tubing into the hole, but I find waxing sufficient provided the hole is finished cleanly and the string runs straight up to the control. If it runs up to the hole at an angle before going vertically to the control, then it will rub on the edge of the hole and is more likely to fray over time, though waxing does delay the deterioration.

Separate eye strings enable the eyes to be operated either together or independently but sometimes the screws in the balls are replaced by a single piece of galvanized wire, appropriately weighted and bent into a 'U' shape. A single string is then used to control them.

If the modelling material shrinks and the eyes jam in the head, this can usually be put right by running a sharp craft knife around the inside of the eye sockets. Otherwise you will need to open up the head to gain access to the eyes.

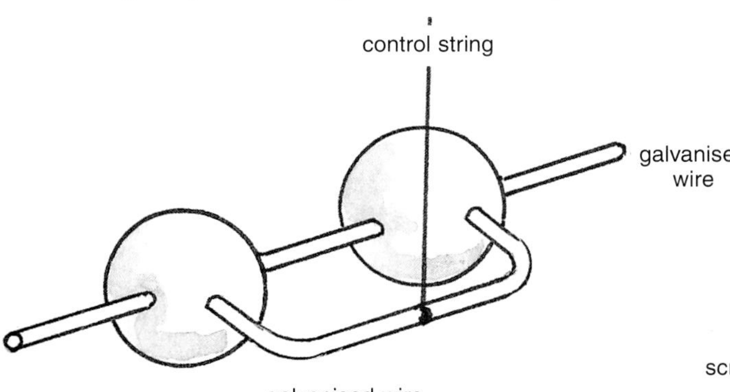

Operating the eyes together rather than singly.

If the eyes are for a carved head, you will need to cut open the back of the head and hollow out the inside to allow the eyes to be fitted. When cutting the eye cavity and hollowing out the inside of the eye socket, take great care. You need smooth surfaces and a good, clean fit so that the eyeball sits securely in the socket without jamming. The actual eye mechanism is the same as for a modelled head.

Swivelling Eyes

In order for eyes to swivel, the wooden balls must be mounted on vertical, rather than horizontal, wires with short dowels or other supports below them to maintain the correct position. Fasten screws into the back of the balls and attach a control string horizontally, securing it to each of the screws. Fix screw-eyes or other suitable fastenings in each side of the head. Thread the ends of the control string up through the screw-eyes and the holes drilled in the head, then attach them to a control bar that is pivoted on the main control.

Rocking the control bar will cause the eyes to swivel. The bar needs elastic attached between it and the main control in order to return the bar and the eyes to the resting position when released.

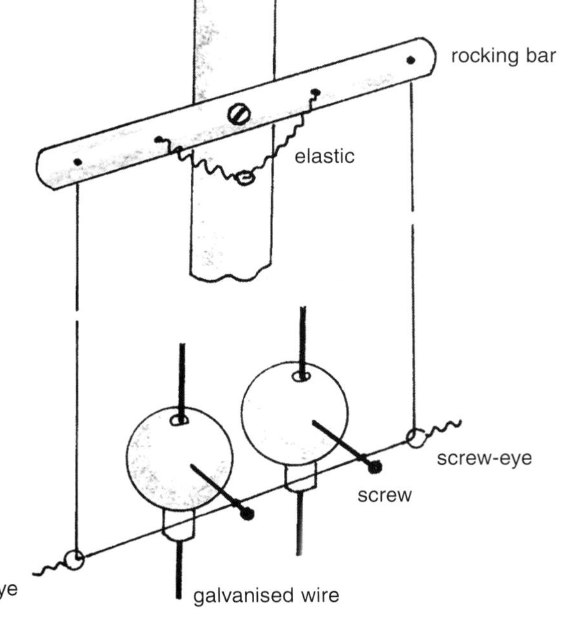

Swivelling eyes.

Cross-Eyes

Although it is possible to amend the swivelling mechanism described above to make the eyes move in opposite directions, an effective alternative is to paint one pair of eyes on the eyeballs when in the open position and to paint a second, cross-eyed set on the eyeballs when in the closed position. To make the eyes cross, just pull the string to 'close' them.

Moving Mouths

Marionettes often do not need to have a moving mouth, even for plays where they have a good deal to say. In fact, trying to keep a marionette's mouth moving in synchronization with speech can look unconvincing and may distract the puppeteer from the general manipulation of the puppet.

I do have a few variety puppets for whom a moving mouth seemed appropriate: a compere who has a little, but not a great deal, to say; a few animals, such as a dog that barks and needs to pick up items with its mouth; a strong man who groans and puffs when trying to lift the weights (his eyes also roll) and one or two characters who actually say comparatively little but perhaps give a gasp of surprise or 'eat' something.

Willie the clown by the author. Cross-eyes are achieved by having a second set of eyes painted on the eyeballs instead of eyelids. Note the run-through string used to raise a hand to the mouth.

Access to Internal Mechanisms

When a head has any internal mechanism there is a risk that you may have to cut it open at some point. To facilitate future access, during construction you can cut away a section at the back of the head under the hairline and glue this back in place. If you need access, run a sharp knife around the join and remove the panel. Replace it when the repair is accomplished.

If the head has a hat secured to it, you could leave the top of the head open and remove the hat to gain access to the mechanism.

A Moving Mouth for a Modelled Head

Model the head over a Plasticine base (*see* pages 23-5). When dry, cut it open and remove the Plasticine. Carefully cut out the lower lip and chin in an 'L' shape and thoroughly clean the inside surface. Cut a wooden block to the required size and glue it inside the chin. Fill any gaps with the modelling material.

Replace the chin in the head and drill a hole through the jaw into the side of the block. The hole should be positioned so that the majority of the weight of the block is to the rear of the hole, not near the chin. If the drill does not reach through the opposite jaw, remove the chin and finish drilling the hole. Replace the chin and insert a piece of galvanized wire right across the head. Use this it to mark the inside of the opposite jaw, which will enable you to align the matching hole accurately.

Pivot the chin in the head on 12 or 14 gauge galvanized wire. If it does not move freely or displays any possibility of dislodging, you may need to add dowelling spacers (drilled through the centre lengthways) on either side of the block to keep it in place. Cut the wire to size and seal the holes in the jaw with the modelling material.

Attach a string to the back of the block for opening the mouth. The string passes through the top of the head up to the control. The weight of the block acts as a counterbalance to close the mouth. A screw weighted with lead may be attached to the back of the block to increase the weight if necessary. Rub the string with beeswax to prevent fraying.

Carving a Moving Mouth

The head must be cut open and the inside hollowed out to accommodate a moving mouth. It may be possible sometimes to saw and chisel out the mouth section and replace this section inside the head, appropriately pivoted, but in most cases it is necessary to cut away the mouth and to construct the replacement block separately.

The block is pivoted in the head and controlled in the same way as described above for a modelled head.

Constructing a moving mouth.

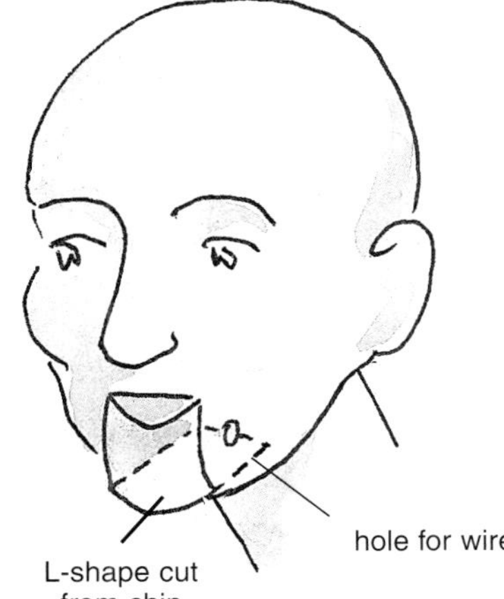

The mouth shape is cut from the chin.

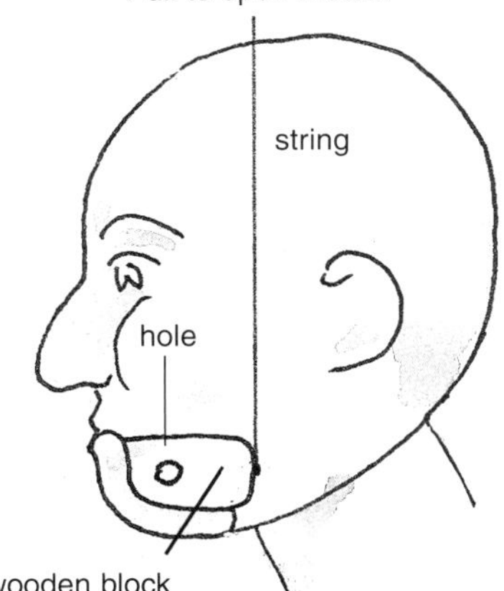

A wooden block used for pivoting the chin and as a counterweight to close the mouth.

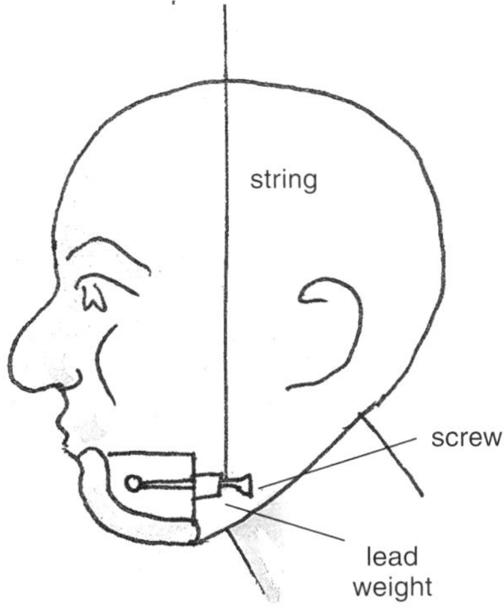

A screw weighted with lead used as a counterweight.

Painting and Finishing

General Principles

In order to match skin tones, paint the head and all areas of exposed skin after the puppet is assembled but before it is costumed. In order to enhance the modelling, faces should be considered in terms of stage make-up and lighting, rather than natural colours, but paint in good natural light so that the true colours are clear.

Generally, receding areas are darker and frontal areas or highlights are lighter; to paint them the opposite way tends to neutralize the modelling and therefore the characterization. It is a good idea to mix a fairly light shade of the basic skin colour for an overall application and then develop this with lighter and darker shades or other colours.

One can purchase ready-mixed flesh colours but they usually need some modification to suit individual requirements. Varying quantities of white, yellow, red and brown help to achieve appropriate skin tones.

Eyeballs can be any colour but mostly they will be white. Pure white can make the eye appear to be staring, so a slightly cream colour may be preferable. Lips can remain matt or be given a satin sheen, and occasionally a darker lip-lining colour may be used.

Materials and Methods

To prepare the surface for painting, wood will need priming and papier-mâché can be sealed with a coat of PVA glue. Apply an undercoat of white emulsion paint, taking care not to leave brush strokes. When dry, lightly sand and apply a second coat to achieve a very smooth surface.

For the actual colouring, avoid using any paints with a gloss or shiny finish as they look unnatural and will glare under stage lighting. If a surface should appear too shiny, dust it lightly with talcum power before it is completely dry. Shake and blow the surplus away and dust off any remaining powder with a very soft, large paintbrush but take great care not to smudge the paint. Continue to add and remove the powder until the desired effect is achieved.

My own preference is for acrylic paints. Although they can be diluted with water, for best results they should be thinned with a matt polymer medium, which produces a good finish. When mixing shades that require large quantities of white, emulsion is a cheap and satisfactory substitute for acrylic paint.

Painting on fibreglass requires polyurethane paints.

When painting on latex rubber it is necessary to mix acrylic paint with the acrylic matt medium, or a mixture

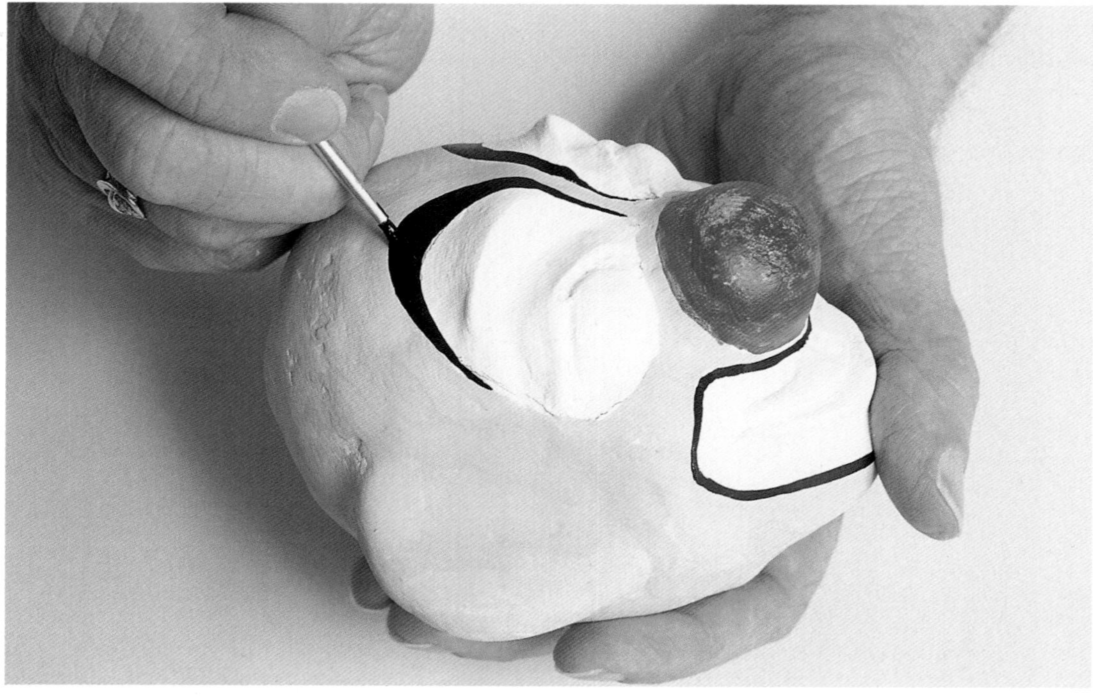

Painting the head: note the clean, simple lines.

of water and medium. Alternatively, mix it with liquid latex in equal proportions, or with PVA glue using one part paint to three parts glue. Do not apply the paint too thickly or it will crack when the rubber flexes. Clean the brushes with acetone immediately after use.

Rubber parts can also be given a base colour by adding proprietary rubber dyes, thick emulsion paint, aniline dyes, or liquid acrylic paint to the liquid latex before it is used for casting. Test it first with a small quantity and note carefully the proportions used, bearing in mind that it may appear a slightly darker shade when dry. Mix the latex and the colouring carefully to minimize air bubbles, as these will spoil the latex part when casting. Leave the latex to stand in a sealed container for at least a day before use to allow any remaining air bubbles to disperse.

For any parts that might need varnishing, such as eyeballs or lips, acrylic varnish is recommended. When wet it has a milky appearance but it does dry clear.

Hair

Hair may be modelled, carved, or created with materials of different textures. Glue such materials directly to the head or make a skullcap from a fairly stiff material and glue or stitch the material to it.

Attach the 'hair' starting at the base of the skull and work upwards and inwards towards the crown. There is a wide variety of suitable materials ranging from string to rug or knitting wools, embroidery silks, crochet thread, synthetic fur fabric, or even ostrich feathers – but not real hair or fur.

String may be used it its natural state or dyed to any colour. Knitting wools may be used as they are, but it is sometimes helpful to cut lengths and fluff them up with a brush or comb.

These materials can also be used for eyebrows but it is usual to paint them. Even if the hair is fair, one usually makes the eyebrows darker or they will not show on stage.

A different style of painting, and hair created from plaited wool.

4 Construction and Costume

It is important to design the whole puppet and be clear about joints required before you commence construction of the body. You need to know the neck, waist, shoulder and hip joints before you start on the body; and the shoulder, elbow, wrist, hip, knee and ankle joints before you embark upon making the limbs. When determining joints, aim for smoothness and flexibility, with restricted movement where appropriate, and try to avoid joints that rattle. Sometimes a small piece of electrical tape or sticking-plaster wound around an offending metal pin or loop will stop the rattle but this should not be at the expense of movement.

Small boy by John Roberts, PuppetCraft. An unclothed figure, except for shoes which are carved and painted. The marionette is jointed to give standard movements, with the addition of a moving mouth. The puppet is a caricature of the young boy for whom it was made.

Heads, Necks and Neck Joints

Heads and Necks

A carved head created with the neck attached provides a fixing point for the joint with the body.

The methods for creating hollow heads with attached necks necessitate plugging the neck with a dowel to

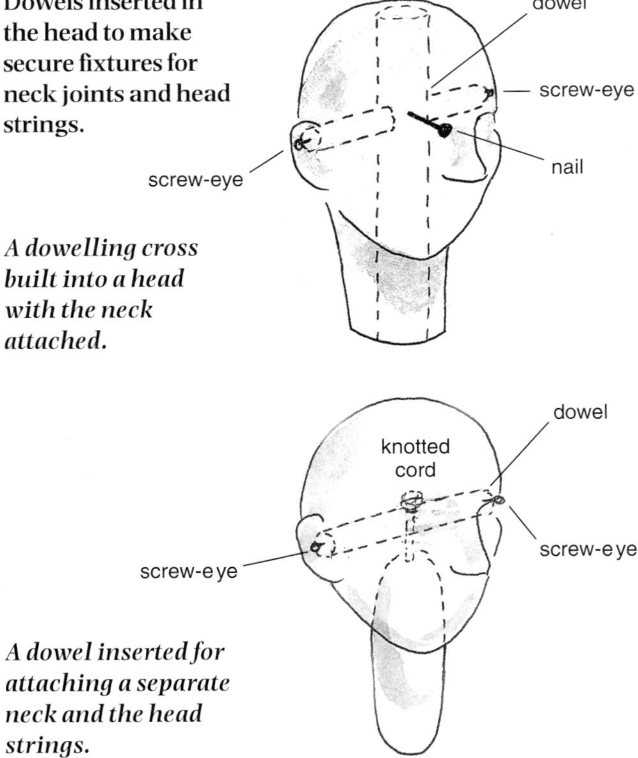

Dowels inserted in the head to make secure fixtures for neck joints and head strings.

A dowelling cross built into a head with the neck attached.

A dowel inserted for attaching a separate neck and the head strings.

provide a means of effecting the joint with the body. Shape the dowel to ensure a good fit and glue it in place. Fill any remaining gaps with more of the head material, which may be extended under the neck plug for extra security.

If the head has any internal mechanism, the plug should be the same length as the neck. If it has no such mechanism, the dowel may extend to the top of the head if required and can be used to support the horizontal dowel described below.

If the ears are not sufficiently strong to support the weight of the puppet or if they are not in a suitable position for the head strings to be attached, secure a dowel across the head and fix screw-eyes into the ends, through the head shell. If a vertical dowel extends the full length of the head, glue the horizontal dowel into a hole drilled in it.

A head with a separate neck may also require a horizontal dowel secured widthwise to effect the neck joint or for attaching screw-eyes for head strings if the ears are not suitable for this.

For the neck joints and the positioning of the head strings you need to identify the point of balance for the head. To do this, hold the head lightly but securely between the tips of your index fingers near its ears, so that it can turn but not fall. Adjust the position of your fingers until you find the point of balance where the head does not dip forwards or backwards. For more precision you might use the points of nails or dividers but take care not to damage the head. Mark the position for future reference.

Neck Joints

When the Neck is Built on to the Head

Join the neck to the body in one of the following ways, as appropriate to the body construction.

- Thread a loop of cord through a hole in the body and through a screw-eye in the base of the neck; knot and glue the ends of the cord. This method is suitable for laminated or latex bodies with a central wooden core.
- Drill two holes in the body, one to each side from the neck to the underarms. Countersink the holes underneath the arms. Thread a loop of cord through a screw-eye in the base of the neck and carefully thread the ends down through the holes. Knot and glue the ends of the cord, pressing them

Neck joints.

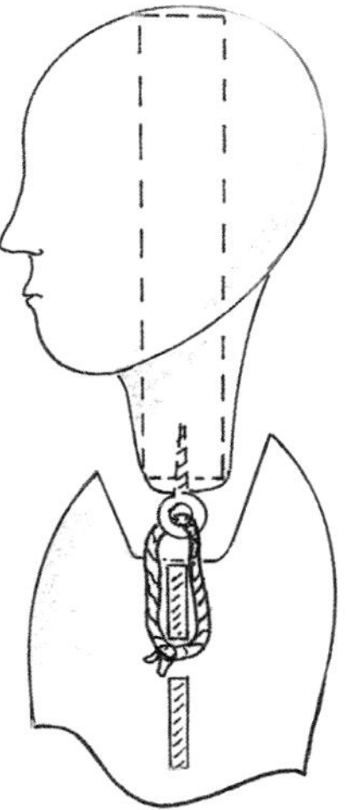

A screw-eye and cord joint with a padded plywood body.

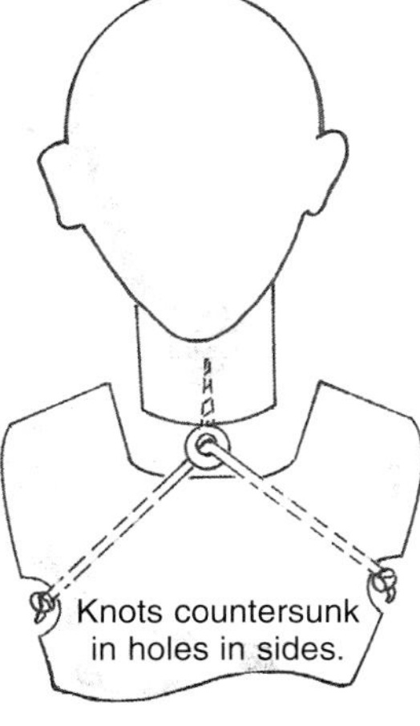

A screw-eye and cord joint with a rigid body.

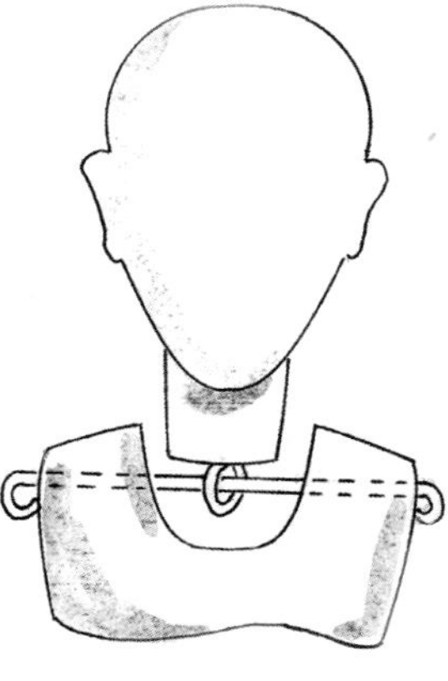

A screw-eye and galvanized wire joint. The looped ends of the wire can be used for attaching the arms.

Neck joints.

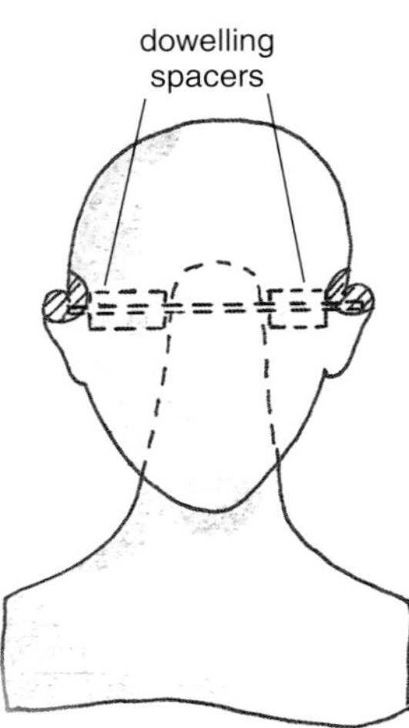

A wire through the neck, secured in the head, restricts head movement to nodding only.

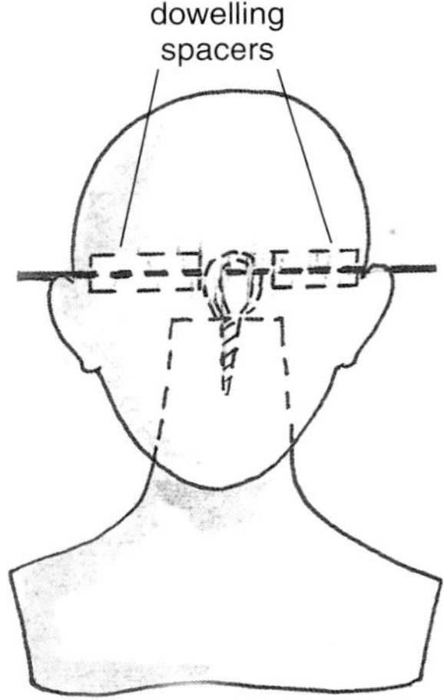

Wire through a screw-eye in the top of the neck permits nodding and some turning.

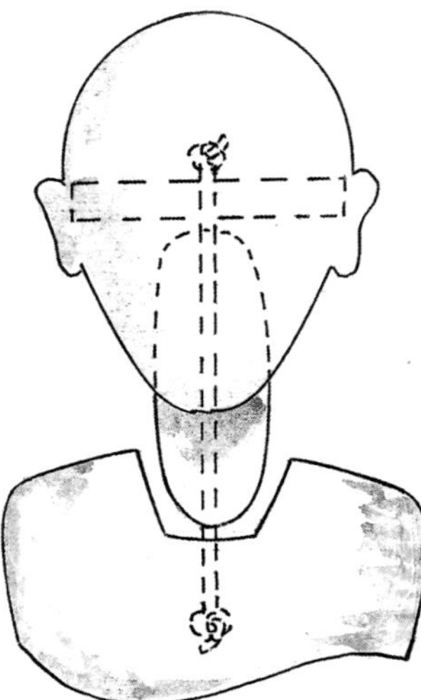

A neck that is separate from head and body, attached by cord, is recommended as it allows very flexible movement.

firmly into the countersunk holes. This method is suitable for solid bodies.

- Secure the neck in the top of the body with a piece of strong galvanized wire, the ends of which can be looped for attaching the arms. To permit turning, pass the wire through a screw-eye in the base of the neck; if you wish to restrict it from turning, pass the wire through the neck. This method is suitable for solid and hollow bodies.

With solid wooden bodies it is possible to have screw-eyes in the base of the neck and the top of the body joined by cord. However, it is not recommended and interlocked screw-eyes are strongly discouraged because of their potential rattling and the possibility of the head becoming locked in an awkward position.

When the Neck is Built on to the Body

When constructing the body, ensure that the neck is sufficiently strong and secure for the joint with the head. This joint is probably best used when the body is carved or modelled on a central core that remains inside the body.

Fasten a screw-eye in the top of the neck if the head is to turn, or drill a hole from side to side through the neck for a restricted neck joint that allows nodding but not turning. Drill a hole in either side of the head at the point of balance.

Insert a length of strong galvanized wire through these holes and through the screw-eye or the hole in the neck. If spacers are needed to hold the neck in position, drill holes through two short dowels and slip these on to the wire on either side of the neck. Cut the wire to length and secure it in the head with glue and more of the head material or filler as appropriate.

When the Neck is Separate from the Head and Body

Carve the neck in wood or use a large diameter dowel shaped with tools or built up with a modelling material. The top and bottom of the neck can be joined inside the head and body using any of the methods described above but the most flexible method, which gives very satisfactory movement, utilizes a cord running through a hole drilled vertically through the neck. Attach the ends of the cord to a dowel inside the head; pass them through a hole in the body, then knot and glue. Alternatively, the cord may be looped with both ends threaded through holes drilled in a solid body, as described above.

Bodies and Waist Joints

Bodies

A Fabric Body

While it is possible to construct an entire marionette from fabric, this is not a common technique. However, occasionally it may be appropriate to fashion the body in the same way as the old-time marionettes, which were mainly carved but with the upper arms and central body made of fabric. Use a strong linen, calico or canvas for the body tube. Pad it with fabric or small pieces of foam rubber and tack it to wooden shoulder and hip blocks. If required, run a drawstring through holes around the body and gather it up a little to form a waist.

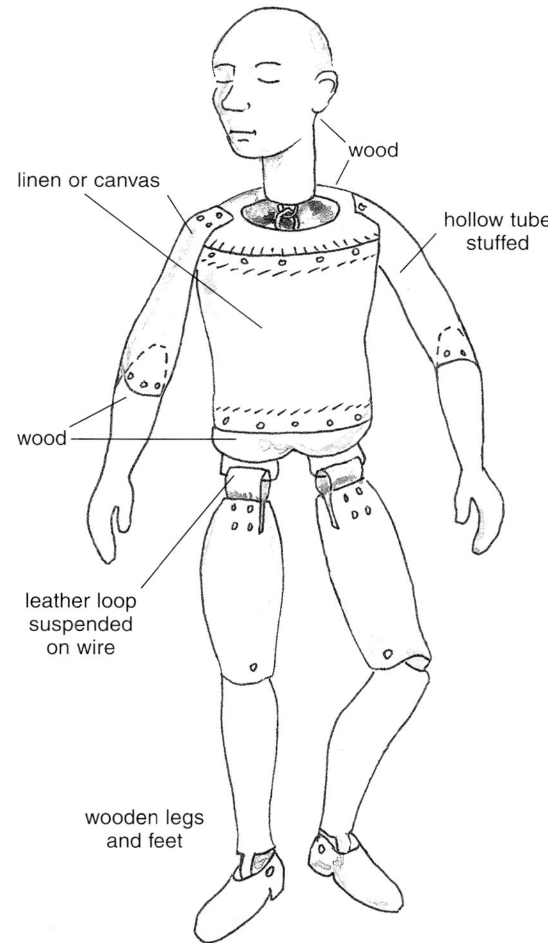

An 'old-time' marionette with a strong linen or canvas body and linen upper arms.

A Carved Body

Carve the body using the techniques described for carved heads (*see* page 21–3). Follow the shapes detailed for bodies throughout this section. You might need to hollow the thorax from underneath in order to reduce its weight but have regard for the waist joint before embarking upon this.

A wood and foam rubber body. Note that balsa wood is a good alternative to foam rubber.

Foam rubber is glued to a plywood centre piece and trimmed to shape.

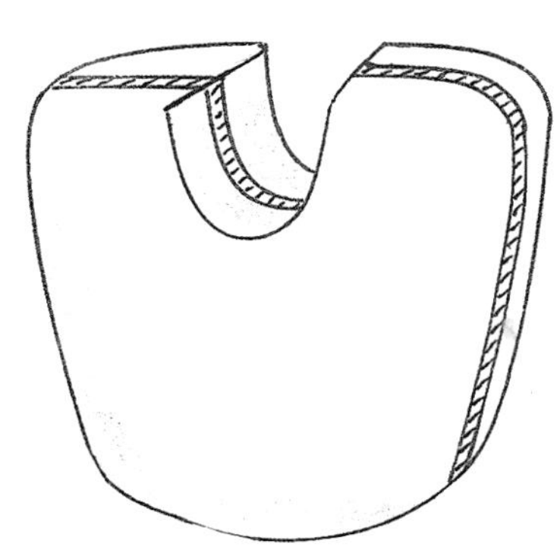

The shaded parts are cut from the wooden block to form the pelvis.

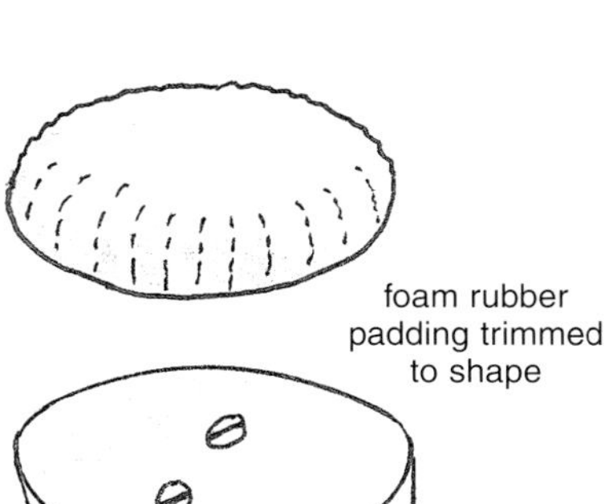

Two pieces of shaped wood are joined and padded with foam rubber for the pelvis.

Normally one would use a wood such as lime or Jelutong but it is possible also to make the body from balsa wood, which is very easy to cut and to shape with rasps. Having achieved the basic shape, complete the detail with glasspaper, finishing with a fine quality grade.

A Laminated Body

Make the thorax in layers over a firm central core of plywood that is cut to shape before applying the additional layers. You will often find it useful at the outset to drill four holes in the core near the neck, waist and shoulders and to secure cords to these for effecting joints later.

Build up the body shape by gluing blocks of foam rubber or balsa wood to the front and back of the plywood. Shape foam rubber with scissors; small snips are better than trying to cut large chunks. Shape balsa wood with rasps and glasspaper.

Make the pelvis in a 'T' shape. Either saw two sections from a block of wood to form the shape and round off the sharp corners, or glue and screw together two pieces of wood in the 'T' shape. Glue foam rubber or balsa wood to this base and shape it as required.

A Modelled Body

Model the body using one of the techniques described for heads (*see* pages 23-9). For extra strength, apply the modelling material to a basic shape of balsa wood or polystyrene, which remains inside the body.

A Cast Body

Model the two parts of the body in Plasticine on dowels and take a plaster cast (*see* pages 30-2). It is a good idea to build out the upper dowel a little with Plasticine on both the thorax and the pelvis to create a slightly wider hole. When the Plasticine is removed from the cast, the dowels will leave holes in the plaster through which latex rubber can be poured and also holes in the body parts that can be used for joining them.

Cast the body in one of the materials described for casting heads (*see* pages 32-3). For latex rubber, Plasticine should be used to seal the joints around the cast and to plug the lower hole in each section. This will retain the latex in the cast and when you wish to drain off the surplus, removal of the plug will facilitate the flow of latex. For the body parts, allow the latex to form a fairly thick layer so that it will maintain its shape when the puppet is assembled.

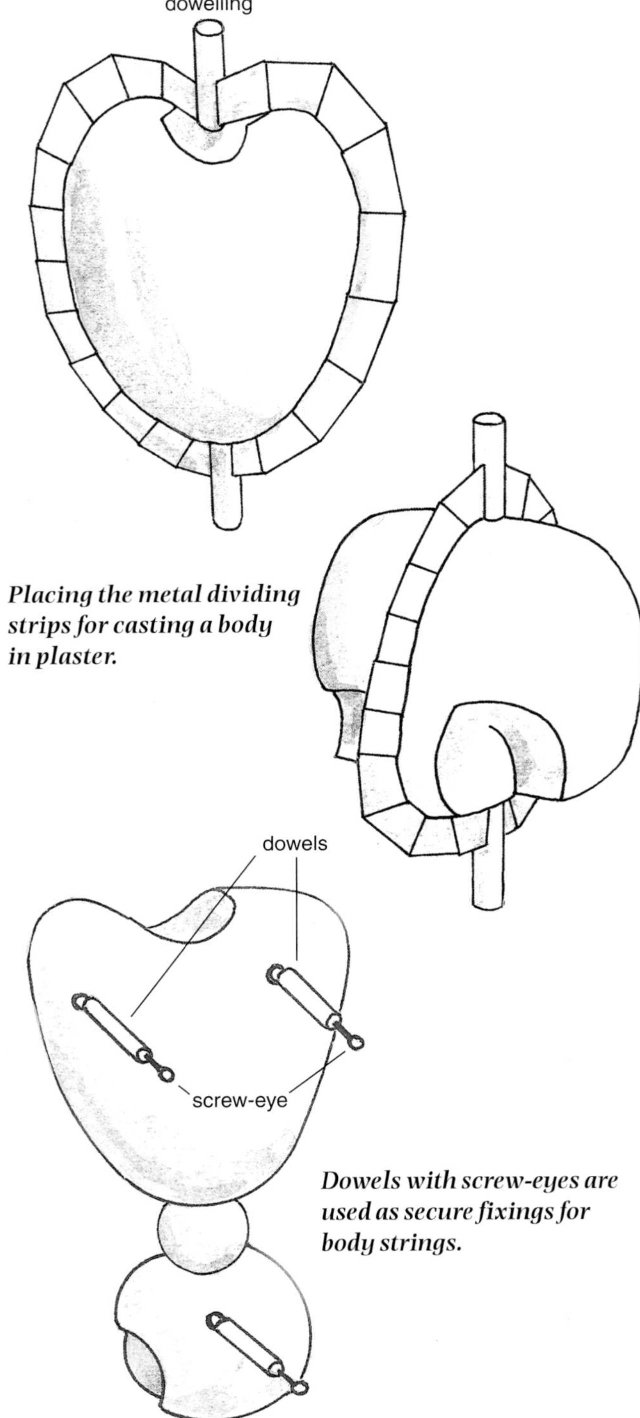

Placing the metal dividing strips for casting a body in plaster.

Dowels with screw-eyes are used as secure fixings for body strings.

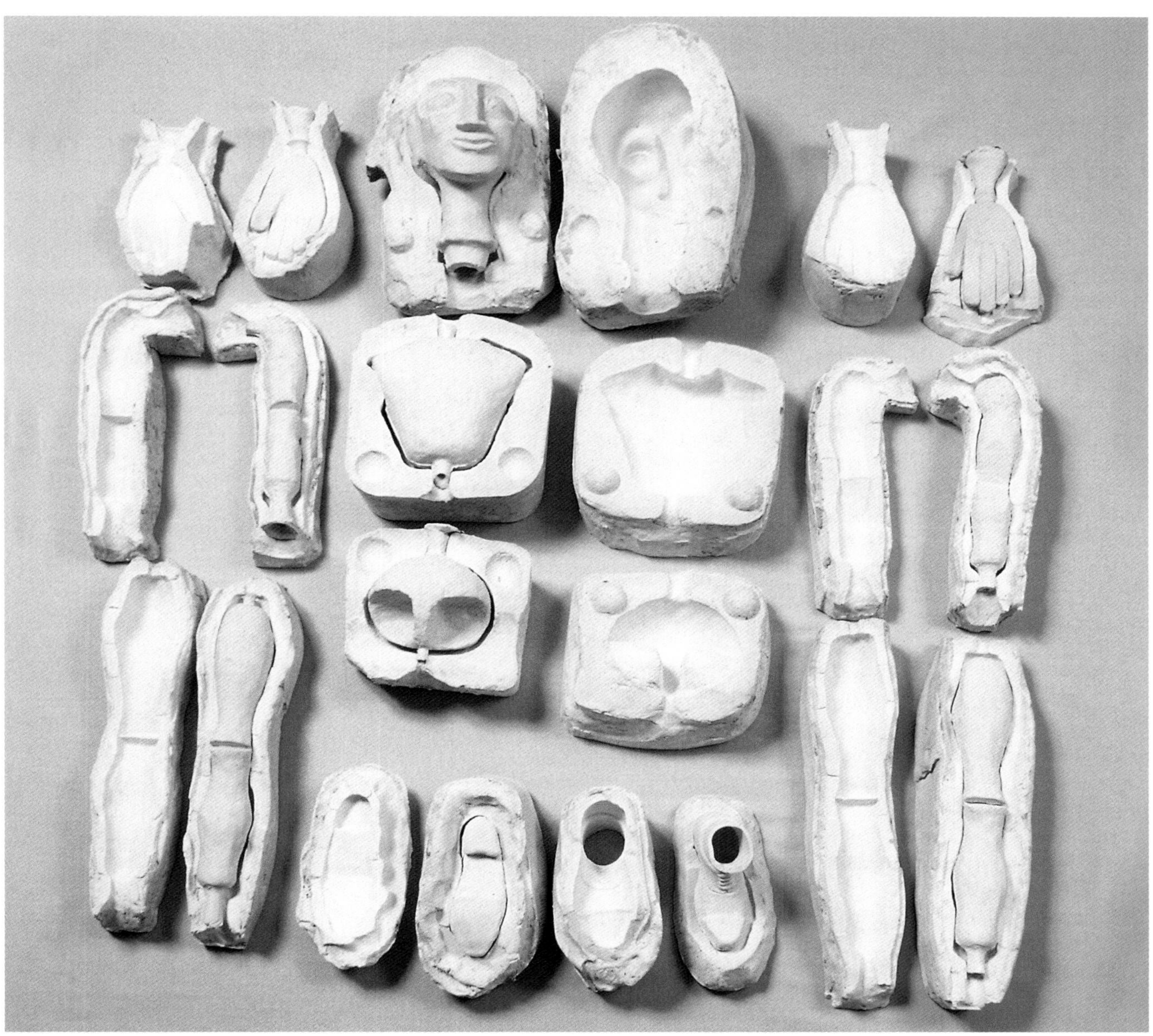

A marionette made entirely from latex rubber and the plaster casts used to create the separate parts.

Fixing Points for Strings

All bodies need secure fastening points for attaching the control strings. Small screw-eyes, which should be glued as well as screwed in place, are suitable for some materials. Others will require additional measures.

The solid core of a laminated body may be drilled to accept the string if the position is suitable.

Padded bodies such as foam rubber or balsa wood may have dowelling inserts with screw-eyes in the ends. Drill a hole in the balsa wood or through the wooden core of a foam rubber body and glue the dowels in the holes. Angle the holes upwards from the outside so that the control strings cannot pull out the dowels. Use the same technique for bodies modelled on top of a core

This marionette, carved by the late John Wright for the Puppet Centre collection, has wedge-shaped segments at the waist with cords running through from the thorax to the pelvis.

that will not retain screw-eyes such as polystyrene or balsa wood.

For latex-rubber bodies, an inner plywood shape may provide a fixing point or screw-eyes can be attached to a strip of wood glued inside the shoulders. Alternatively, attach the string to a small button and use a needle to pull the string and button through the hole where the neck joins. Push the needle out through the body at the rear of the shoulders, leaving the button inside as a fixture. If this is not possible, or to replace a string, insert the string and button through a slit cut into the back and reseal the slit with glue afterwards.

Waist Joints

There are several methods for making waist joints, but the one method that is not recommended is interlocked screw-eyes.

Cord Joints

Two versions of a simple cord joint work very well, especially with carved or modelled bodies. One uses cord, in effect, to suspend the pelvis from the thorax (see the 'small boy' on page 42). Drill two holes in each side of the thorax, one close to the front and the other near the back; angle the holes downwards. Drill two more holes down through each side of the pelvis and countersink the lower end of the holes. On each side of the body, insert the ends of a loop of cord through the holes in the thorax and the pelvis, and knot the ends.

Alternatively, suspend the pelvis in the same way but insert wedge-shaped segments between the thorax and the pelvis. Arrange them so that the thick end of the wedge is at the back and the thin end at the front.

Ball Joints

Marionettes often move more effectively if a wooden ball is built into the waist to give a little more flexibility between thorax and pelvis. Always allow for the size of the ball to be used when determining the size of the thorax and pelvis. Use a pre-drilled ball or carefully drill a hole through the centre of the ball. Thread cord through the ball and through holes or a screw-eye in the body sections. Knot the cord and seal with glue. This method is suitable for laminated bodies.

To join latex-rubber body parts, thread two small wooden balls or large beads on to a length of cord, one on either side of a larger wooden ball. Knot and glue the ends of the cord. Glue one bead into the base of the thorax and another into the top of the pelvis.

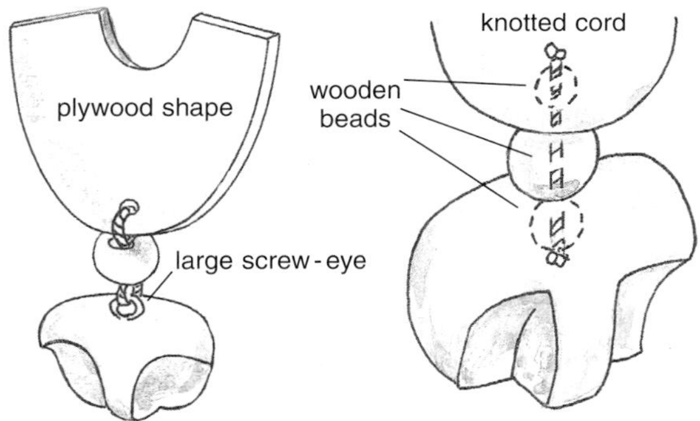

Ball joint at the waist.

A ball joint for latex-rubber bodies.

For carved and modelled bodies, make the body with holes or indentations in the pelvis and thorax to accommodate a large wooden ball. Drill two parallel holes down through the ball with the distance between them roughly equivalent to the radius of the ball. Drill matching holes up through the pelvis, emerging at the sides, and down through the pelvis, emerging near the tops of the legs. Countersink the holes. On each side, thread a cord through the body sections and the ball; knot the ends of the cords where they emerge from the body. Sink the knots in the body and seal them with glue. Fill the holes if the body is to be unclothed.

Ball joint at the waist.

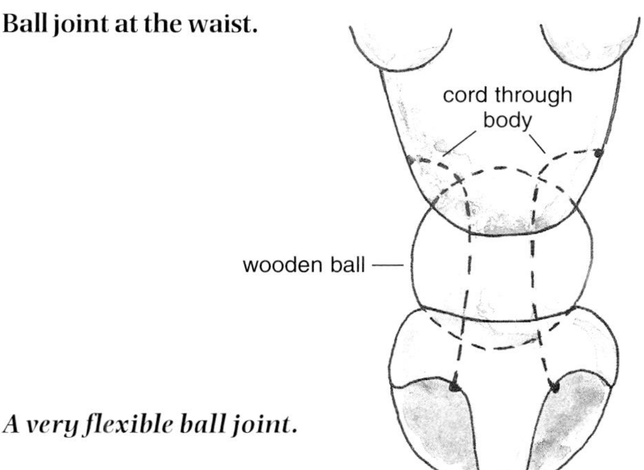

A very flexible ball joint.

Leather Joints

Leather, real or synthetic, produces a smoothly moving joint for bodies that do not require any twisting movement at the waist. Use with solid bodies or bodies that have a firm central core of plywood.

For solid bodies, cut matching slots in the two sections to be joined. Cut a strip of leather to the required size. The length should be exactly the combined depth of the two slots plus the intended space between thorax and pelvis. It should be a little wider than the body so that you have something to hold when making the joint. Apply glue to the front and back of the part of the leather that is to fit inside the thorax. Holding the edges of the leather, slide it into the slot in the thorax; it should be a snug fit. Repeat the process for the pelvis with the other end of the leather. Secure the leather further with nails and trim away the waste leather at the sides with a sharp blade.

For a more restricted joint, permitting only forward bending, use the above method with the following differences. Cut away a wedge shape from the front of the thorax and pelvis. Cut the leather the combined depth of the two slots so that when it is glued and nailed in place, the rear of the thorax and pelvis are in contact with each other.

A variation of the leather joint can be used to make waist and hip joints with a single piece. Cut a strip of leather long enough to run the entire length of the body and, if required, to extend beyond this to make the joints with the legs. Glue the front and back of the thorax and pelvis to the leather and slit the leather below the pelvis to create two strips for attaching the legs.

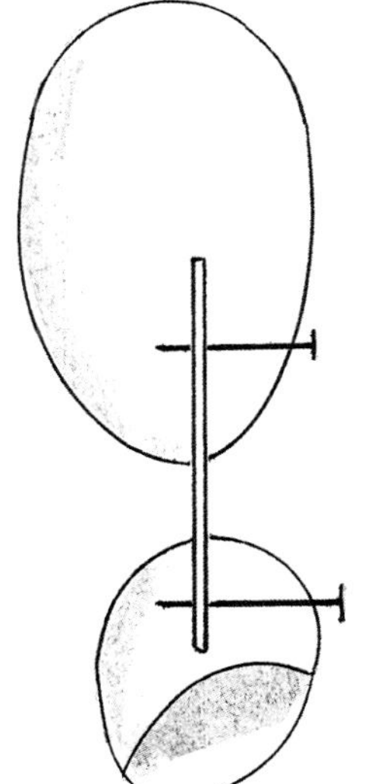

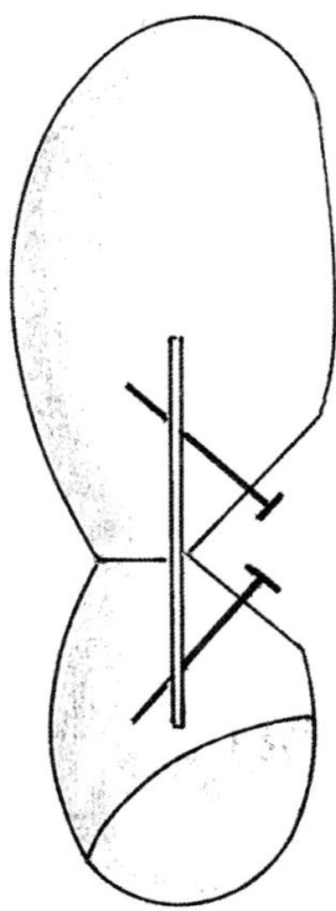

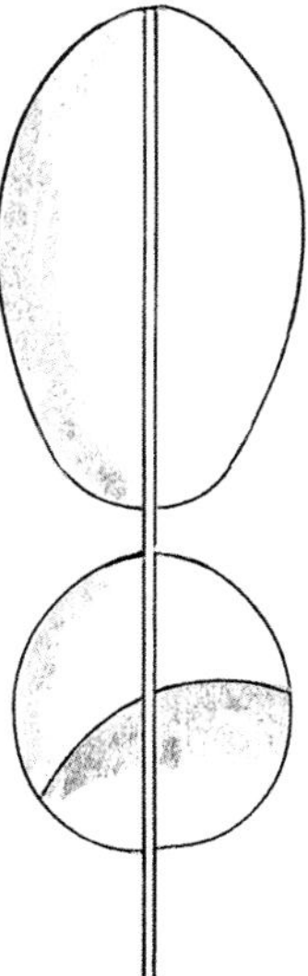

Leather waist joints. Left: ***A leather joint that permits forward and backward movement but not turning.*** **Middle:** ***A restricted joint that allows only forward movement.*** **Right:** ***A central strip of leather used for both waist and hip joints.***

A Body in Three Parts
This joint, which allows only sideways movement, is most often used for humorous effect in a novelty act. Make the body in three sections: chest, pelvis, and a larger central section incorporating the waist. Leave the chest and pelvis hollow and shape the top and bottom of the centre section to fit into the other two parts. Insert the ends of the centrepiece into the chest and pelvis and join the three sections with two long nails so that the body is free to pivot sideways.

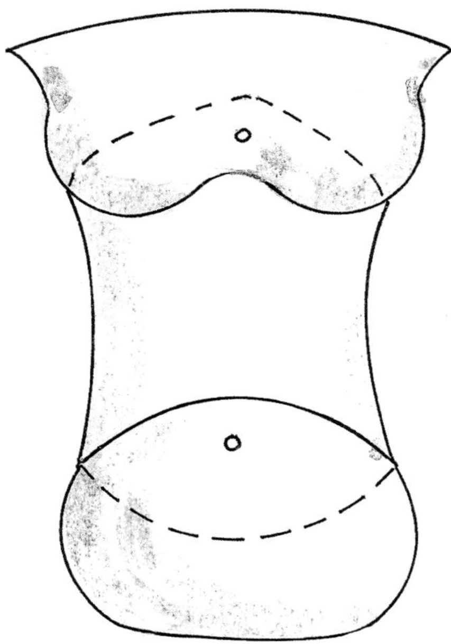

A body in three sections.

Arms, Elbows and Shoulder Joints

Arms

Arms can be made from stuffed tubes of cloth, and have even been made from very thick rope that remained visible to the audience. However, they are generally made by one of the methods described below.

Latex-Rubber Arms
Cast the arms in latex rubber as described for heads (*see* pages 30-4). When you make the plaster cast, insert dowels into the Plasticine models at the wrist and at right angles at the shoulders. Remember to make one shoulder dowel turn to the left and the other to the right. To facilitate bending, make a 'V'-shaped groove in the Plasticine model across the back of the elbow. To divide the model for casting, follow a line along the inside and outside of the arm when positioned as if the palms were forward facing.

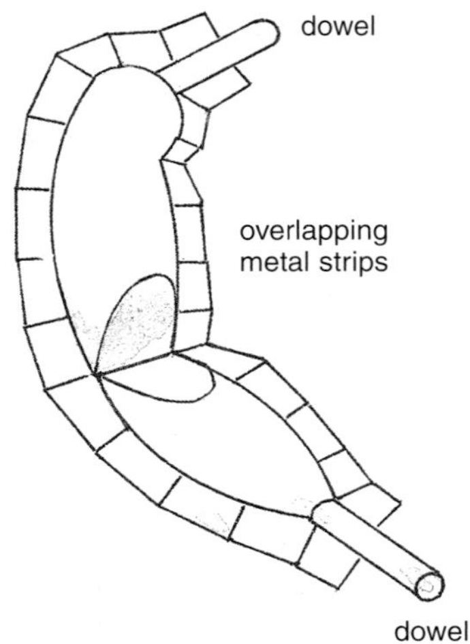

A plasticine model with metal dividers inserted for making a plaster cast.

Having cast the rubber arm, use a sharp blade to make a slit in the groove across the back of the elbow joint in order to allow the arm to bend. Take care not to cut the rubber at the front of the joint. Provided the latex is reasonably thick (quite firm but still somewhat flexible), the joint will last for many years. I have cast rubber limbs that are good after twenty years, though quite thin puppet parts have perished or become brittle and cracked over this period.

Wooden Arms
Arms are best carved from the same type of wood as used for carving the head and body (*see* pages 21–2) but they may also be made from dowelling, which is shaped by paring away or by adding a modelling material. Do not use

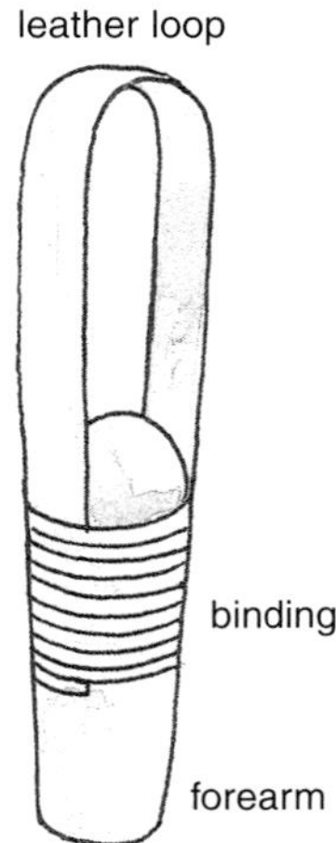

A solid forearm sometimes has a leather or fabric upperarm. Here a strip of leather is glued and bound to the forearm.

dowels of small diameter, as they will not have sufficient bulk.

For a very flexible alternative to a full wooden arm, use a wooden forearm with either a leather or a fabric upper arm. Glue and bind a loop of leather to the forearm or make a tube using a strong fabric such as calico or canvas and tack it to the forearm (*see* illustration of the old-time marionette on page 45).

Elbow Joints

The recommended elbow joints for wooden arms are an open mortise and tenon joint or a leather joint. In all cases, it is important to leave sufficient wood at the back of the elbow on both forearm and upper arm to prevent the joint bending in the wrong direction. Latex-rubber arms are cast with a built-in elbow joint (*see* page 50).

An Open Mortise and Tenon Joint

This joint comprises a protrusion or 'tongue' on the forearm that is pivoted in a deep groove in the upper arm. If the arm is carved, shape the tongue as part of the forearm. Ensure that the top is rounded and that it will extend far enough into the upper arm to be secured. Saw and chisel out the groove in the upper arm. It should be just wide enough to permit the lower arm to move freely but without wobbling.

When both parts are carved and sanded smooth, insert the tongue in the groove. Holding the parts in place very securely, drill a small hole across the joint. Remove the lower arm and enlarge very slightly the hole made in the tongue so that it will turn freely on the nail that will complete the joint. Sand lightly the inside surfaces of the groove and the sides of the tongue to remove any burrs caused by the drilling. Replace the tongue in the groove, insert a nail to act as the pivot and add a spot of glue to the head of the nail to secure it.

The tongue may be cut from a strip of aluminium; this is more appropriate with arms shaped from dowelling. Cut the aluminium to shape with tin-snips; it may be square at one end but the top of the tongue should be rounded and the sides cut to the profile shape of the forearm. File the edges smooth. Place the forearm in a vice and saw down into it, cutting a slot into which the aluminium will fit snugly. If it is difficult to achieve a sufficiently wide slot with a saw alone, slice a little more wood away with a craft knife. Glue and insert the aluminium into the slot and secure it with small nails, having first drilled guide holes.

Open mortise and tenon elbow joints.

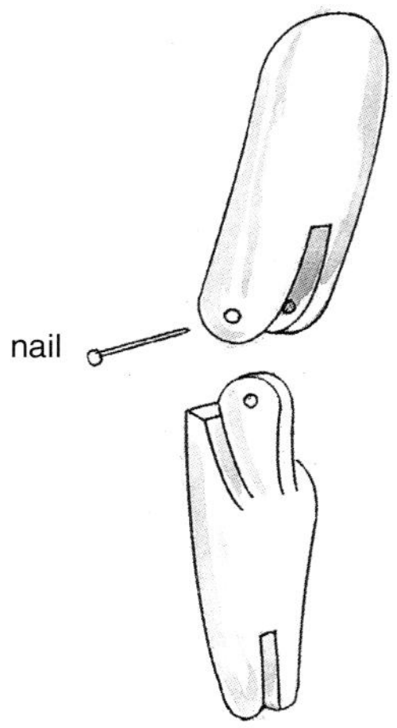

The elbow joint is carved as part of the arm.

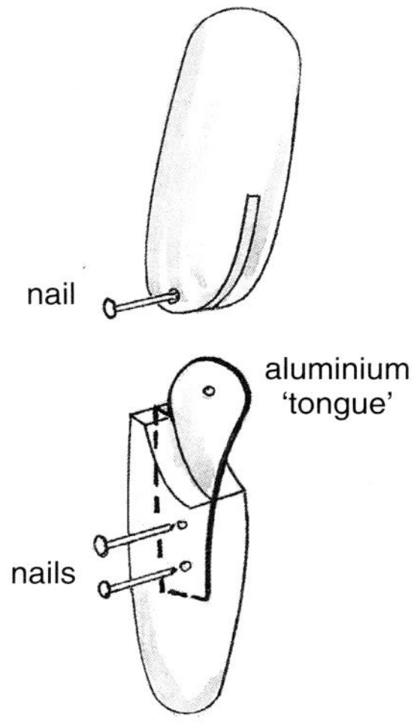

A shaped strip of aluminium is used to form the tongue for the joint.

Cut a narrow slot in the upper arm to accommodate the tongue. The slot should be just wide enough for the tongue to turn freely but not wobble. Assemble the parts and drill a hole across the elbow for the pivot, as described above. Remove any burrs with glasspaper and a file, reassemble the joint, insert the pivot nail and add a spot of glue to its head.

Leather Joints

Leather elbow joints are the same in principle as the restricted leather waist joint. Use a saw to cut matching vertical slots in the upper arm and forearm at the elbow. In each arm section, cut or file away a wedge shape at the front of the elbow; the angle of the wedge determines the degree of movement at the elbow. For each arm, cut a strip of leather a little wider than the arm and no longer than the combined depth of the slots. Glue the leather and slide it into the slots; ensure that the backs of the elbow are in contact and that the arm is accurately aligned. Allow the glue to dry, then secure the leather further with small nails and finally trim the waste leather with a sharp blade.

An alternative leather joint, often favoured by professionals who carve their figures, involves 'stapling' to the upper arm a loop of leather that fits into a slot in the top of the forearm. To cut the slot in the forearm, drill a line of small holes very close together and clean out the waste with a sharp craft knife. Glue the ends of the leather loop into the hole; it should be a close fit with just a little of the loop protruding, so you will probably need to ease it in with a small tool. Secure the leather further with tiny nails.

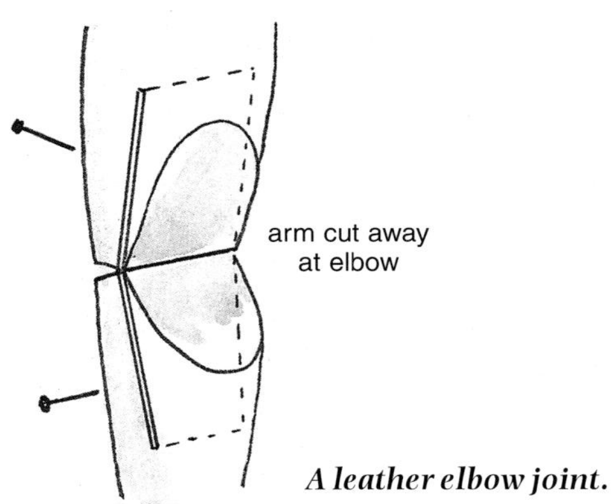

A leather elbow joint.

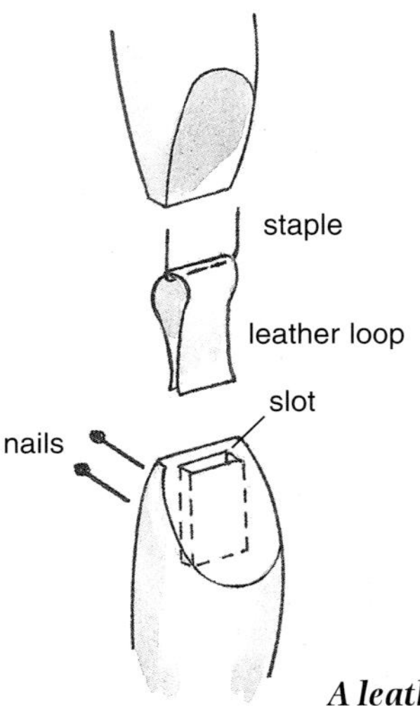

A leather and staple joint.

Bend a piece of galvanized wire into a square-cornered staple and drill small holes in the upper arm to accommodate the wire. Insert the wire through the leather loop and glue the staple into the holes in the upper arm. The arm should move freely without bending in the wrong direction.

Shoulder Joints

The nature of the shoulder joint will be determined in large part by the material and method of construction of the body and the arms. Select the appropriate joint from the following possibilities.

Cord Joints

A range of simple but effective shoulder joints can be achieved with strong cord. Knot one end of the cord, thread the other end through a countersunk hole in the top of the arm then proceed in one of the following ways.

- Thread the cord through a hole in the body and tie it securely, either in the neck cavity or to a plywood insert in the centre of the body.

Shoulder joint.

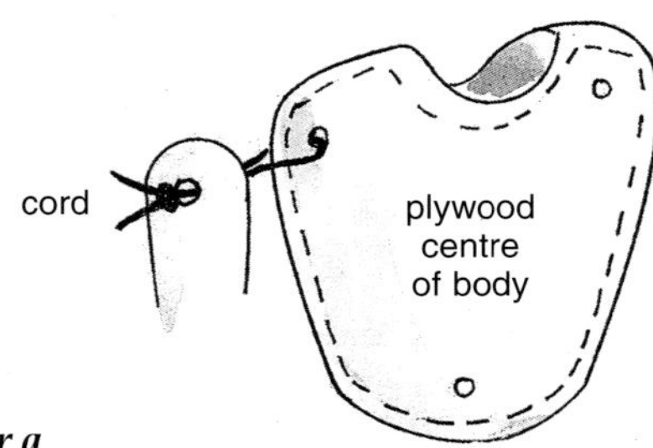

A cord joint for a hollow body.

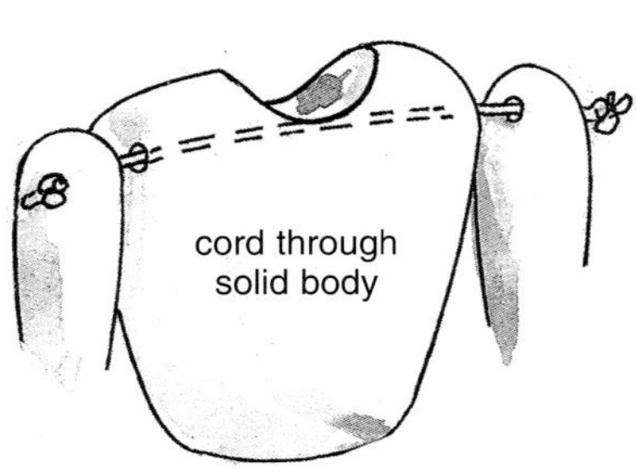

A cord joint for a solid body.

- Thread the cord through a hole right across the body, through the opposite arm, and knot it.
- If the body is not suitable for attaching the cord, insert a piece of galvanized wire across the body and loop the ends for attaching the cord.

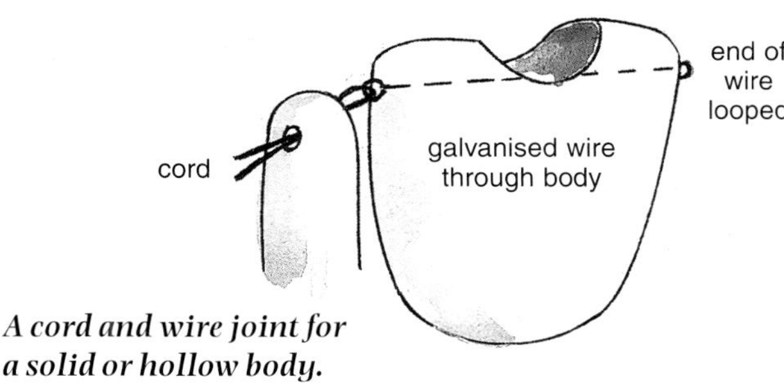

A cord and wire joint for a solid or hollow body.

A Leather Joint

The leather loop and staple joint described for elbows (*see* page 52) is also suitable for the shoulder joints of wooden arms and bodies, provided the loop of leather is sufficiently loose to permit a full range of movement.

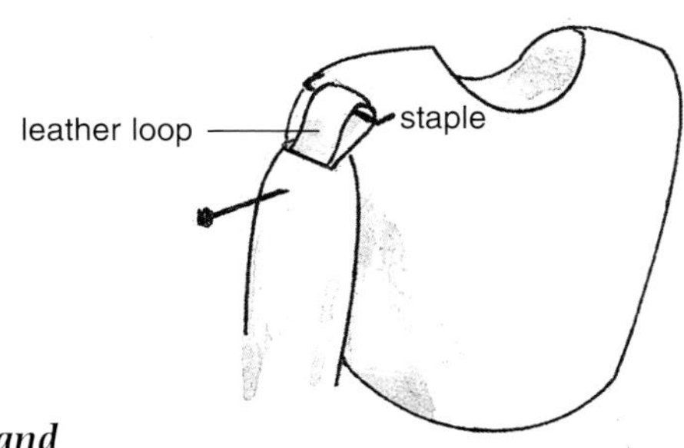

A leather loop and staple joint.

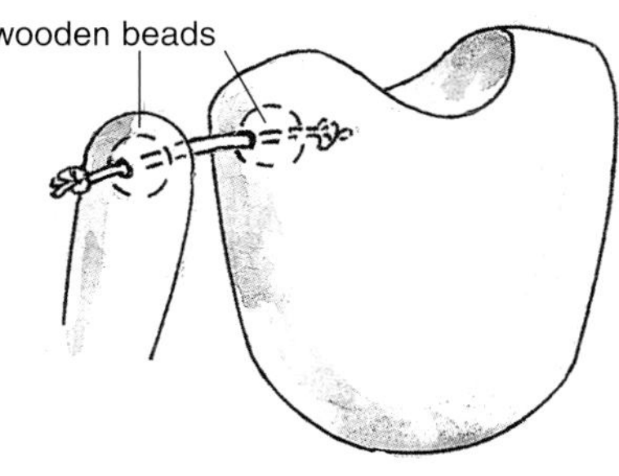

Cord and beads used to join latex-rubber puppet parts.

Make the slot for the leather in the top of the arm, then glue and insert the linked galvanized wire staple into holes drilled in the shoulder.

A Cord and Bead Joint

Wooden beads linked by cord make a useful shoulder joint for latex- rubber parts. Thread two beads on to the cord and knot each end. The distance between the beads determines the degree of arm movement. Make a slit in each part to be joined, insert the threaded bead and reseal the slit with glue.

A Concealed Joint

When the body or limbs are to be unclothed you do not necessarily have to conceal the joint, but there may be

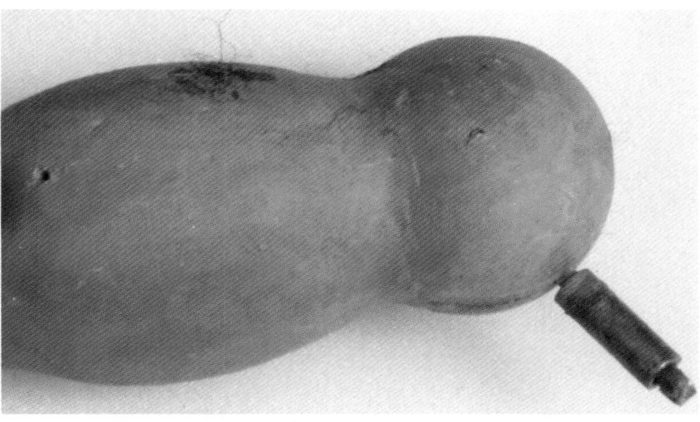

A concealed shoulder joint. ***A strip of metal pivoted in a slot in the arm and inserted in a metal tube.***

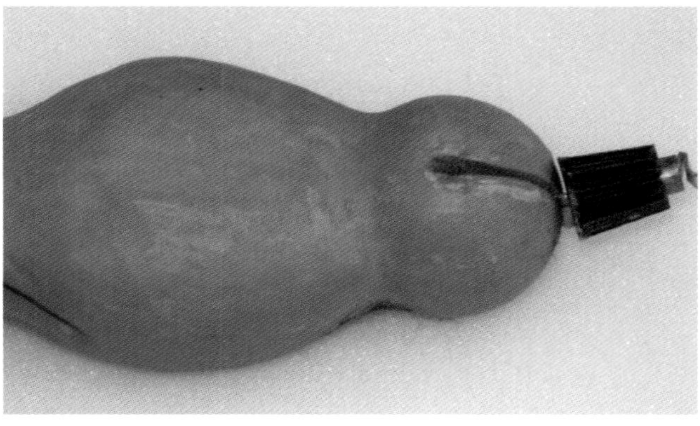

A concealed shoulder joint. ***The end of the metal strip is bent to prevent it coming out of the tube and it is secured into a larger sleeve for insertion in the shoulder.***

A concealed shoulder joint.

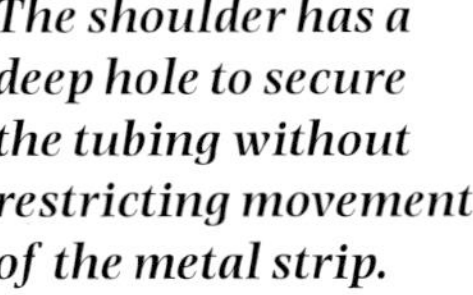

The shoulder has a deep hole to secure the tubing without restricting movement of the metal strip.

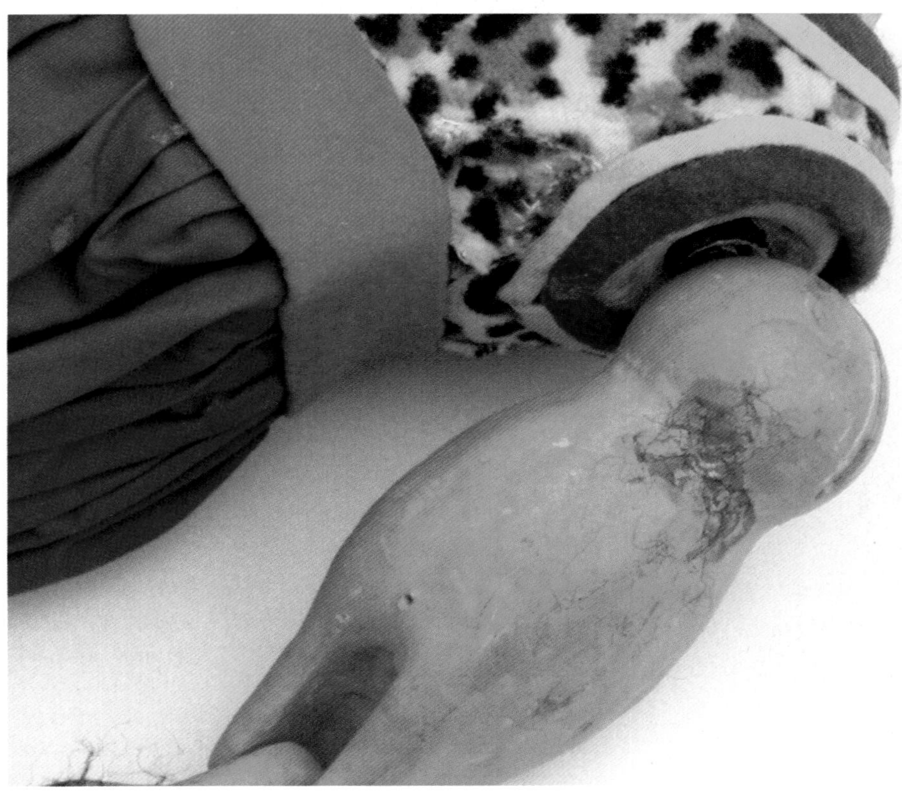

The assembled shoulder joint allows movement in all directions.

occasions when you wish to do so. A concealed shoulder joint is rather more complex than a similar joint for a knee, because the shoulder joint requires movement in most directions.

The joint is made using a narrow metal strip with one rounded end. This end fits into a slot in the top of the arm and rotates on a nail through the arm. Cut the slot across the top of the arm, insert the metal strip and drill a hole through the arm and the strip. Separate the joint, enlarge slightly the hole in the metal, and use a file to remove any burrs. Replace the strip in the arm and secure it with a nail.

Insert the other end of the strip into a short metal tube with an internal diameter just large enough to let it turn freely. Bend the end of the metal strip to prevent it coming out of the tube. In order to ensure that the metal strip can turn freely without the bent tag on the end snagging, glue the metal tube into a piece of dowelling with a hole drilled through its length, or into an improvised plug. Glue this plug into a suitable hole at the shoulder.

The slot allows the arm to be raised away from the body while the tube allows forward and backward movement.

Hands and Wrist Joints

Hands

Hands help to establish character and puppet hands should be expressive. Look at your own hands as you gesture or when relaxed: they are not stiff and flat but form interesting and sometimes animated positions. Notice that your fingers are not held in the same plane and that the thumb is set in a different plane from the fingers. Detailed modelling will not show, except to an intimate audience or on video, so they are often simply shaped or stylized. Like cartoon characters, puppets sometimes have only three fingers and a thumb.

Some puppet makers, concerned at the prospect of snagging a string, do not separate the fingers but cut deep grooves instead. However, most puppeteers find a

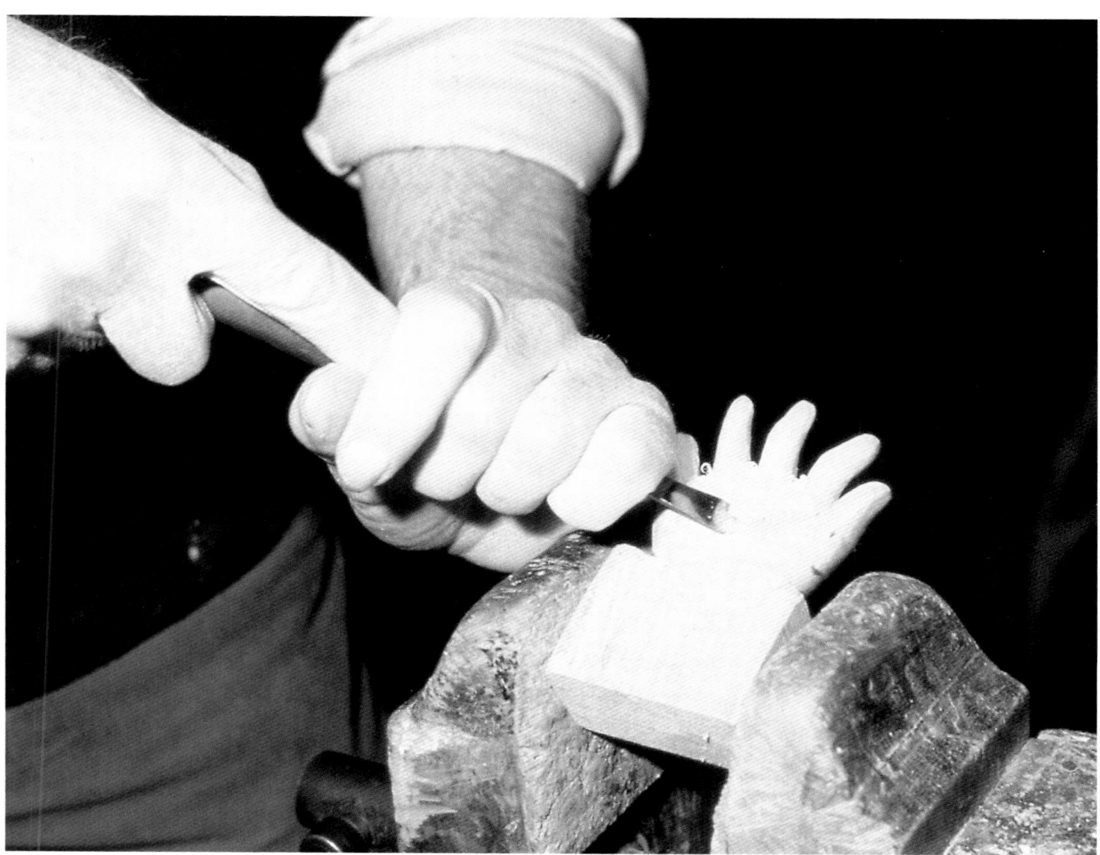

John Wright carving a hand. Note how the chisel is held against the heel of one hand while the other hand guides the blade.

way of resolving any problems that may arise. For example, where a hand with thin, knobbly fingers might catch on a string, it is possible to run a piece of very fine wire between the tips of the fingers to prevent snagging.

Before making the hand, determine the wrist joint you intend to use because some methods for making this joint have fixtures that are built into the hand while it is being made.

Carved Hands

Carve the hands following the same principles described for carving a head (*see* pages 21–3). The block of wood needs to be long enough to allow spare at the wrist for securing in the vice.

On the block of wood, mark the hand shape and make saw cuts to establish the separate fingers. Carefully shape the individual fingers and hollow out the palm of the hand. When the carving is complete, gently cut away any waste at the wrist and smooth the hand with increasingly fine pieces of glasspaper.

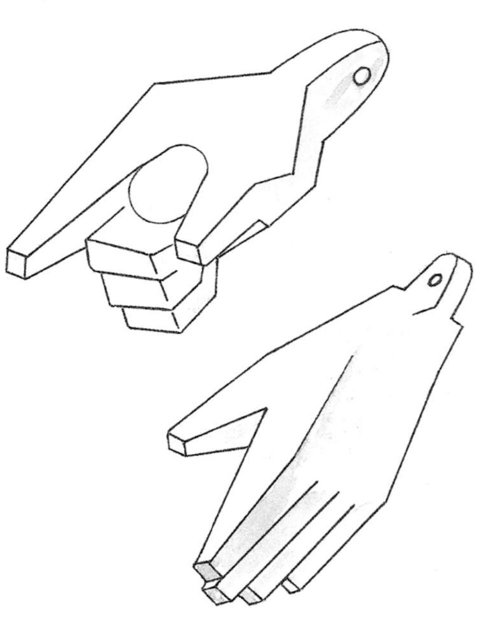

The main cuts when carving the hands.

Modelled Hands

To model the hand, first establish a basic shape by intertwining pipe-cleaners and bending them into position. Build upon this base using one of the modelling materials previously described (*see* pages 27–9). Those with good adhesive properties will stick directly, for others you need to cover the pipe-cleaners with an all-purpose adhesive.

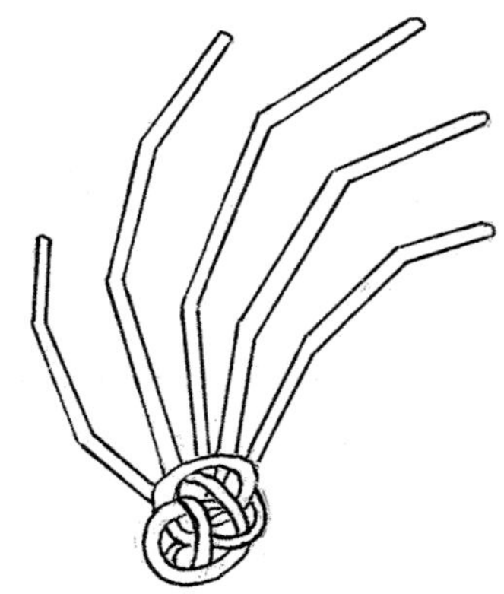

A pipe-cleaner base for modelling a hand.

You will find that some materials are best applied to individual fingers. Others work better if used in fairly large pieces: apply these across the fingers, snip between the fingers with a pair of scissors, and finally model the shape of the fingers. Sometimes one approach works better than another, not because of inherent differences in the materials but because it suits the individual modeller.

When the hand is thoroughly dry, complete any additional shaping required and smooth the hands ready for jointing and painting.

For some wrist joints, preparatory work prior to modelling can make jointing much easier later. For example, you might build a dowel in with the pipe-cleaner base so that there is a good fixing point for a screw-eye.

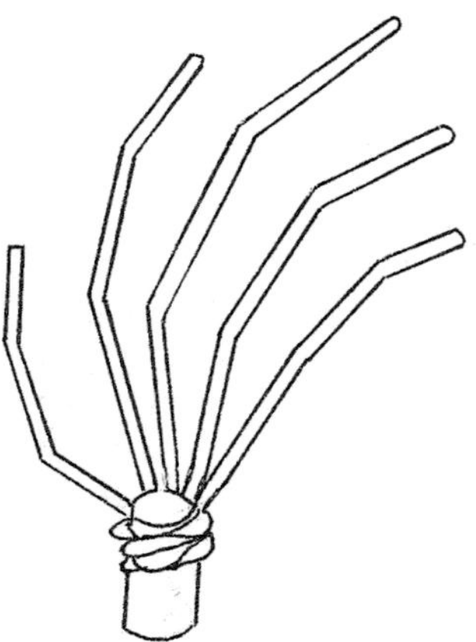

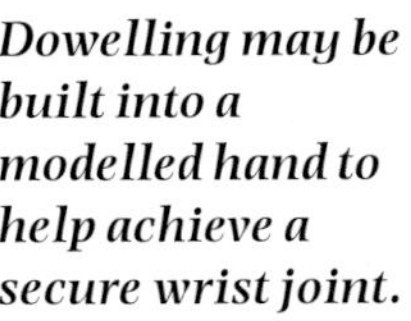

Dowelling may be built into a modelled hand to help achieve a secure wrist joint.

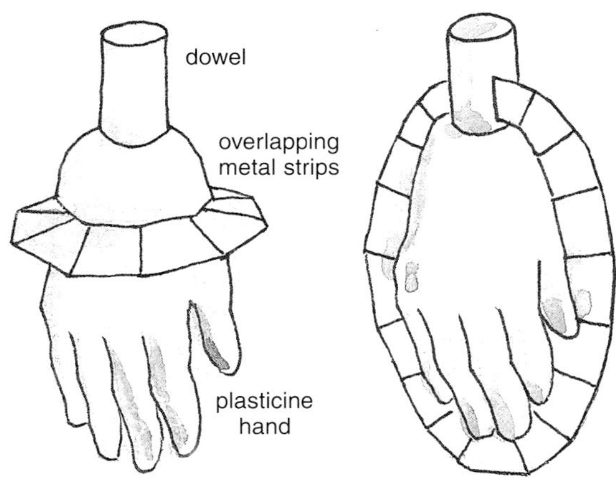

Alternative positions for the metal dividers when casting a hand in plaster.

Inserting a strip of aluminium, a leather strip or a loop at the start can save you a more fiddly job of securing these in a finished hand. Take care not to damage any leather inserts when working on the hand.

Latex-Rubber Hands

Latex-rubber hands are moulded in the same way as latex heads (*see* pages 30–4). When inserting tin dividers in the Plasticine model to prepare for making the plaster cast, you can either follow a line up the sides of the hand and over the tips of the fingers or make a division across the back of the hand and the palm. You would be wise to make this division at the widest part of the hand so that you can remove any part that becomes too thick and therefore less flexible.

If you are making a rigid hand, it is best to make the division between the front and the back or you will not be able to remove the shaped fingers without breaking the plaster cast.

Cloth Hands

Cloth hands are not common on marionettes but they are sometimes used for a particular effect. Albrecht Roser of Stuttgart, for example, has Clown Gustaf whose hands are made of tightly padded fabric with one row of stitches at the main knuckles. This not only gives some amusing flexibility when playing the piano, but a string raises an index finger and waggles it at the audience when they begin to applaud too soon. This is so simple yet so effective. The fingers are not even rounded: they are cut square at the tips.

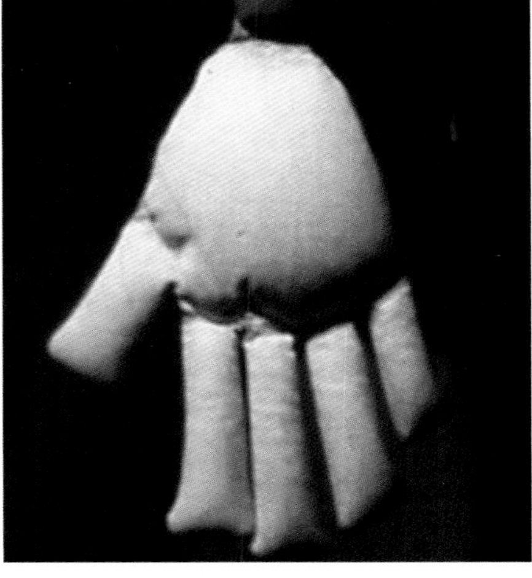

A stylized fabric hand of Clown Gustaf by Albrecht Roser.

To make the hands, use a template to cut out the matching shapes, leaving sufficient waste. Stitch around the edges, trim the waste as close to the stitching as is safe and turn the fabric the right way. To prevent puckering, you might need to snip into any tight corners before turning. Leave a strip of fabric at the wrist to glue into a slot in the arm for the wrist joint.

Wrist Joints

The wrist is an important joint of a marionette. There will be occasions when the movement of the wrist is deliberately restricted to facilitate a particular movement but usually it will require a flexible, smooth action. If you hold an arm horizontally and then turn and tilt it in various directions, the hand should move or drop smoothly and without hesitation.

The following joints are suitable for the wrist. The choice will depend on the degree of restriction required and the materials used for the hand and arm.

A Rope Joint

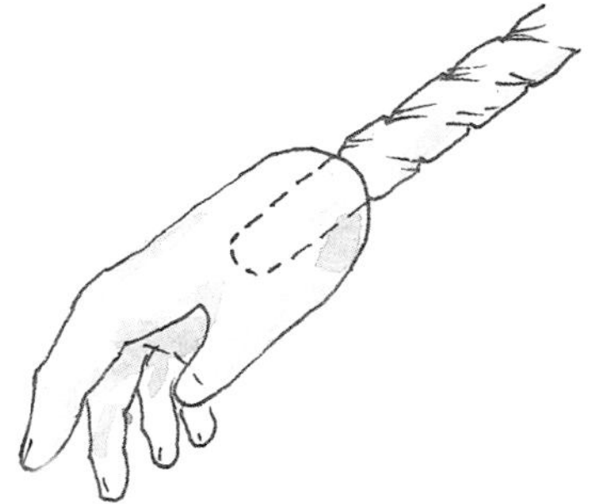

A rope arm and wrist joint.

In the exceptional case of an arm being made from rope, glue it into a hole in the heel of the hand. Assuming it is sufficiently thick, you might secure it further with a couple of tiny nails inserted through the palm.

Leather Joints

To restrict movement somewhat, glue and nail a strip of leather into a slot cut in the arm and in the hand. The degree of movement permitted depends upon the thickness and the width of the leather.

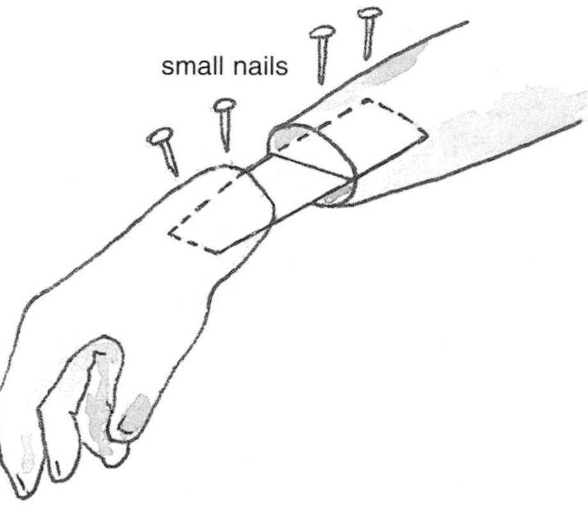

A strip of leather, glued and nailed into slots cut in the hand and forearm.

To achieve a more flexible leather joint, cut a slot in the hand. Glue and pin into the hand the ends of a loop of leather, approximately 6mm (¼in) wide. Drill a 6–8mm (¼in) hole upwards into the forearm, insert the leather loop into the hole and secure it with a nail. The hand should be close to the end of the forearm but not so close that it interferes with movement. This is a very smooth and flexible joint often used by professionals for carved puppets.

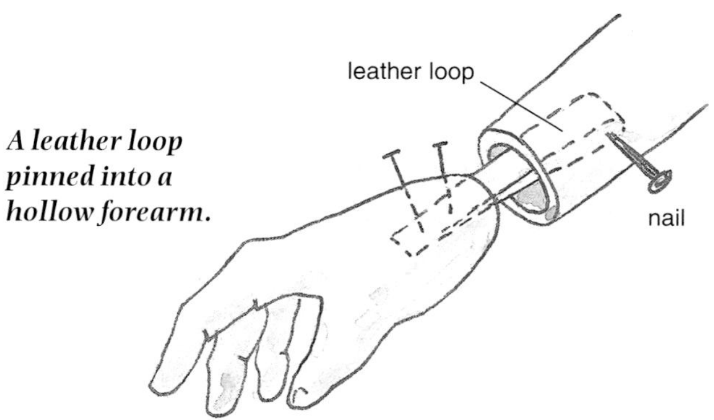

A leather loop pinned into a hollow forearm.

A Tongue and Groove Joint

This is a good joint for restricting movement in one plane, for example for a pianist. The tongue is a strip of aluminium that is secured in the hand and pivots in a slot in the forearm. Build the aluminium into the hand when it is constructed, or cut a slot in the hand and glue the aluminium into it.

Saw a slot in the forearm just a little wider than the thickness of the aluminium. You might need to make two saw cuts and trim away the waste with a sharp craft knife. Normally you will want the hand to have a little upward but much more downward movement. To achieve this, angle the saw cut(s) in the forearm so that the slot reaches just a little way back at the top but much further back on the underside.

Position the aluminium tongue in the slot and drill a small hole across the slot and through the aluminium. Remove the tongue from the slot, enlarge the hole very slightly and remove any burrs with a file. Replace the tongue in the forearm and secure it with a nail through the hole. Put a spot of glue on the head of the nail.

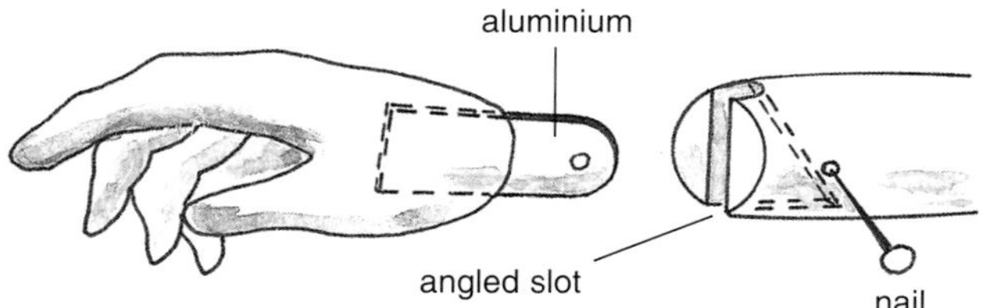

A strip of aluminium secured in the hand and pivoted in a slot in the forearm.

Screw-Eye Joints

Screw-eye joints are not recommended but there are times when they may be useful or provide a solution to a problem. Interlocked screw-eyes are best avoided at all times; not only do they rattle but they can also catch in awkward positions. On the rare occasions when this method might be necessary, I would embed them deeply into both of the parts to be joined and build around them with a modelling material so that the parts near the threaded shaft are covered, as this is where they are most likely to snag. The following joints are less problematic.

- Screw and glue a screw-eye into the heel of the hand. Attach it to the forearm with cord threaded through a small hole drilled across the arm.
- Attach the screw-eye to the hand and drill a fairly large hole upwards into the forearm. Insert the screw-eye into the hole and secure it with a nail across the forearm; pre-drill a guide hole for the nail so that the arm does not split.
- If the hand is made from latex rubber, insert and glue a dowel into it as an attachment for the screw-eye. The dowel can also provide a helpful fixing point later for a control string for the hand.

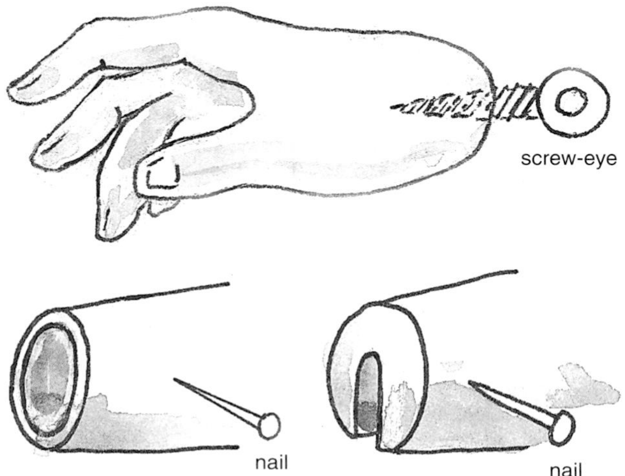

A screw-eye pivoted in a hole or a slot in the forearm.

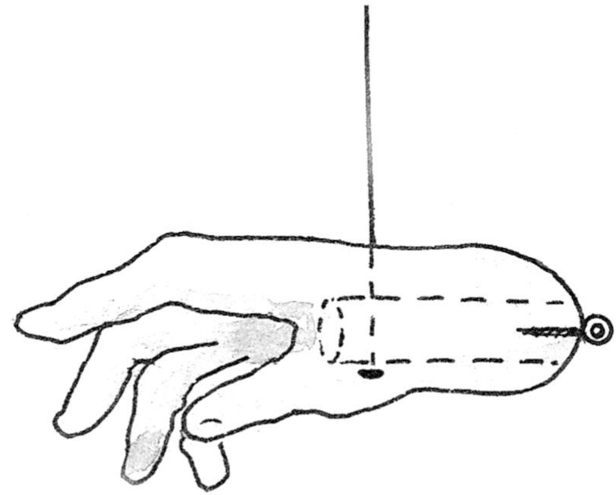

A dowelling insert provides a secure fixing that is useful for modelled and moulded latex-rubber hands. It also offers a fixing point for the control string for a latex rubber hand.

A Cord and Bead Joint

Hollow rubber hands and arms may be joined with cord and wooden beads. Knot one end of the cord and seal the knot with glue. Thread two beads on to the cord and knot the other end, allowing the required amount of space between the two balls. Insert one bead into the hand and the other into the forearm through the holes left from the casting of these parts.

If the rubber is not too thick, it should flex enough for you to push the beads in through somewhat smaller holes. Tug the hands a little to see if the beads will be released; if they are not sufficiently secure, squeeze a little glue into the holes to fasten them. If you cannot insert the beads through the holes, slit the rubber a little, insert the beads and glue the slit together again.

As an aid to flexibility, you may want to thread an additional bead on the cord to fit between the hand and the forearm. You must plan to do this from the outset so that you can adjust the length of the forearms accordingly or the puppet's arms will look more like those of an ape.

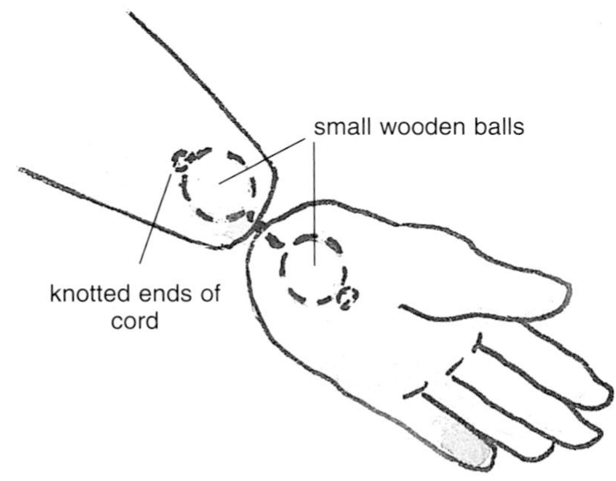

A cord and bead wrist joint for latex-rubber parts.

Legs, Knee and Hip Joints

Legs

You must decide on the hip and ankle joints to be used before making the legs.

Carved and Dowelling Legs

Legs may be carved or made from dowelling that is shaped down or built up with a modelling material such as Wood-Form.

Plywood Legs

Laminated plywood shapes make strong, freely moving legs, provided the plywood used is not too thin. There are two options available: making the leg entirely in plywood, or using a core of plywood that is padded with foam rubber or balsawood, which is helpful if there is a need to reduce the weight.

Latex-Rubber Legs

Rubber legs are cast in one piece using the procedure described for heads (*see* pages 30–4). When creating the Plasticine model for making the plaster cast, shape it with wedge-shapes cut from the back of the knee and a small 'V'-shaped groove across the front of the knee to permit bending. Take care to ensure that sufficient Plasticine remains in the centre of the knee joint to create a gap for the latex rubber to flow into the other half of the leg.

When inserting the tin dividers ready for casting, follow a line up the sides and around the top and bottom of the leg. When the cast has been created and the rubber legs have been made, use a sharp knife to make a slit across the groove in the front of the knee joint to allow it to bend. Take care not to cut the rubber at the back of the knee as this forms the hinge. Provided the legs are cast fairly thickly, the hinge will last for many years.

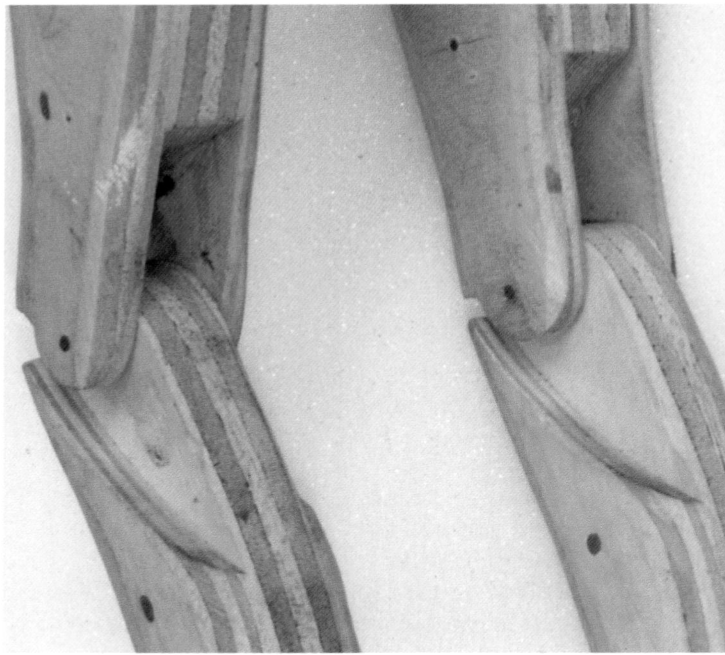

The knee joint for laminated plywood legs.

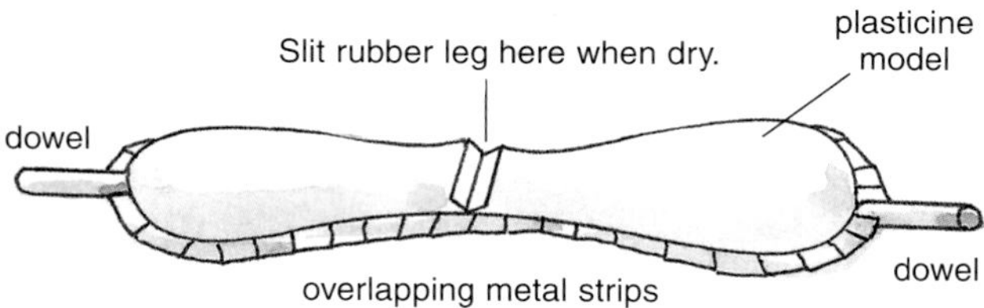

A Plasticine model with metal dividers inserted ready for making a plaster cast of the legs. Note the 'V'-shaped groove at the knee to permit bending.

Joints

The best joints for carved and dowelling legs are a standard open mortise and tenon joint cut into the legs, a similar joint that uses an aluminium tongue, or a leather joint. For plywood legs, a mortise and tenon or a leather joint are the most suitable. Latex-rubber legs are cast with a built-in knee joint (*as described above*).

An Open Mortise and Tenon Joint

Suitable for carved and dowelling legs, this joint is cut into the leg, not added later, so you need to allow for the overlap of wood at the knee when determining the length of each piece of wood.

Cut an angled slot in the lower leg, at the knee. Shape the wood on each side of the slot: first use a saw to remove a small rectangular block at the front of the knee to create a ridge. The ridge will butt against the corresponding ridge in the upper leg to prevent the leg bending the wrong way. Round the remaining wood at the top of this leg section.

The thigh section has a protruding tongue that fits into the slot. Cut away a small block at the front of the knee to correspond to that cut from the lower leg. Make angled saw cuts on each side of the intended tongue and then saw down to these cuts from the sides of the legs to remove the waste. Round the end of the remaining tongue.

Place the tongue into the slot with the knee in the locked position. Holding it securely in place, drill a small guide hole across the leg and through the joint. The hole should be aligned with the two ridges. Separate the parts and enlarge slightly the hole in the tongue so that it will turn freely on the nail used as a pivot. Smooth the sides of the tongue and the groove with glasspaper, removing any burrs.

Reassemble the leg and insert a nail to secure the joint. If the knee joint does not move smoothly and freely, trim or sand any offending part, then replace the nail and secure its head with a spot of glue.

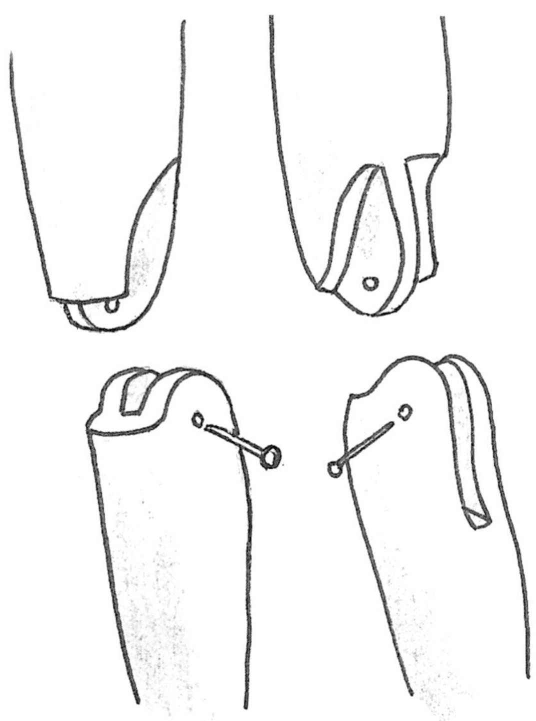

An open mortise and tenon knee joint for wooden legs.

Aluminium Mortise and Tenon Joint

In this alternative form of the open mortise and tenon joint, the wooden tongue is replaced with a strip of aluminium, which is also used for a concealed joint for a bare leg. If the joint is not to be seen, the additional shaping described to conceal it is unnecessary. The joint is essentially the same as that described previously for an open mortise and tenon elbow joint (*see* page 51). When carving or modelling the leg, shape it at the knee so that a 'ball' on the top of the lower leg fits into a 'socket' in the thigh section.

Shape a strip of aluminium to round off one end, then glue the other end into a slot cut in the lower leg. Drill guide holes through the leg and insert two small nails to secure the aluminium. In the thigh section, cut a slot to accommodate the aluminium tongue. Do not let the slot pierce the front of the knee: the wood that remains at the front blocks the movement of the aluminium, preventing the knee from bending in the wrong direction.

Assemble the leg with the knee in the locked position and drill a guide hole across the knee and through the

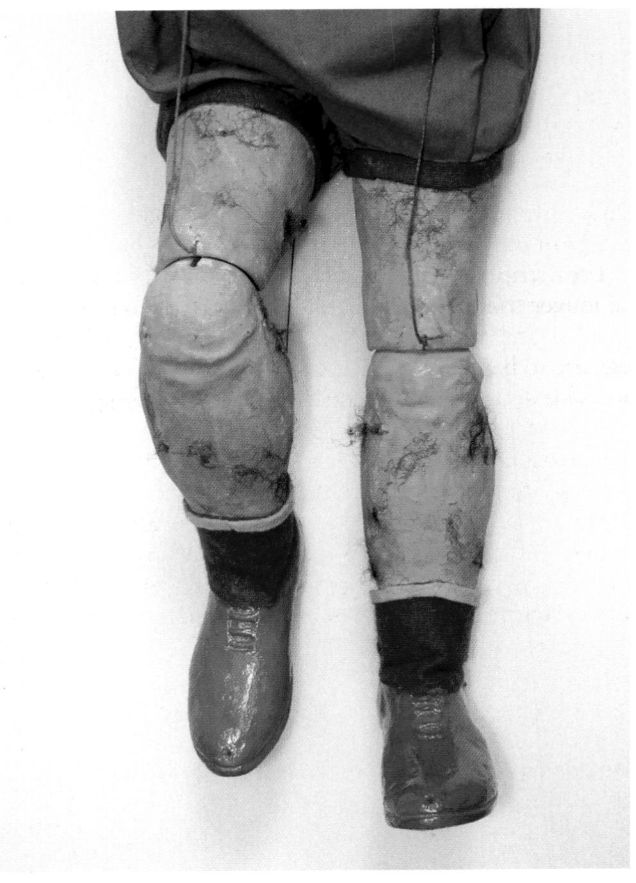

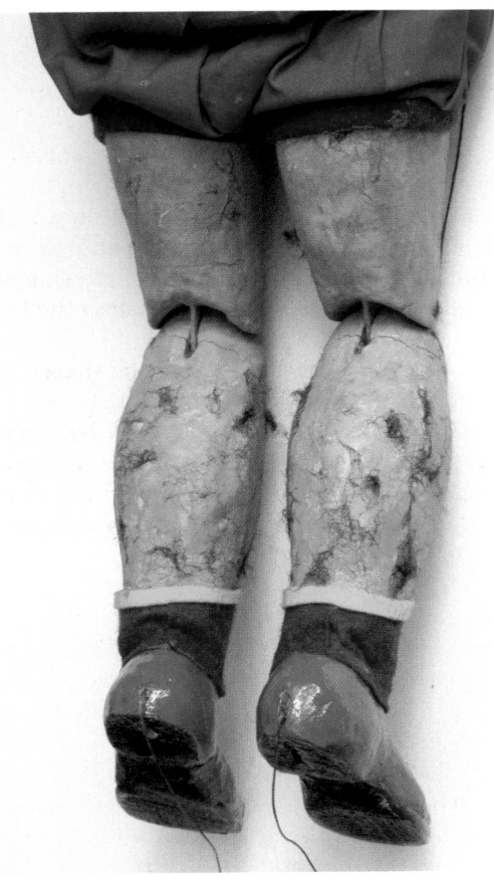

A concealed knee joint using an aluminium tongue pivoted in a slot in the lower leg.

aluminium. Remove the aluminium and enlarge the hole in it. File off any burrs and sand the inside of the slot. Reassemble the knee and insert a nail for the pivot. Seal the nail with a spot of glue. If any further shaping is required, it can be completed with a modelling material.

Plywood Mortise and Tenon Joints

The joint is made from six plywood shapes. Make the centrepiece of the lower leg long enough to insert into the foot for the ankle joint. For the lower centrepiece, either use very slightly thinner plywood than the centrepiece in the thigh or sand down the top of the tongue it creates, so that the finished knee moves freely.

With a coping saw or a band saw, cut out the six leg shapes (*see* 'A' and 'B', shown right). Glue together the three thigh sections and the three sections of the lower leg, creating a tongue and a groove. Insert the tongue into the

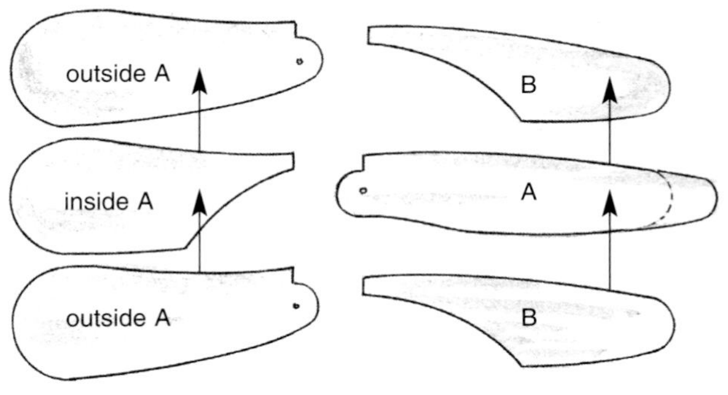

Plywood leg shapes.

Constructing laminated plywood legs.

groove and, holding the leg with the knee in the locked position, drill through the joint at the centre of the overlapping parts (see illustration below). Enlarge the hole in the tongue, smooth the tongue and groove with glasspaper, and reassemble the joint using a nail as the pivot. When it is moving freely, seal the head of the nail with glue.

Shape the plywood to round the leg. If necessary, add a modelling material, or glue on foam rubber or balsawood and trim it to shape. Ensure that any additional modelling or padding does not restrict the leg movement.

The alternative method uses three plywood shapes 'A' for the thigh and only the one centre shape 'A' for the lower leg. All of the plywood may be thinner than that used for the leg made entirely in plywood. The bulk of the leg, including the outer two sections of the lower leg, is created in foam rubber or balsawood that is glued on, then shaped.

Leather Joints

Leather makes a very good hinge for a knee joint and is suitable for plywood, carved and dowelling legs. Cut matching slots in each leg section at the knee: the slots should be just thick enough for the leather to fit snugly. Remove a wedge shape behind the knee with a saw, a chisel or a rasp. The angle of the wedge determines the degree of movement of the leg.

Use a strip of leather that is a little wider than the legs and no longer than the combined depth of the two slots. Glue both sides of the leather, avoiding the centre strip where the legs are to bend. Hold the leather by the spare at the sides and slide it into the slots. Check that the legs are aligned and meet properly at the knees. If the leather is too short and pulled too far into the slots, it will not straighten fully. If it is too long, the legs will bend in the wrong direction.

Leave the glue to dry before proceeding in case you displace the alignment. When the glue is dry, drill small guide holes into the leg, through the leather. Secure it further with small nails. Finally, trim off the waste leather with a sharp craft knife.

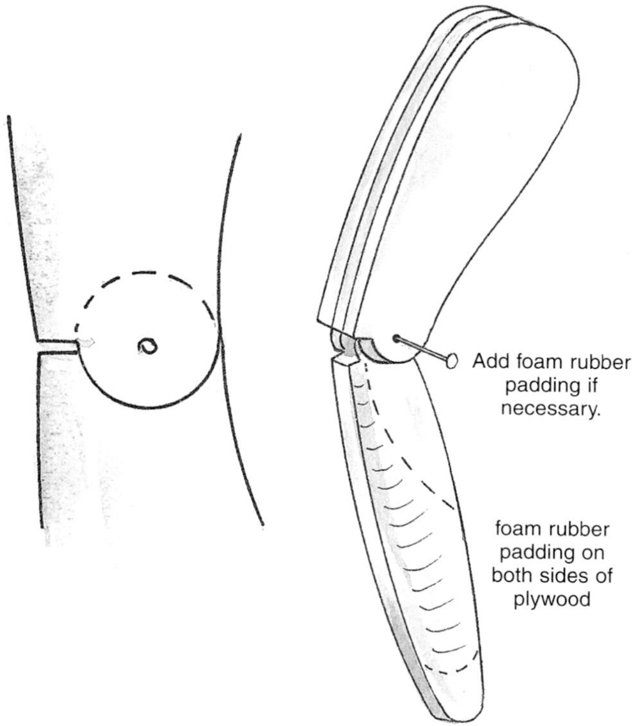

ABOVE LEFT: ***The position of the hole for jointing.***
ABOVE RIGHT: ***The leg assembled, showing foam rubber padding used as an alternative to the plywood outer sections of the lower leg.***

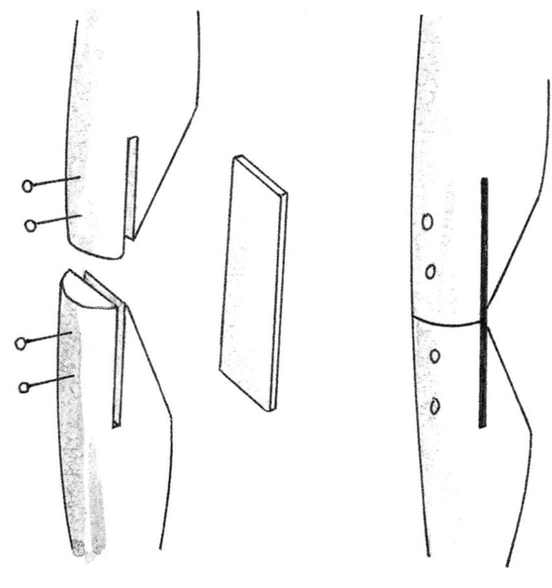

A leather knee joint.
ABOVE LEFT: ***Slots are cut for the leather, and the rear of the leg sections are cut away to permit bending.***
ABOVE RIGHT: ***The leg assembled with the leather glued and pinned in place.***

An alternative leather joint for plywood legs is sometimes used to reduce the weight of large puppets. Design and cut out the plywood shapes full on, not in profile. Glue the leather hinge to the back of the leg with the plywood sections touching at the knee. When the glue is dry, stick blocks of foam rubber or balsa wood to the front and back of the plywood. Cut away wedge-shapes behind the knee and trim the remainder of the blocks to shape. If you are also effecting the hip joint with leather, you should do this before you add the padding to the legs.

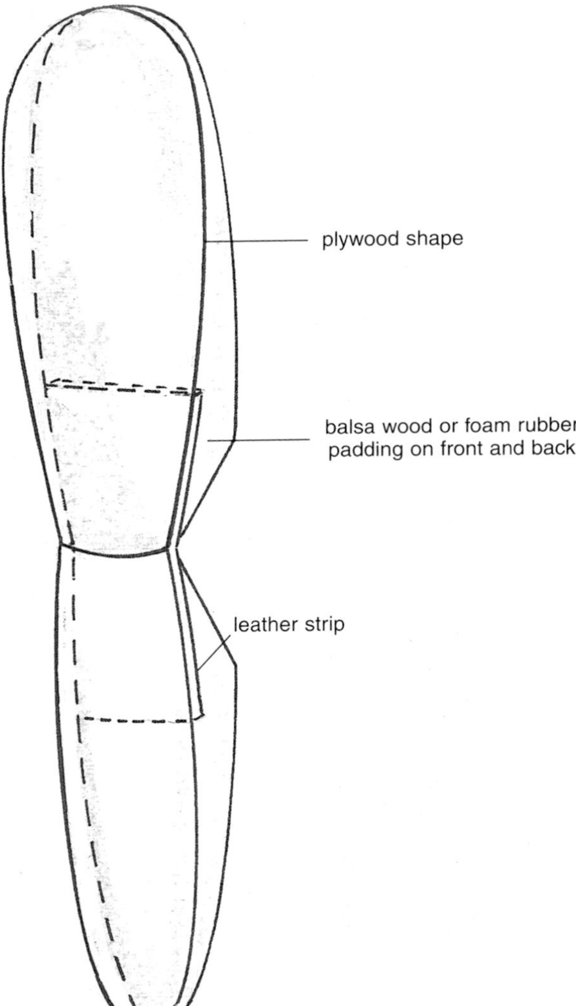

Plywood shapes, joined with a strip of leather and padded with foam rubber.

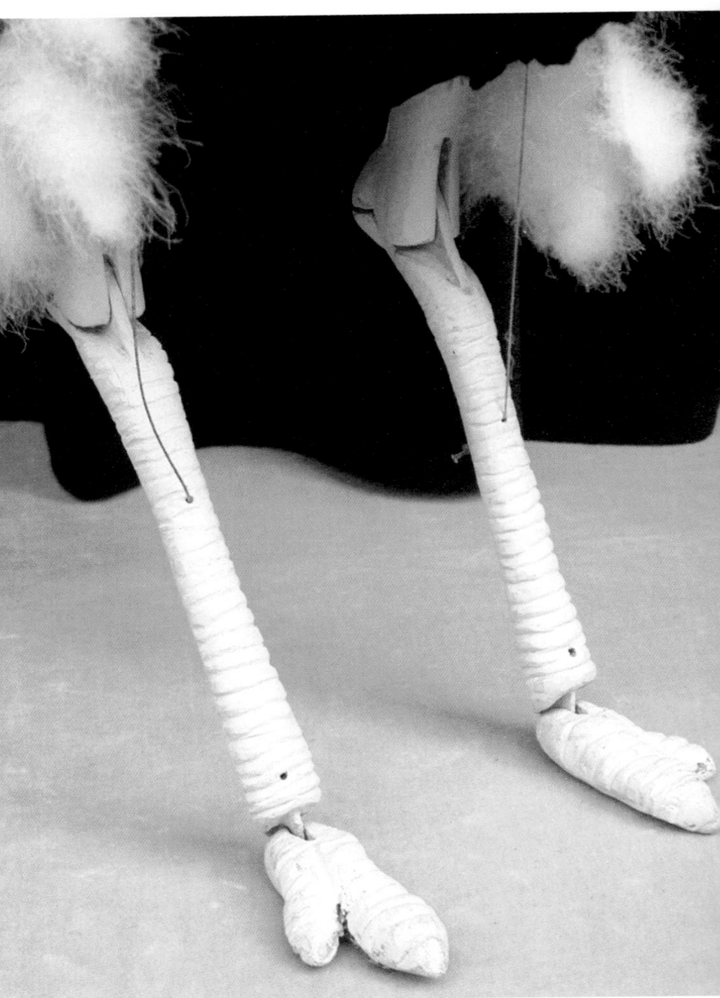

This puppet has a wooden knee joint but, for the ankle, a strip of aluminium is used instead of a wooden tongue.

Hip Joints

The hip joint selected depends on the materials used for the legs and the pelvis as well as what the puppet is to do and how it is required to move. Some puppets have a good deal of movement both backwards and forwards while others need to be more restricted. Sideways movement is generally quite limited or the legs will be more difficult to control, but, of course, there will always be exceptions. For sculpted legs, all of the following methods are possible; for other legs the leather methods are not suitable, with the exception of the plywood leg with a leather knee joint.

Galvanized Wire Joints

This is my preferred joint, where it is appropriate. Suspend the legs from a piece of strong galvanized wire. In the pelvis drill three holes for the wire, one through the leg-divider and one into each hip. Drill a hole across the top of each

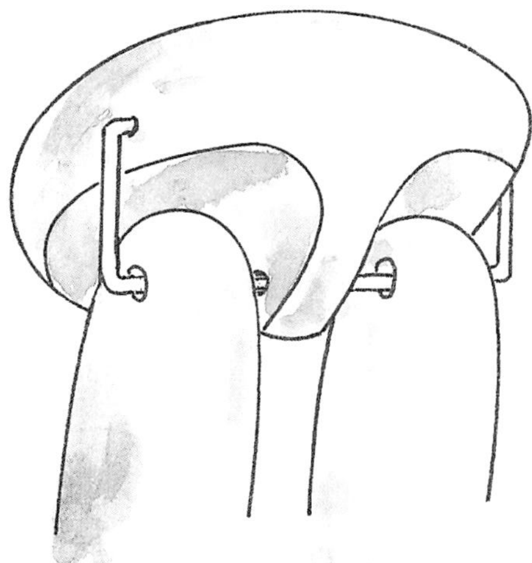

A wire hip joint.

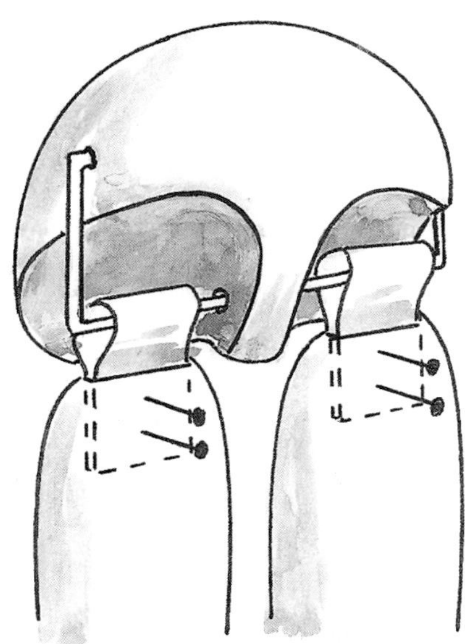

A wire and leather loop hip joint.

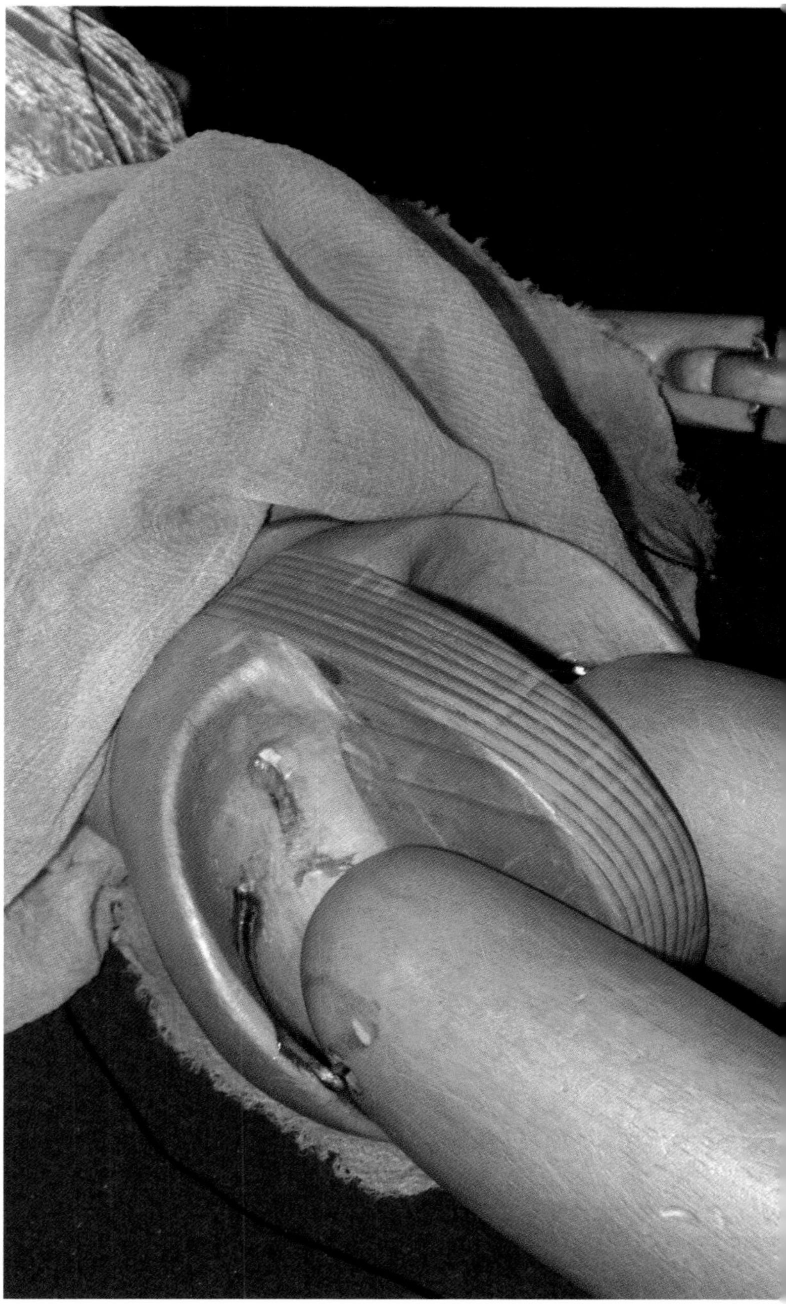

Looped wire, attached inside the leg socket of the pelvis, is soldered to a horizontal wire that passes through the tops of the legs and the leg divider.

thigh and insert them on to the wire on each side of the leg-divider. Use pliers to bend each end of the wire up at a sharp right angle. If the wire is curved, the legs might jam in an awkward position. Bend the tips of the wire inwards to fit into the holes in the hips. Secure the wire with glue and add staples if necessary. If you use thick wire to suspend the legs, it may not bend sharply, so use two lengths of wire. Pass one horizontally through the legs and pelvis. Bend the other (which may be thinner) into a loop with the sides pressed close together. Attach it vertically down the outside of the pelvis or concealed within the socket for the leg, the top curing into the pelvis. Solder the horizontal wire securely to the end of the vertical wire loop (*see* illustration on page 65).

Alternatively, glue and pin a loop of leather into a slot in the top of the thigh and suspend the loop from the galvanized wire. This is useful when you cannot drill a hole across the leg but are able to make a slot or to build the leather loop into the construction process. However, in order to prevent the leg rotating too far sideways on the wire, the loop itself needs to be fairly small.

A Cord Joint
Drill a hole across the top of each thigh and up through the pelvis. Thread strong cord through the legs and pelvis, then knot and glue the ends.

Leather Joints
Glue and nail one end of a strip of leather into a slot cut in the leg and the other end into another slot cut in the

Leather hip joints.

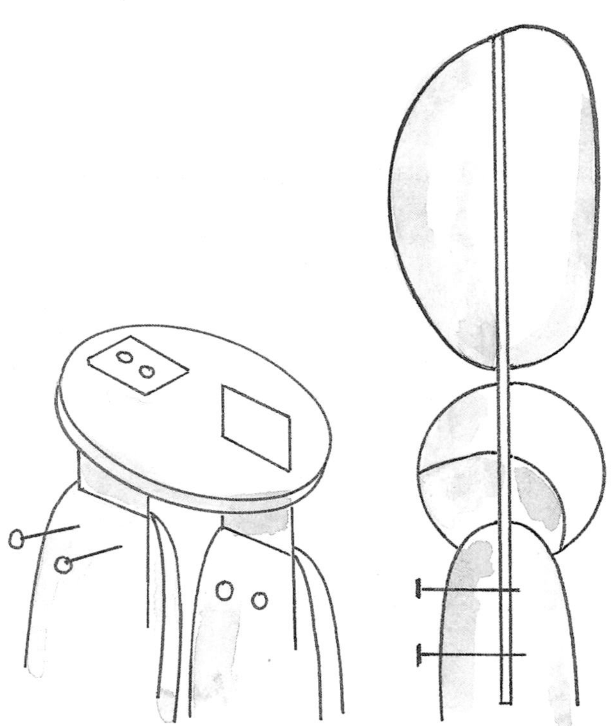

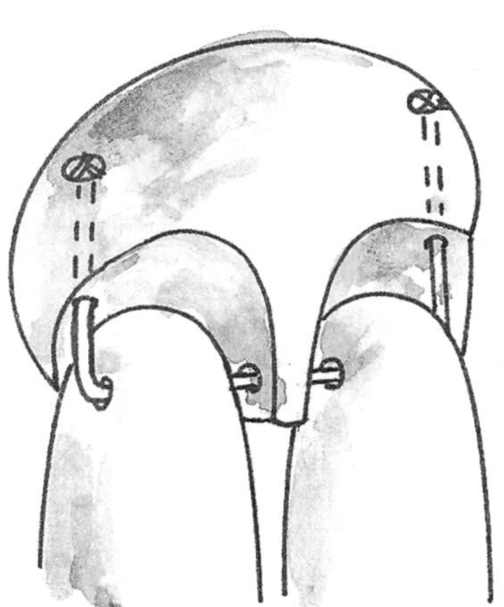

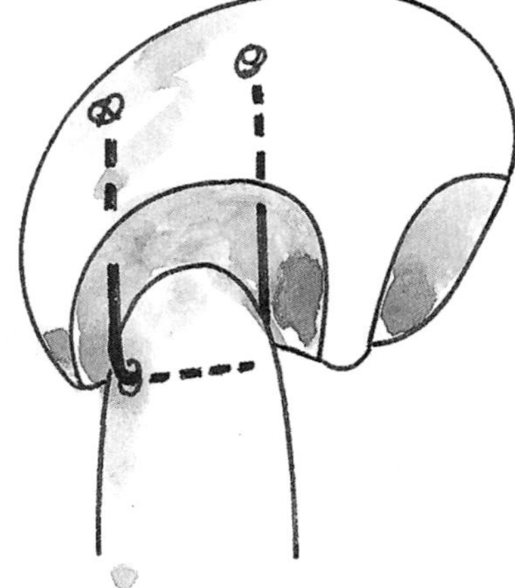

Cord hip joints.

pelvis. An alternative method uses a strip of leather throughout the entire body and into the top of the thigh. The end of the leather is split for the separate legs and is secured with glue and small nails.

Feet and Ankle Joints

Feet

Create carved, modelled or cast feet using the materials and methods described in Chapter 3. When modelling a foot, it is often preferable to build upon a base of balsa wood or polystyrene that does not need to be removed later. If Plasticine is used, cut off the sole to remove the Plasticine and then glue the sole back on to the foot. Ensure that the foot has sufficient weight for good movement, but without being too heavy.

Have regard for the ankle joint when making the foot as this will often be built in rather than added later. For example, you might build into the foot a slot, or a tongue made from plywood or aluminium, ready for the joint.

To facilitate a good walking action, it is recommended that ankle joints are cut with the feet pointing very slightly outwards to avoid the feet catching each other, and that the degree of vertical movement at the ankle is limited to prevent the toes dragging. If the feet make too much noise on the stage floor, glue a piece of felt or, preferably, chamois leather to the soles.

Latex-Rubber Feet

Rubber feet are cast in the same way as a rubber head (*see* pages 30–4). When dividing the Plasticine model to make the plaster cast, insert the metal strips around the sole.

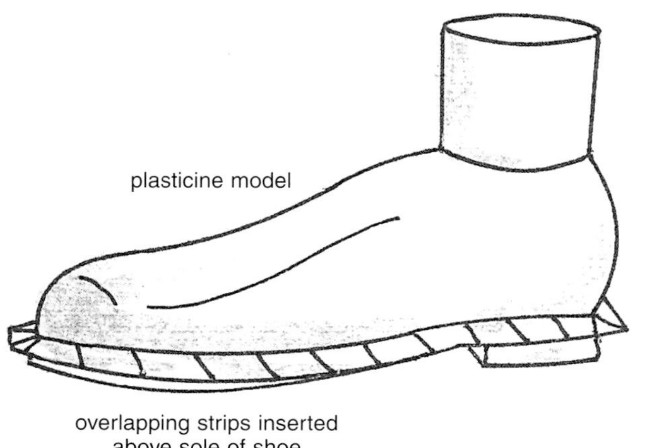

Making a plaster cast from a Plasticine model.

You can cast the foot and the bottom of the leg in one piece so that the lower leg fits into this 'tube'. If it is a tight fit, you can glue it in place but this will prevent any flexibility at the ankle. If the tube on the foot is larger than the leg, use a nail across the assembled parts to form a pivot and allow ankle movement.

Alternatively, make a fairly thick strip of rubber by pouring a quantity of latex into a small container such as a tin or a mirror surrounded by a retaining barrier made from Plasticine. When it has set, peel off the rubber strip and trim it to the required size. Glue the strip into a slot cut in the leg and insert the other end of the strip into the foot. Pour liquid plaster of Paris into the heel and the bottom of the leg to secure the strip. Make a small slit in the calf to pour the plaster in and keep the foot tilted backwards so that the plaster remains in the heel and does not fill the entire foot.

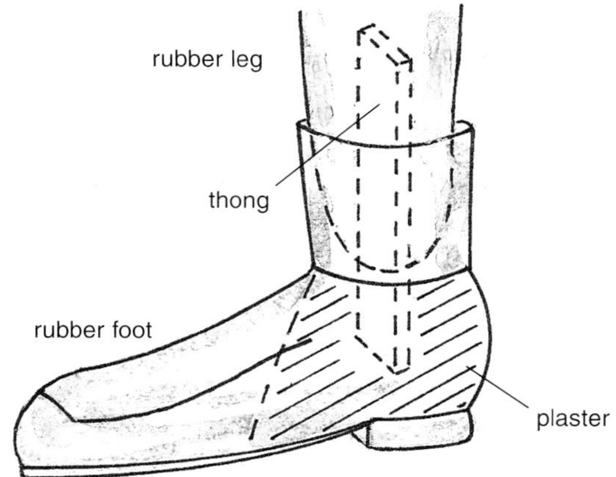

An ankle joint for latex-rubber puppets.

Ankle Joints

Latex-rubber feet are cast with built-in ankles (*see* above). The open mortise and tenon joint is recommended for carved, modelled and cast feet.

Open Mortise and Tenon Joints

This joint has a tongue built on to the bottom of the leg that fits into a slot in the foot. To make the slot, either build it into the foot during construction or drill a series of holes in a straight line and clean out the waste with a craft knife or a chisel. The length of the slot determines the degree of

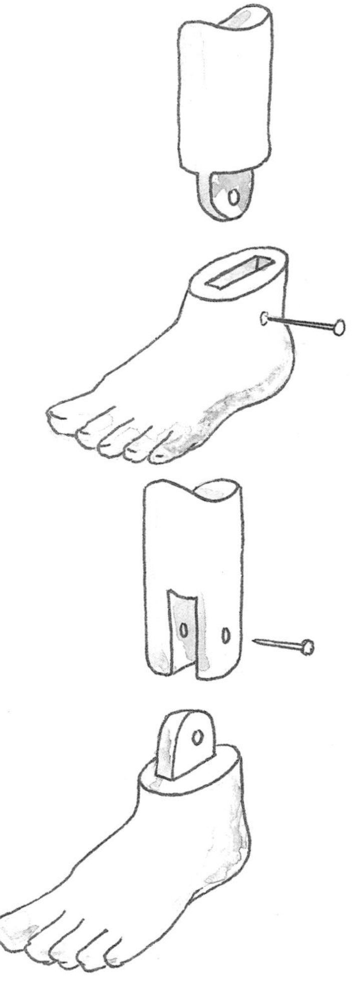

Tongue and groove ankle joints; the recommended joint has the slot in the foot and the tongue on the leg.

movement at the ankle. Insert the tongue into the slot and drill a guide hole through the foot, across the joint. Remove the tongue and enlarge the hole slightly. Clean the tongue and the groove, reassemble the joint, and secure it with a nail. Glue the head of the nail to retain it.

If you need the groove to be in the leg and the tongue to be on the foot, it is best to build this in during construction. In order to restrict movement at the ankle, cut the groove at an angle so that it is higher in the front and lower at the back of the leg. This will prevent the toes dipping too far.

An alternative to the wooden tongue uses a strip of aluminium, glued and pinned into one section and pivoted in the other section on a nail.

Sir Fool's Quest ***by John Roberts, PuppetCraft. Large string puppets for a modern version of the King Arthur legend. Puppets designed and carved by John Roberts. Costumes by Maria Liljefors: it took three attempts to get the making of the leggings correct to allow knee and ankle movement.***

COSTUME

Selecting Fabrics

Just as puppet design focuses upon the essence of the character, so the costume should capture the theme or period and reflect this without becoming too fussy. Select materials that will stand up to wear but are fairly soft and lightweight. Fabrics that drape well, such as jersey fabric cut on the cross, make good, flowing robes. Avoid those that restrict movement or that let light shine though.

Using only one type of fabric can lead to a rather dull appearance; mixtures of colour and textures generally prove more successful. Consider how the costumes look from a distance and how they appear under stage lighting. Coloured lighting can enhance or kill the appearance of a costume, so take swatches of the fabrics

Opposite: ***Bullfighter by John Wright.***

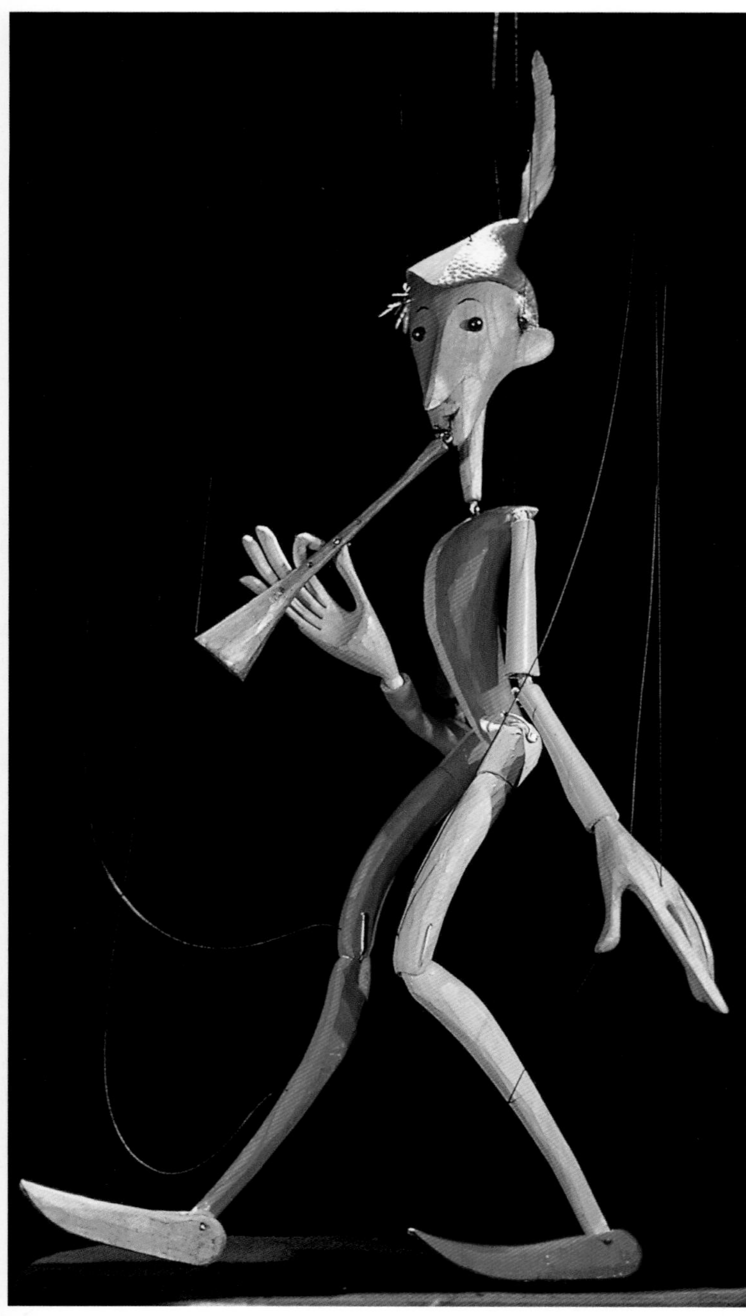

Pied Piper *by John Roberts, PuppetCraft. Carved in limewood and 50cm (20in) tall, this marionette is about as thin as is possible for a marionette of this size. The clothes are simply painted onto the wood. Leather and a feather are used for the hat.*

to test under stage lighting before you purchase them. Black tends to look flat as a costume so you might substitute a dark shade of blue, green or brown. Explore different shades of one colour and contrasting colours: use one colour to accentuate another rather than using contrasting colours in equal parts.

You can dye fabric to the required colour before making it up into the costume, but always dye spare material to allow for errors in making or for modifications as you proceed. Avoid large prints as these are unsuitable for puppets; you might add your own design with textile paint or diluted acrylic paint. Puppeteers also keep collections of trimmings – felt, braid, fringing, lace, ribbons, feathers, beads, costume jewellery, embroidery silks, knitting wools – in fact, all manner of odds and ends that might come in useful for a costume.

Making up the Costume

You need to dress the puppet before attaching the strings. Sometimes you might need to secure the hands and feet after dressing the puppet, depending how you go about making the costume. You can stitch the costume together as if for a doll and then dress the puppet, but many people, especially beginners, end up with costumes that are too tight and restrict movement. A good alternative is to stitch or glue the costume directly on to the puppet.

The main sections for costume construction.

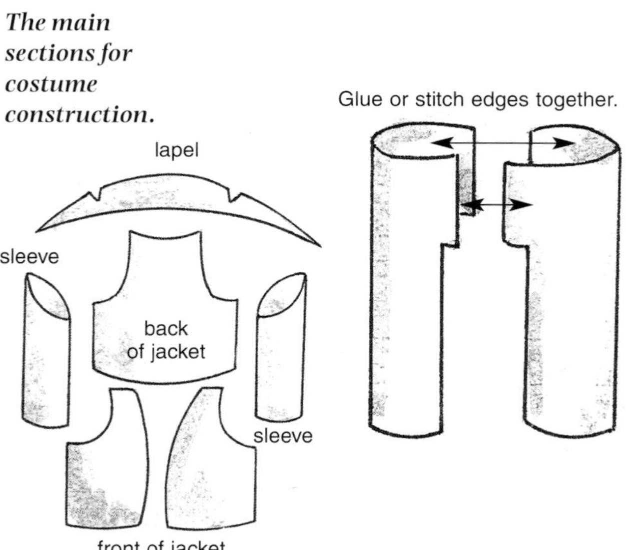

Gluing is usually quicker and avoids having seam edges inside the costume as these can hinder movement, but parts that are subject to strain might need a few stitches for security. The choice of glue depends on the fabric; fabric adhesive is usually best but clear, multi-purpose contact adhesive is possible for many materials. To create a hem, smear the glue sparingly and evenly along the edge, then turn it up and press down firmly, or smear glue along the fabric and trim it clean when the glue is dry. The use of glue for a turned-up hem may be unsuitable for fabrics that are to flow loosely in folds as the glue may stiffen them too much.

Trousers are created from two tubes of fabric joined at the top. First establish the hems, and then make each tube by gluing one edge of the fabric over the other. Lay the fabric flat and fold the inside edge towards the centre; smear glue along the overlapping edge, up as far as the crotch, then place this over the inner edge and press down firmly. Snip a little into both edges at the crotch so that the fabric can be opened out at the top to meet the matching fabric from the other leg. With the trouser legs on the puppet, glue together the two pieces of fabric down the fly front, under the crotch and up the back of the trousers. A stitch in the crotch may be helpful. To make a waistband, glue a strip of material into a narrow tube shape. Press it flat with the join inside and glue it on to the trousers.

The front and back panels of shirts and jackets are glued to each other; collars and lapels are glued on separately. The sleeves are made from two tubes of material cut at an angle at the top and glued or stitched on to the shirt or jacket. The ends of the sleeves may be hemmed or you can add separate cuffs.

Dresses usually require front and back panels for the bodice and separate sleeves. The skirt can be cut in one piece or in separate panels. However you can achieve very effective costumes by draping the fabric and stitching or gluing it in place, rather than making up an actual dress. You can also add further layers of fabric of different colour, texture, or transparency to achieve the desired effect.

FOR SALE
WARNING

5 CONTROL AND MANIPULATION

MARIONETTE CONTROL

Strings attached to the puppet are normally joined to a wooden control, sometimes called a 'crutch' or a 'perch', that is constructed and manipulated so as to move the puppet in the desired fashion. The essence of marionette control, more than for any other three-dimensional puppet, is to let the puppet do the work: use the natural movements, and the momentum of these movements, to assist you. Therefore you should design your controls to achieve the required movements or effects as simply as possible.

The *Kathputli* marionettes of Rajasthan are often controlled with just a loop of string, the ends of which are attached to the top of the head and the back of the waist, sometimes with another loop to the hands. A combination of the intrinsic movements of the marionette and the dexterity of the puppeteer produce an amazing degree of control and variety of movements. A typical Burmese control has only a few strings attached directly to it; instead there are loops of string that sit in grooves in the control when not in use. This type of control also depends on the puppeteer's ability to deal with the various loops simultaneously.

However, some of you may remember having been given, as children, marionettes that were frustratingly difficult to manipulate, despite the simple controls. Often the figures had insufficient structure or weight to move well, the costumes sometimes proved a further limitation, and, paradoxically, the controls were too simple. They were not only simple but in a sense they were inefficient because they did not do the work for you; mostly they supported the puppet and you had to operate individual strings to make something happen. A good control may appear more complicated but it will be much easier to operate the marionette with less direct string pulling.

Although there are a number of good basic designs, these will need to be adapted or supplemented with individual features to suit the particular puppet and what it is required to do. In my entire collection of marionettes, including those I have made myself, I do not have two controls that are exactly the same. Controls for puppets that are characters in plays have a greater degree of similarity than those that perform variety-style acts with tricks and transformations, which may require a good deal of inventiveness when the control is designed.

Plan the control at the same time as planning the marionette, but be prepared to adapt your plans even as you string the puppet (*see* pages 84–6) in the light of how effectively it moves (*see* pages 88–95). The marionette must be dressed before you start to string it.

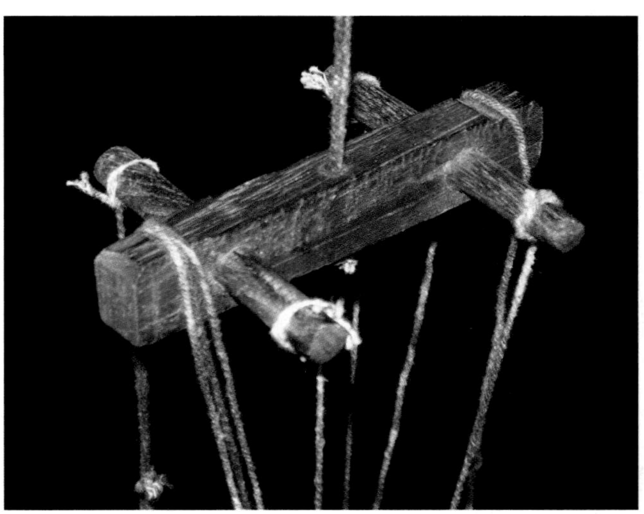

***ABOVE:* This apparently simple control for a Burmese marionette takes a good deal of skill to operate. The front crossbar carries the head strings and the rear crossbar carries the body strings, which are attached close together just behind the neck. The three looped strings sitting in the front groove operate the upper arms, hands and legs; the loop of string in the rear groove operates the heels.**

***LEFT:* Paul Doran, operating open-stage style. Normally he wears black cotton gloves to perform but omitted these for the photograph.**

Most marionette controls require two-handed operation, the most common being the upright control and the horizontal control; the latter is sometimes called the 'aeroplane' or 'paddle' control. Unless the puppet's actions require otherwise, the tendency in the UK is to use the upright control for human characters, and the horizontal control for animal puppets. However, in some countries, the horizontal control is used extensively for both. Some controls of each sort have the walking action built into the main control whilst others have a separate leg bar, which is generally preferable for human figures.

The use of screw-eyes is not recommended for attaching the strings to the control; they tend to catch in the strings of other puppets, especially when removing the figures from a hanging rack. In the middle of a performance this can bring the other puppets crashing to the ground. It is better to drill small holes through the appropriate part and use the edge of a triangular file to make a fine groove around all parts of the control where a string is to be attached. Lightly sand the control to remove any roughness, snags, or sharp edges, then thread the strings through the holes, wind them around the grooves and tie them.

The dimensions for the controls described below are intended purely as a rough guide. The length of each rod or bar will be determined largely by the size and proportions of the puppet; the width, thickness or diameter will be determined by what feels comfortable and, more particularly, by the dimensions needed to effect any joints required without weakening the control. Equivalent metric and imperial measures are approximations to the nearest common size.

The Upright Control

The basis of the upright control is an inverted cross shape; the upright is the main bar and the crosspiece the head bar. To the main bar are attached a dowelling shoulder bar at the rear, a detachable leg bar at the front near the top, and wires just below the leg bar to operate the hands. Further attachments are made as required.

The main bar is made from a 22.5cm (9in) length of 20mm (¾in) square section timber or a dowel of 20mm diameter. The head bar is either 20mm square section timber or 10mm (⅜in) diameter dowelling, each a little longer than the width of the puppet's head. Attach a

LEFT: The Burmese marionette in action.

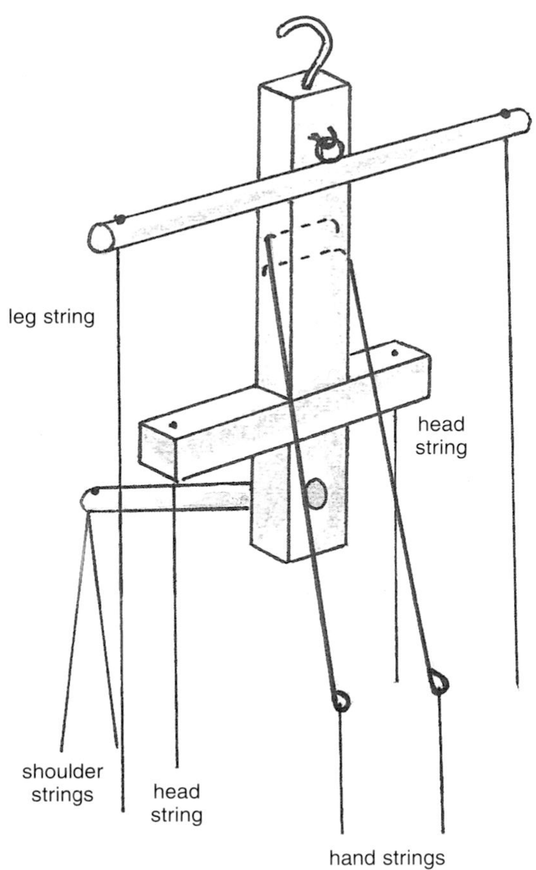

LEFT: The basic upright control.

dowelling head bar by drilling a hole across the control and gluing the head bar into it. Secure it with a nail through the upright. Attach the square section timber with a cross-halving joint. Make two saw cuts half-way through each piece of wood and then chisel out the waste so that the two pieces can be glued, interlocked and screwed together.

The length of the shoulder bar is determined by whatever is necessary to hold the shoulder strings clear of the head. Approximately 12.5cm (5in) should suit a 60cm (24in) marionette, but you might leave the bar longer than required and cut it to length later when you are sure where the strings need to go. It will operate better if the bar is angled 30–40 degrees downwards. To attach the shoulder bar, drill a hole in the rear of the control below the head bar and glue the dowel into the hole so that it sticks out at the back. This dowel must be a tight fit. It will carry a good deal of the marionette's weight so secure it further with a small nail.

As an alternative to a dowelling shoulder bar, it can be made of galvanized wire, which enables it to be folded up for packing. Drill a hole across the main bar just below the head bar. Pass the wire through the hole, bend each end backwards to form a loop of the part through the control, and bind together the two halves of the wire with strong thread. Bend the ends of the wire into a small loop for attaching the shoulder strings. If

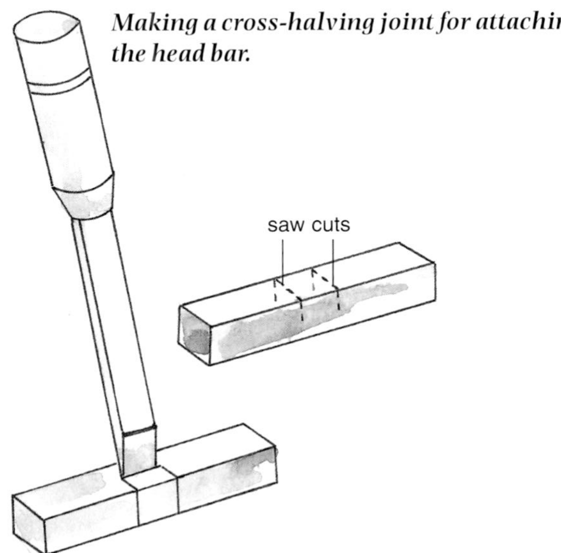

Making a cross-halving joint for attaching the head bar.

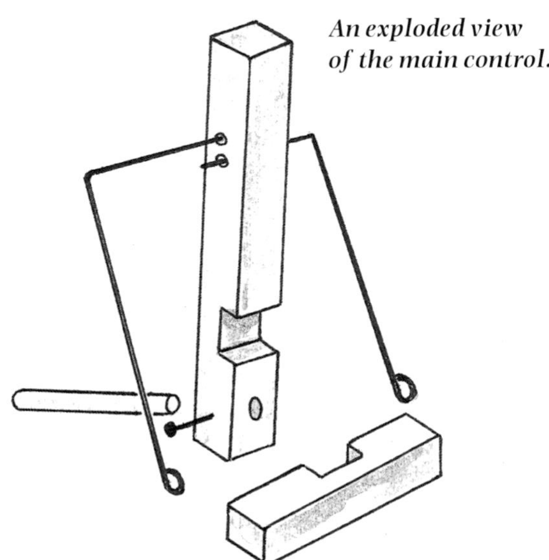

An exploded view of the main control.

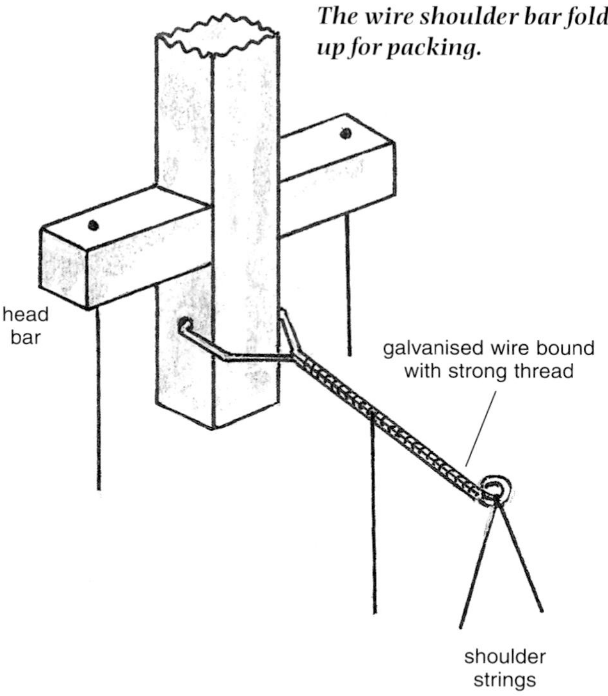

The wire shoulder bar folds up for packing.

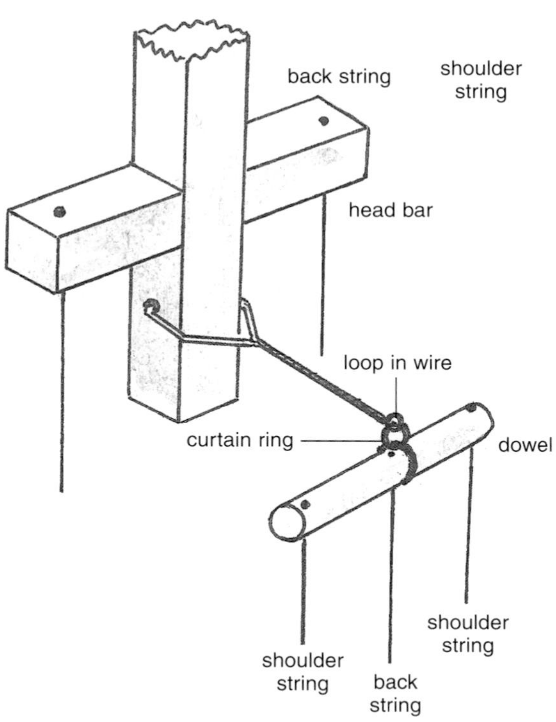

A dowel attached to the shoulder bar to hold the strings clear of the head.

necessary, to keep the shoulder strings well clear of the head, attach them to the ends of a separate dowel and suspend the dowel by a curtain ring or screw-eye from the loop in the end of the wire.

To attach the leg bar, tie a curtain ring or twist a screw-eye into the centre of a 20cm (8in) dowel and suspend this from the top of the control by a small hook. I prefer to use the curtain ring as it is slightly larger and the attaching thread, which must be strong, lets it flex. This helps when you are trying to replace it quickly on the hook. To ensure the ring does not slip, drill a small hole through the centre of the dowel for attaching the thread.

Heel strings are not normally required but, if they should be needed, either attach them to a second leg bar on the rear of the control or attach them to the shoulder bar. If you have a number of such attachments on the shoulder bar, or elsewhere for that matter, you need ways to identify them quickly while performing. For example, tie a small coloured bead on to the string just below the control, or attach a short white thread between the control string and the control.

The hand wires are made from galvanized wire and attached to the main control far enough below the leg bar so as not to interfere with it when you raise the hand wires. How you hold the control will be a factor when determining the position for the hand wires. My preferred method is to hold the control with my little finger under the head bar and my other fingers above it, but some puppeteers place all their fingers above the head bar. Hold the control as you would to operate it and mark the position for the holes. I find a convenient position for the lower hole to be 1cm (⅜in) above my index finger and the upper hole 8mm (5/16in) above that, with the hook for the leg bar at least 3cm (1¼in) higher again.

Bend one end of each wire into a fairly sharp right angle using pliers. Insert the long straight pieces of wire through the holes in opposite directions; carefully bend the long ends downwards. They should not be too tight to the upright or they will not move freely but you need quite sharp corners, as wide curves will let the wires wobble about. They also need to be angled outwards slightly, not pointing straight down. To obtain a sharp angle, hold the wire with pliers and, as you bend the wire down, keep firm pressure upwards on the piece of the wire that is across the control. This takes a little practice to achieve.

Cut the wires to the same length, loop the ends for attaching hand strings and seal the closures of the loops with glue. The hand wires usually reach at least to the bottom of the control and a little beyond. For puppets of 60–75cm (24–30in) in height, I find that hand wires of 16–17cm (6½in) in length when finished are usually sufficient to achieve the degree of hand movement required.

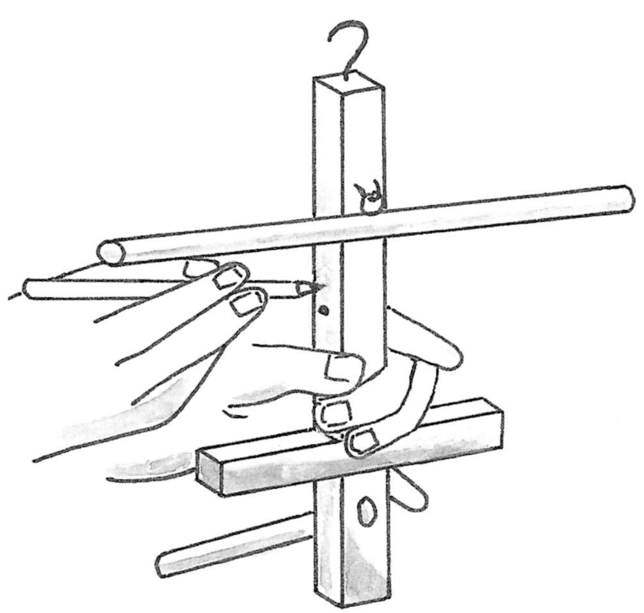

Marking the position of the hand wires.

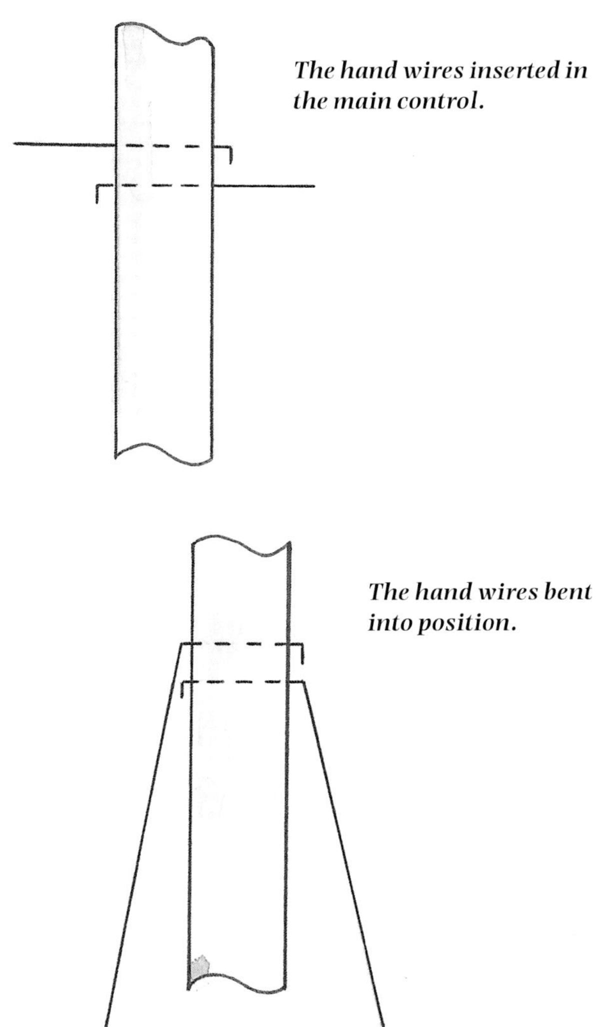

The hand wires inserted in the main control.

The hand wires bent into position.

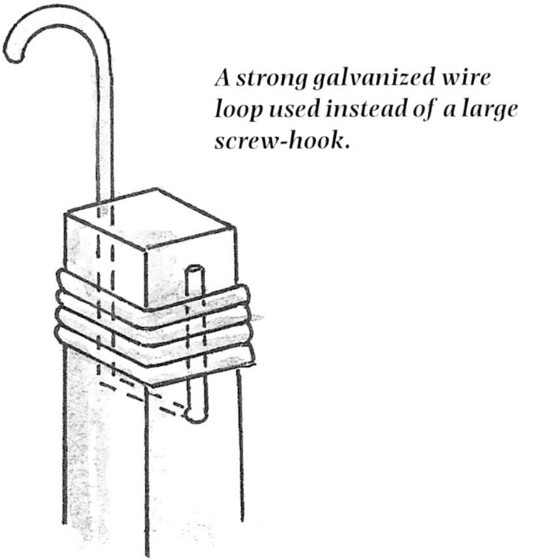

A strong galvanized wire loop used instead of a large screw-hook.

If the puppet has a back string and/or a chest string, leave them a little slack so that they do not interfere with normal movement. Attach the back string to some part of the shoulder bar, and the chest string somewhere along the head bar, or to a dowelling insert on the control, to help to guide the string away from the front of the face.

Add a large screw-hook for hanging up the control. Alternatively, make the hook from strong galvanized wire: insert it through a hole drilled across the control, bend the ends upwards along the control and bind it securely with cord.

Mouth and Eye Strings

If fixtures are required for mouth and eye strings, attach to the control short dowels of about 6mm (¼in) diameter. Drill two holes in the front of the control above the head bar and glue the dowels into the holes. Space the dowels so your second finger can fit under one dowel and your third finger under the other.

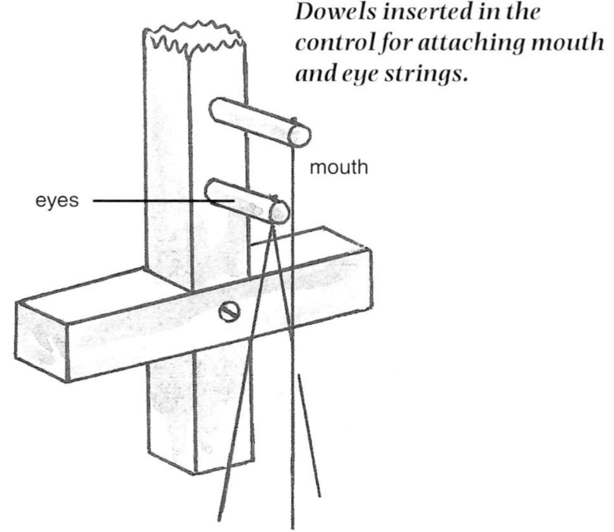

Dowels inserted in the control for attaching mouth and eye strings.

Rocking Bars

A rocking bar enables you to walk the puppet with the hand holding the main control. It is used most often when you need to free your other hand for some particular purpose, such as operating a specialized feature of the puppet. However, the leg action is not usually as good as when a separate leg bar is used. There are two common types of rocking bar for an upright control: one made of shaped wood, the other comprising a straight wooden bar with a wire thumb loop.

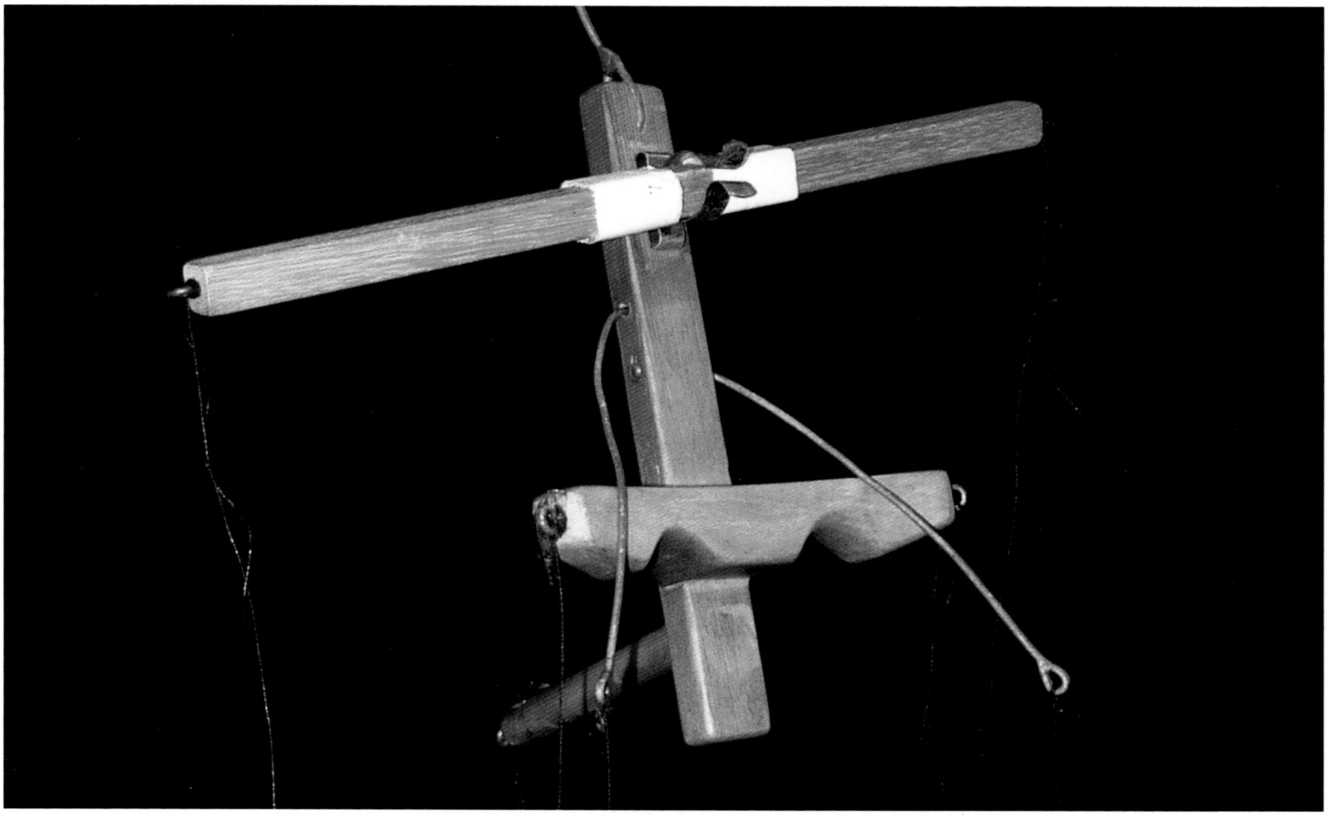

A variation on the basic upright control by the late John Wright. The head bar is grooved for the little finger of the supporting hand and a spring clip is used to hold the leg bar.

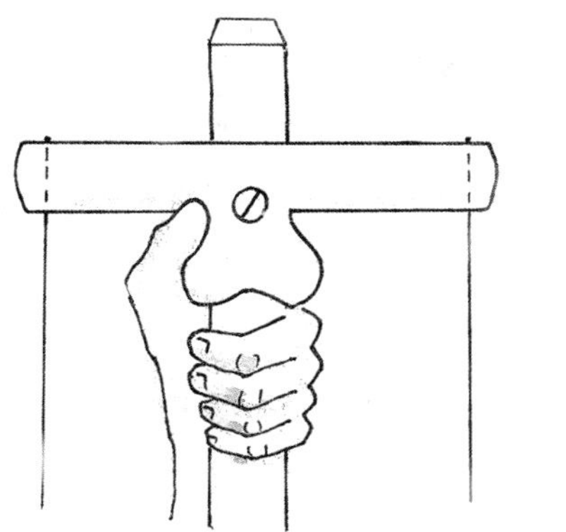

A shaped wooden rocking bar.

Cut the shaped wooden leg bar from strong plywood with two large notches for your thumb or finger to fit into. Drill a hole through the centre of the bar and screw it to the main control bar at a position where you can reach it comfortably with your thumb and index finger. Screw it sufficiently tight to permit a smooth and free rocking action without wobbling. If you find it makes manipulation more comfortable, you can insert a short dowel between the rocking bar and the main control.

For the alternative control, drill two holes up through a straight leg bar and push the ends of a loop of wire through the holes. Bend the ends of the wire along the top of the bar, then glue and bind them with strong thread. Drill a hole through the centre of the leg bar and screw it to the main control where you would normally hang the leg bar, with a dowelling spacer if required. Hold the control and slip your thumb or index finger into the wire loop to move the bar.

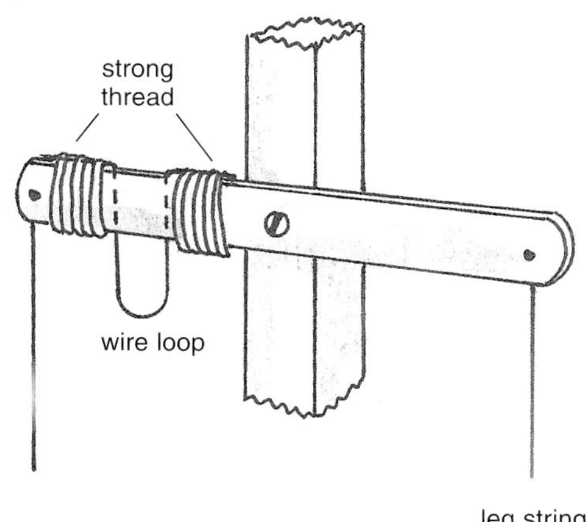

A wooden rocking bar with a wire thumb loop.

The Horizontal Control

This type of horizontal control is used for human figures; the animal control is described in the following chapter (*see* pages 109–12). The control consists of a wooden main bar 20cm (8in) in length and 25 x 25mm (1in x 1in) in width, to which are attached the dowelling head, shoulder and leg bars and a removable hand bar. The dowels are approximately 7–10mm (¼–⅜in) in diameter.

The head and shoulder dowels are a little wider than the respective parts of the puppet. They are suspended from the main control so that you can walk the puppet without rocking the head and body from side to side. Drill two holes down through the main bar, one approximately in the middle for the head, the other near the back for the shoulders. Drill a hole through the centre point of each dowel rod. Thread a strong cord through each hole and the corresponding dowel and knot the ends.

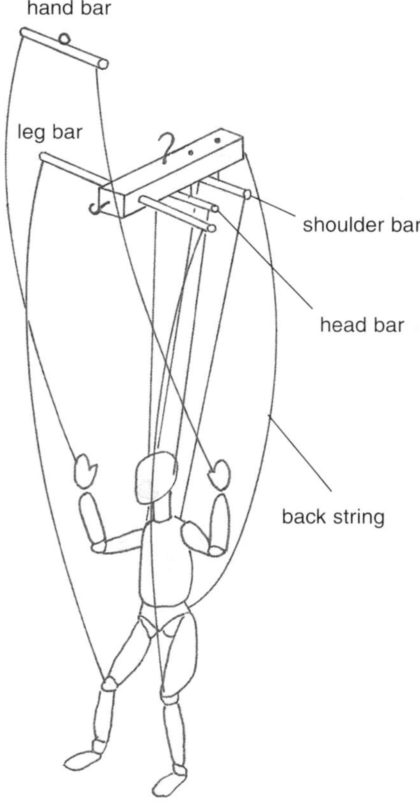

The standard horizontal control and stringing.

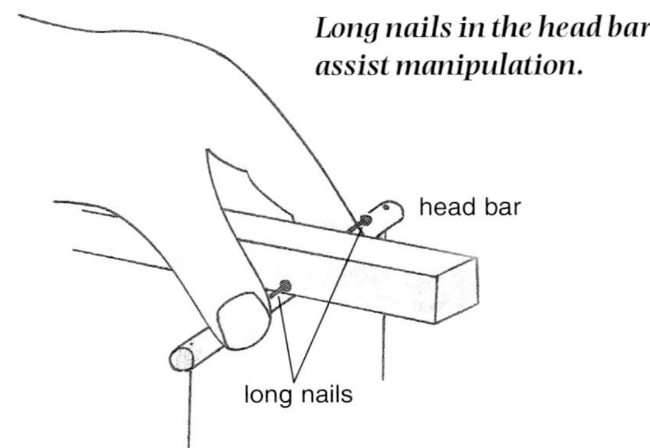

Long nails in the head bar assist manipulation.

To assist manipulation of the head, you can glue into the top of the head bar long nails that can be gripped with your thumb and forefinger of the hand supporting the control. Ensure that the string by which the bar is suspended is not too long or you will be unable to reach the head bar.

Attach the leg bar near the front of the control by one of the following methods.

- Glue the dowel into a hole drilled across the main bar. Drill a small hole down through the main bar and the dowel, and insert a small nail for added security (*see* illustration on page 79).
- Use a round file to make a groove across the top of the main bar. Make the width of the groove the same as the diameter of the dowel and the depth the same as the radius, so that the dowel will fit snugly inside. Glue and screw the dowel into the groove.

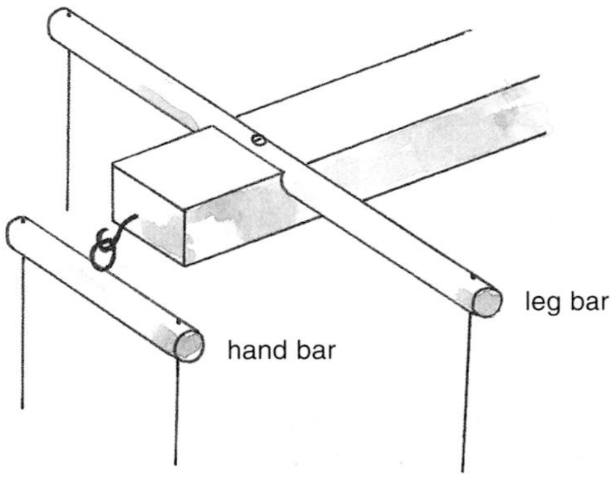

An alternative means of attaching the leg bar is to glue and screw it into a groove in the control.

- Instead of dowelling, square section wood can be used for the leg bar, glued and screwed to the top of the main bar. If this method is used, the main bar should have a section chiselled away for the bar to sit in, which prevents it coming loose and turning during use.

To attach the hand bar to the main control, drill a small hole through the mid-point and tie a small curtain ring to the dowel with strong thread through the hole. Screw a small hook into the front end of the main bar and hang the hand bar from it.

Alternatively, use a screw-on spring clip (terry clip) to hold the bar. The width of the hand bar depends upon what the puppet is to do, whether the hands are simply to gesture or to perform a particular task.

To attach a back string, drill a hole down through the rear end of the control.

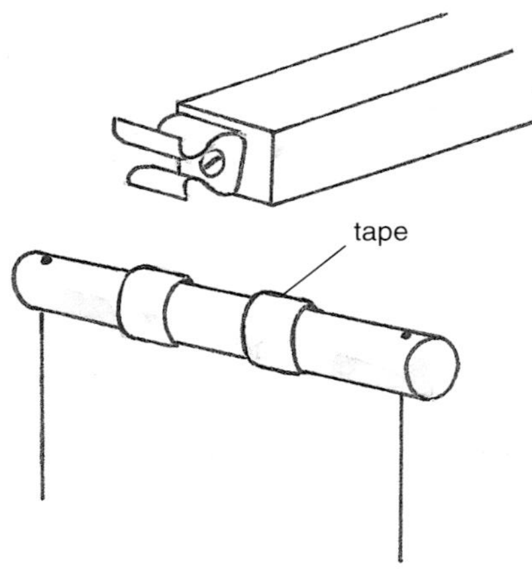

A spring clip used to hold the hand bar.

Some puppets need heel strings. Attach these directly to the control or to a removable heel bar or a lever. The heel bar is a dowel rod that sits on a smaller dowelling peg glued into the top of the control near the rear end. Drill a hole in the heel bar so that it fits snugly, but not too tightly, on to the peg. For a lever mechanism, pivot a strip of wood at the back of the control, so that it can be raised by pressing it with the heel of the hand holding the control.

Add a large hook for hanging up the puppet. Use a large screw-hook or shape the hook from strong galvanized wire and attach it with knotted cord, or bind it securely in place.

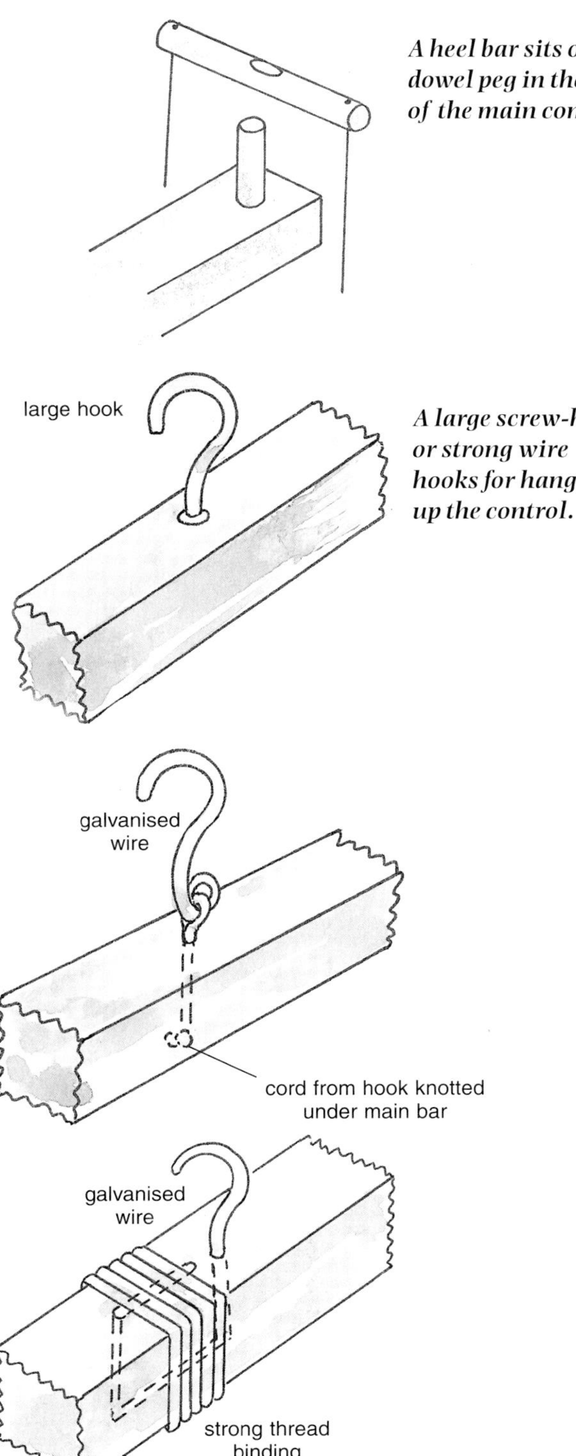

A heel bar sits on a dowel peg in the end of the main control.

A large screw-hook or strong wire hooks for hanging up the control.

Mouth and Eye Controls

If the puppet is to have a moving mouth (or eyes), the control string is fixed to a wire lever attached to the main control. Make the lever from a piece of 12 or 14 gauge galvanized wire with each end bent into a loop. Cut a slot in the control just behind the head bar – an easy way is to drill a series of touching holes in a straight line and carefully trim out the waste with a chisel or a sharp craft knife. Fix the lever in the slot by a nail through one of the loops. The mouth or eye string(s) is tied to the other loop and operated with the thumb or middle finger of the hand holding the control.

If the marionette has both moving eyes and a moving mouth, you can have two of these wire levers, one operated by your thumb and the other by your middle finger. However, this is tricky to operate and in inexperienced hands can increase the risk of dropping the whole control.

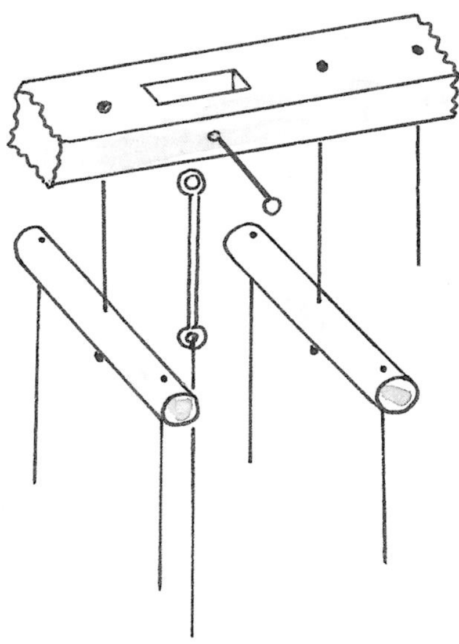

A control lever for eye or mouth movements.

An alternative is to have one wire lever and to use the hand bar to control the other moving feature. A string from the mouth or the eyes runs up through a small screw-eye that is fixed into the front of the control. The string is attached to the hand bar with sufficient slack to permit the hands to be operated without pulling this extra string taut. By pulling the hand bar a little way from the main control, the attached feature is moved.

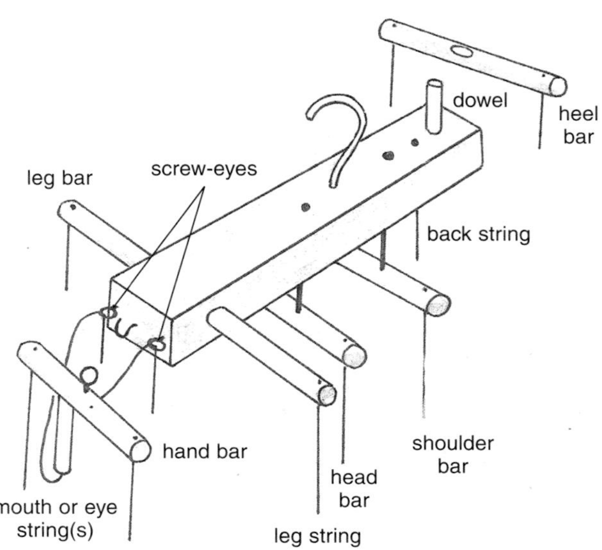

Although the hand bar used to control the eyes or mouth has limited applications, it is useful for a puppet such as a weightlifter.

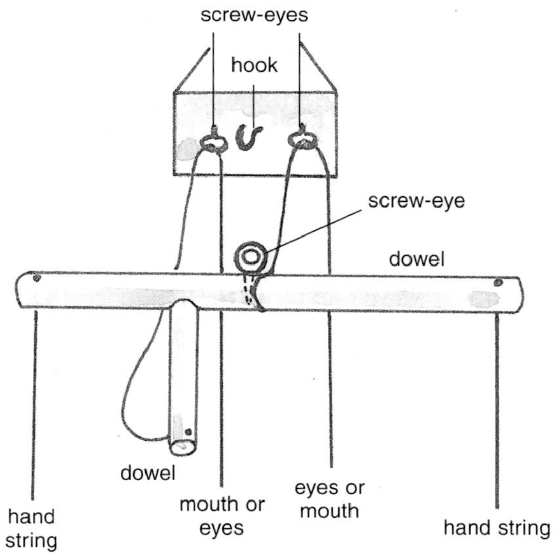

An arrangement for the hand bar to control the mouth and the eyes.

Another possibility, if mouth and eyes move, is to attach both control strings to the hand bar. Drill a hole in the hand bar to accommodate a dowel of smaller diameter. Glue it in place to form a 'T' shape. It should face downwards and slightly rearwards when the hand bar is hanging on the main control. Attach either the mouth or the eye strings directly to the hand bar as described previously and attach the other string(s) to the end of the additional dowel. Rotating the hand bar a little causes the extra dowel to operate the feature attached; pulling the hand bar away from the control operates the other feature. Rotating and pulling simultaneously operates the mouth and the eyes.

Before finally securing the strings, experiment with the optimal amount of slack in the mouth and eye strings to permit the required hand and arm movements with and without moving these features.

Rocking Bar

A rocking bar is sometimes helpful for a horizontal control, although it is more useful for the upright control. Screw the rocking bar on to the front end of the control and move it with your thumb and index finger whilstholding the control with your other fingers. Of course, you will have to place elsewhere any other controls that would have been attached at this point.

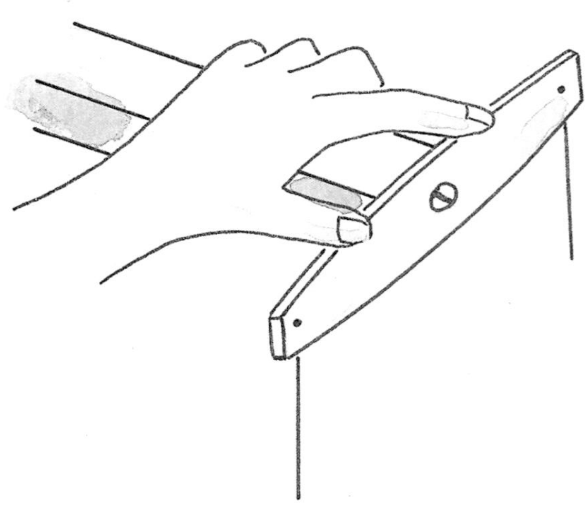

A rocking bar for a horizontal control.

Rotating Controls

A rotating control allows the puppet to be spun round. Screw to the top of the control a cotton reel or a similar sized dowel with a hole drilled through the centre. Use washers on top of and underneath the cotton reel and ensure that the screw is secure, or it will unscrew when you turn the control. Hold the reel with one hand whilst turning the control with the other.

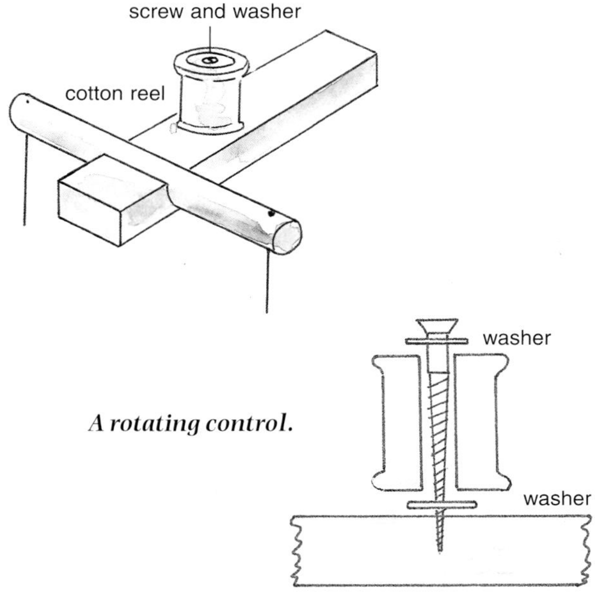

A rotating control.

Strings or Control Bars Attached to Elastic

It is sometimes useful to attach certain strings to the control with a strip of thin elastic to allow a degree of built-in movement. For example, a tightrope walker's hands, which may be held raised away from the body, would be able to move naturally without direct control from the hand wires.

Strong elastic is occasionally used to suspend the head bar from a horizontal control. The marionette's head is tilted forward by slight downward pressure on the head bar.

An Alternative Head Control

Instead of the normal head bar, it is possible to attach the head strings to the corners of a triangular plywood plate. It is suspended from the control by a hook and a screw-eye so that it can be operated independently of the main control. One string attaches at the back or the front of the head (preferably not the nose) and the other two at the sides. This will give control of the head in many directions.

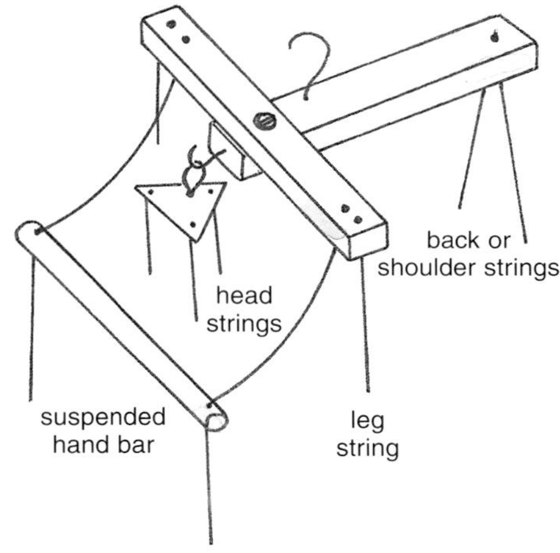

An alternative head control with three strings attached to a triangular plywood plate.

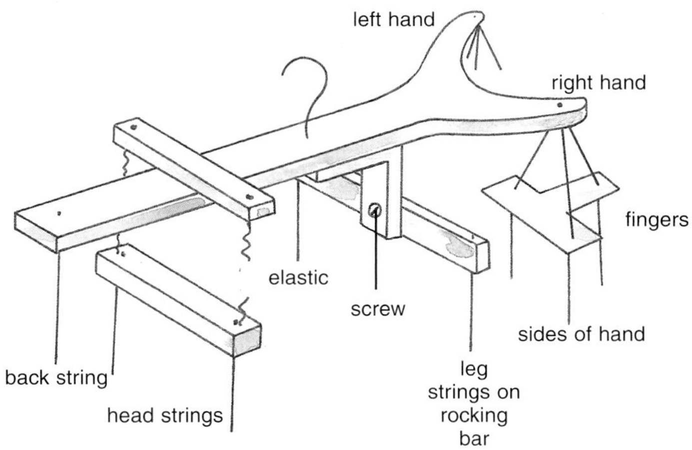

An old style of control that has a 'T'-shaped, three-point hand control, a head bar suspended on elastic, and a form of rocking bar to operate the legs.

Alternative Hand and Leg Controls

A variation of the horizontal control exchanges the position of the hand and leg controls. A detachable leg bar hangs from the front of the control, and the hands are controlled by a single loop of string that runs through a hole drilled across the main bar, near the front, where the leg bar would otherwise be. The limitation of this method is the difficulty of manipulating the hands whilst walking the puppet.

It is possible also to have a 'T'-shaped hand control with three strings to each hand. This is an old style that would now tend only to be used for a specific purpose rather than as a standard method.

Stringing the Marionette

In the West there is the tendency to minimize the visibility of the strings: most performers tend to string their puppets with dark green or black thread. However, many Asian marionettes have fairly substantial strings, often white, and it is interesting that this does not seem to interfere with the enjoyment of the performance or the suspension of disbelief. Similarly, many marionette performers work in an open-stage style in full view of the audience, which is also accepted. This suggests that one should not worry unduly about whether one colour of string is going to show more than another.

In the past many puppeteers strung their marionettes with dark green No.18 carpet thread, but nowadays this can be difficult to find. I use black Dacron braided nylon fishing line (strength 4.5kg/10lb or higher). You can use an appropriate substitute but avoid clear, shiny nylon thread because it may stretch, retains crinkles after being wound up, and glistens distractingly under stage lighting.

We always used to rub the carpet thread with beeswax before use and from time to time thereafter to prolong its life. I do not really know if this makes much difference to the Dacron thread but I continue to use it anyway, just in case. Place the thread over the beeswax block, hold the thread down with your thumb and draw the thread through the wax with the other hand. Repeat this two or three times to ensure all-round coverage, but do not press too hard, nor draw the thread too quickly, or your thumb will suffer. When the puppet is in use, rub the wax block up and down against the taut strings; pull slack strings taut to wax them.

String the puppet so that you can hold it comfortably to operate it, which will usually be with the bottom of the control at about elbow height. The length of the strings depends upon whether you are to stand on the same level as the puppet or to operate from a raised platform or a bridge over the stage. You will find that operating from a bridge with 2.4m (12ft) strings is very different from working at floor level with 75cm (30in) strings.

The strings of any removable control bars, such as a leg bar, must be just long enough to allow the bar to be unhooked without moving the puppet.

String the puppet when it is supported in a standing position. In practice, you can use any means of hanging the control with a chain or a loop of cord while the puppet is standing on a firm surface but it is usually more convenient to stand the puppet on a table or a workbench and suspend it from a 'gallows'.

Constructing a Gallows

A gallows is helpful for stringing puppets with moderate-length strings. It consists of a work surface to which is attached a vertical post, preferably adjustable in height, and a top horizontal bar from which a length of chain is suspended.

Use a substantial piece of wood approximately 50 x 25mm (2 x 1in). Attach an upright of 1.5–1.8m (5–6ft) to the work surface with three shelf brackets. Alternatively, use two overlapping pieces of timber for the upright. Drill a series of equally spaced holes in each piece and join them using bolts with wing nuts so that you can adjust the height.

Screw a 30cm (12in) length of wood to the top of the upright at right angles and use a shelf bracket to support it. Screw a hook into the end of this horizontal bar and hang a chain from the hook.

If the strings are to be very long for working from a bridge, make a similar arrangement from the bridge with the puppet standing on the stage floor or make a temporary rig elsewhere.

Attaching the Strings

Attach strings directly to the puppet or to fixtures on the puppet designed for this purpose, not to the costume or body padding. When attaching the strings to the control, thread them through the pre-drilled holes, wind them in the filed grooves and knot them, loosely at first, so that adjustments can

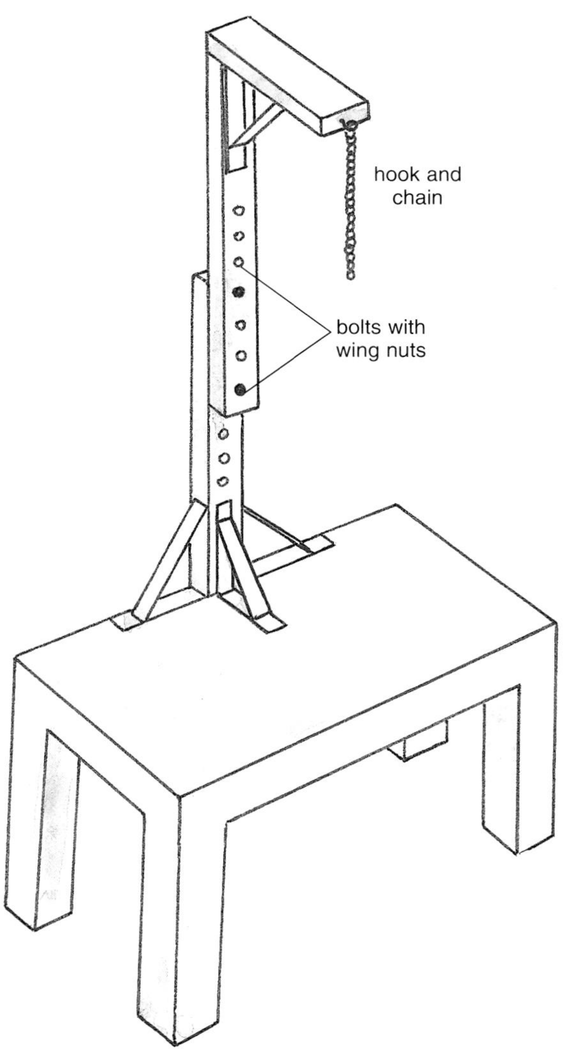

A gallows for stringing marionettes.

be made. The waxing of the strings seems to help them grip in the grooves during this procedure. String the puppet in the following sequence.

1. With the control suspended at the required height from the work surface, connect the head strings (with an animal, the back strings) so that the puppet stands without floating or sagging at the knees. Attach each head string to a hole drilled in the ear. If the ear is not strong enough or in an unsuitable position, use a small screw-eye fastened in a dowel that is built into the head at a position for appropriate balance (*see* pages 42–43).

2. Attach the shoulder strings (with an animal, the head strings), using a needle to thread each one through the costume. Suitable fixing points include holes drilled in a solid body or in the plywood core of a padded body, and small screw-eyes in a solid body. Alternatively, tie the string to a button inside the body.

3. Attach the other ends of the shoulder strings to the end of the shoulder bar. Adjust the tension so that, when at rest, the head sits at the required position in relation to the body.

4. Drill a hole in each hand for the hand strings. The position of the hole depends on how you want the hands to be held and how the weight is distributed. You will not normally want hands to be fully palm-downwards unless they are to play the piano, nor looking as though they are about to clap. Look at your own hands when they hang loosely by your side; they are usually angled with the knuckle of your index finger the most forward point of the hand. This is a good general position for a marionette hand, for which you would attach the string between the knuckles of the thumb and index finger or on the line of the metacarpal bone of the index finger, which runs from the knuckle down the back of the hand. Sometimes you will attach the string to the thumb, centrally on the back of the hand, or even with the palm facing upwards, as appropriate to the required action.
   Countersink the hole in the hand to hide the knot, thread the string through the hole and knot the end. Tie the other end of the hand string to the looped end of the corresponding hand wire or to a hand bar, as appropriate. Ensure that the hand strings are not slack, but long enough for the hands to hang by the puppet's sides when you are not holding the control.

5. Attach the leg strings. Drill a hole in each leg just above the knee, from front to back. If necessary, countersink the hole so that the knotted thread will not impede movement at the knee. Use a needle to

insert the thread through the costume and through the hole in the leg, and then knot the thread. To ensure that the fabric does not pull or pucker when tension is applied, insert the needle through the costume just a little above the hole in the leg. You sometimes have to make more than one attempt to get the position just right. Attach the other end to the leg bar with the string just long enough for the bar to be unhooked without moving the leg.

6. Marionettes do not naturally look upwards just by tilting the main control so a chest string is necessary if this action is required. Attach it to the torso; the point at which it is attached determines how far back the puppet can bend. For the upright control, attach the other end of the thread somewhere along the head bar to help to guide the string away from the front of the face. If the puppet needs a back string, attach it to the base of the torso or the top of the pelvis. Attach the other end to some part of the shoulder bar. Leave the chest and back strings a little slack so that they do not interfere with head movement. For the horizontal control, attach these strings at convenient points near the back and front of the main bar.

7. Attach any additional strings required. Make the final adjustments to the tension of the strings. Tie all the knots securely and seal them with a clear contact adhesive. Trim all the loose ends of the threads close to the knots.

Marionette Manipulation

The difference between puppet theatre and 'dolly-waggling' is akin to the difference between a concert pianist and someone who simply presses the right notes in the right order, or perhaps the right notes but in the wrong order.

This section outlines general principles to enhance movement, together with practical advice about the handling of marionettes, and then explains the mechanical aspects of marionette manipulation.

Principles and Practicalities

The puppeteer is an actor who acts through the puppet, so concentration is essential: focus on your puppet and look where your puppet is looking. Aspire to achieve clean, precise movements and do not slur them together. Develop a variety of gestures rather than jiggling the puppet, and do not jerk or jiggle the puppet to every syllable of speech.

I make no apology for repeating in all my books invaluable advice given by the late John Wright, 'Every line should have an action and every action should have a meaning. Never put in unnecessary movement.' He also advised, 'New moves on new thoughts'. The puppet may appear to think, move and deliver a line almost simultaneously, but the three elements actually follow in sequence so that the movement anticipates the word rather than following it.

Marionettes should make their entrances and exits in character, like a live actor, so start manipulating them before the audience can see them and do not swing or float them on and off the stage. Give listening figures subdued, watchful movements to focus attention on the puppet that is speaking.

Rehearse thoroughly. You might use a mirror occasionally to see how the puppet looks and moves but avoid over-dependence on it, because you will not have it to rely on when you perform. You will begin to know instinctively when the puppet is moving well; you will feel when its weight is just transferred to the floor, or when it is floating or sagging. Use video to record and review your manipulation, and invite someone to watch your live performance and give constructive feedback.

It is important not only to practise manipulation but also to ensure that you have rehearsed under performance conditions. Many years ago I had prepared a number of cabaret acts with 1m (3ft) high marionettes and ultraviolet lighting. Having performed with marionettes for many years and used UV with other types of puppet, I was confident that I knew what I was doing and not concerned that I had been unable to rehearse the items in total blackout. The controls were painted black, the strings were black and I wore black, including black gloves. Everything was going smoothly until a string became caught in an awkward position as I brought a puppet on stage, the kind of hitch that would have been sorted in a second or two normally. I looked down to deal with it and suddenly realized that

***OPPOSITE:* Mr Herbert, by Gordon Staight, loses his glasses, which are on top of his head. When he looks up, with the aid of a string to the torso, they fall into position on his face.**

A back string is required for bowing or bending forwards.

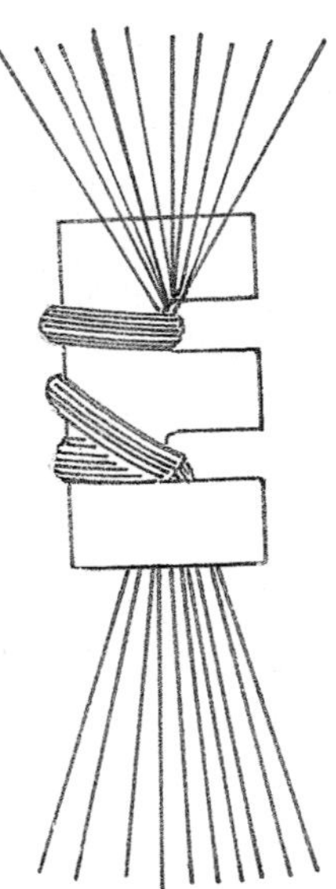

A plywood winder used to prevent tangling when transporting marionettes.

I could not see what was wrong. In fact, I could see nothing except the puppet; I could not even see my hands in front of my face. Fortunately, I was able to feel what the problem was and retrieve the situation, but it could have been different. So always undertake a certain amount of rehearsal under performance conditions and practise until you can deal with the control with your eyes closed.

Buttons are also a source of snagging of strings, so consider what you wear to perform. Stages and scenery can have all manner of potential snagging points too, so try to identify and avoid these. However careful you are, emergencies will arise – keep calm, be prepared to improvise, and carry a puppet 'first aid box' containing a few basic items such as scissors, small screw drivers, stapler, needles, thread, tape, glue, beeswax, and so on. You do not need a lot but I carry a biscuit tin full of odds and ends – just in case!

If you drop the marionette, lift the control (not the puppet) gently; keeping the strings a little slack, undo any loose tangles. If the control takes the weight of the puppet, the tangles will be pulled tighter. If there are

OPPOSITE: Operating the standard upright control. Note the slightly different thumb positions on the hand wires; which one is used depends on individual preference. The free hand operating the leg bar is used also to manipulate individual hand strings.

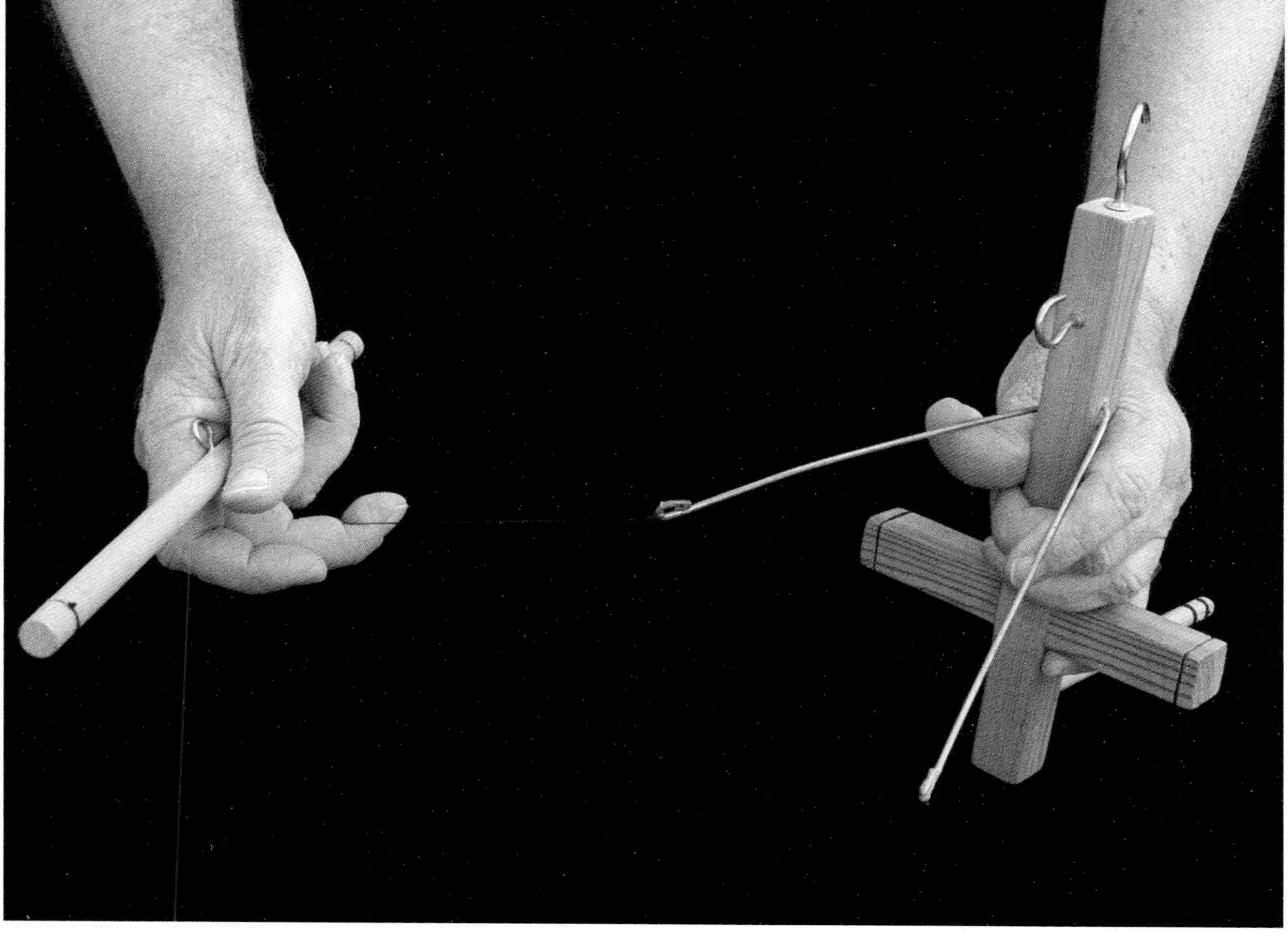

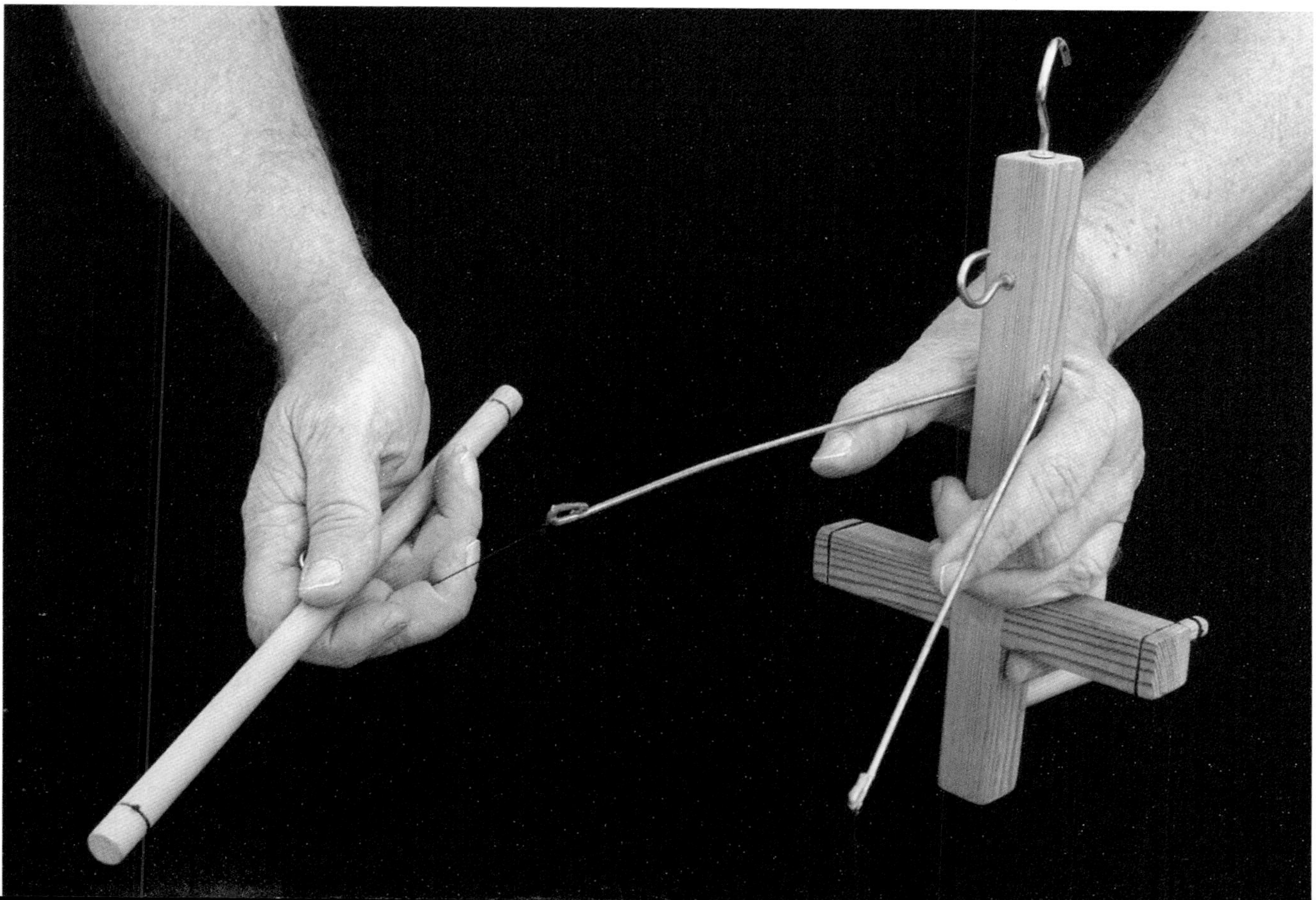

any difficult tangles, for example if the control has tumbled over, trace the strings up from the puppet in a systematic manner, twisting or turning the control as necessary.

To avoid tangling the strings when storing or transporting marionettes, wind the strings round 'winders', pieces of plywood or hardboard in which two slots have been cut to take the strings. Smooth the slots and edges of the winders thoroughly before use.

When marionettes are not in use, protect them from dust and damage by keeping them in bags made of calico or a similar strong fabric. Make the bag long enough for the puppet to remain upright and secure it with a draw cord in the top hem.

Finally, when you are not manipulating the marionettes, you will need some form of hanging rack, sometimes called a 'perchery'. You can construct this yourself with timber uprights that support horizontal metal tubing, but a much simpler method is to use a garment rail designed for use in the home, not the commercial sort because the rails of these are generally too large.

The Upright Control

Hold the main control in one hand. Take the weight of the control with your little finger under the head bar and your second and third fingers above it if this is comfortable. Alternatively, you can place your little finger above the head bar but the former method is recommended as more secure and supportive.

Use your index finger and thumb to manipulate the hand wires for general control of the hands. With your free hand, unhook and operate the leg bar. Use this hand also to manipulate the hand strings when you want to achieve movements not possible with the hand wires alone: with the leg bar resting in your palm and held securely by your thumb, third and fourth fingers, use your index and second fingers to operate the individual hand wires.

To nod or bow the head, or to tilt the head sideways, angle the control in the appropriate direction. To turn the head, tilt the control very slightly forward, just enough to take the weight on the shoulder strings, while simultaneously turning the control.

To bow the body, pull the back string taut to take the weight, tilt and lower the control. If you keep the control vertical while lowering it, the head will remain upright as the body bows.

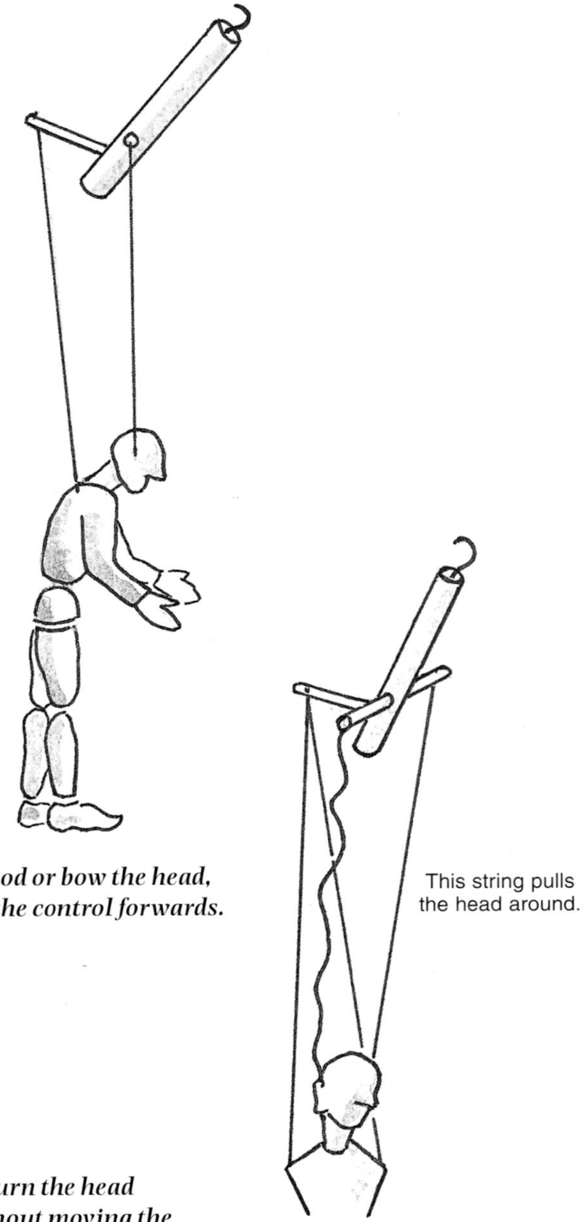

To nod or bow the head, tilt the control forwards.

To turn the head without moving the shoulders, tilt the control very slightly and turn it.

To walk the puppet, use your free hand to unhook the leg bar and manipulate it with a forward moving, see-saw action. Do not drag the legs ahead of the puppet, nor let it

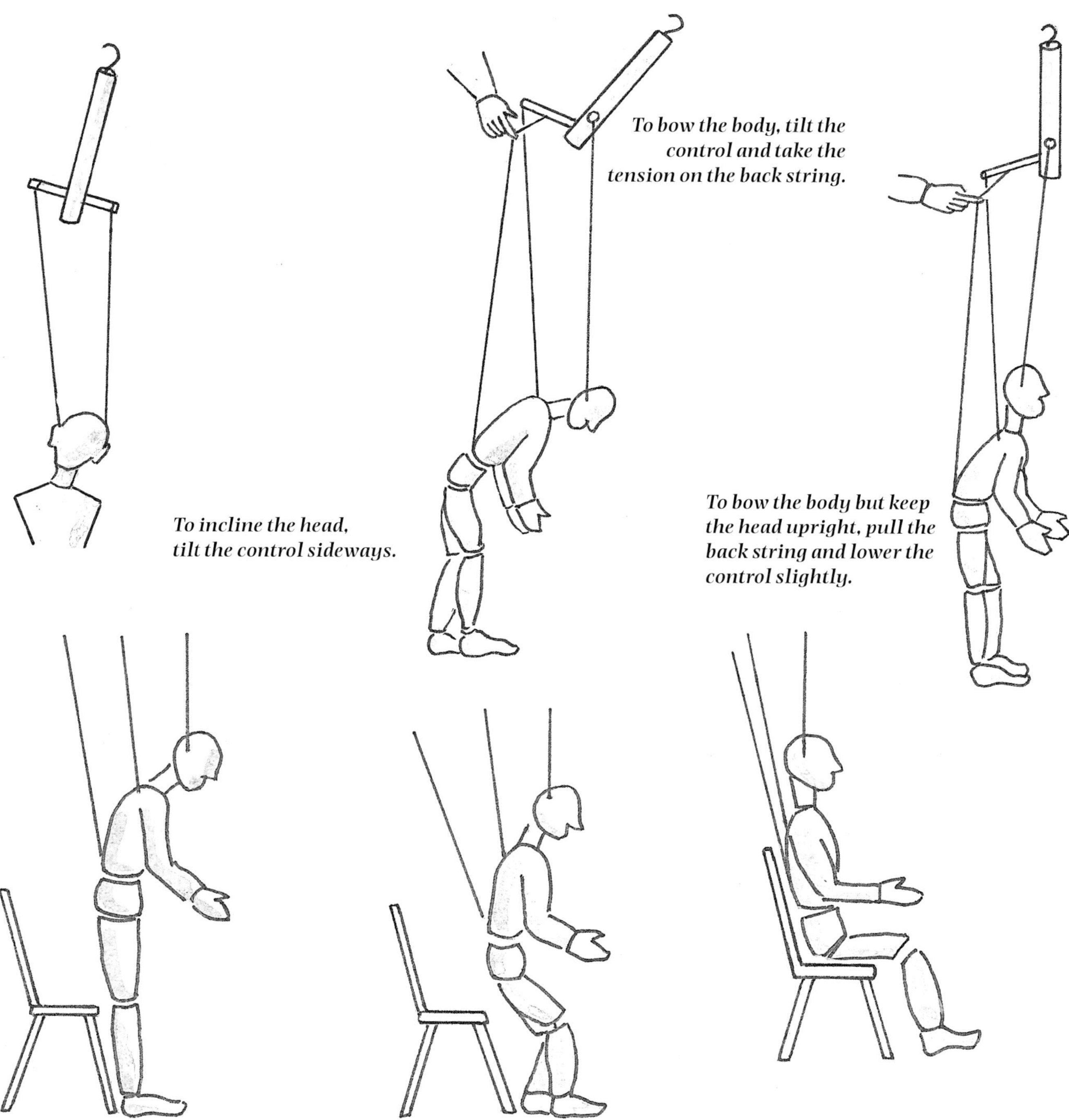

To incline the head, tilt the control sideways.

To bow the body, tilt the control and take the tension on the back string.

To bow the body but keep the head upright, pull the back string and lower the control slightly.

To seat the puppet, tilt the control slightly and take the tension on the back string; bend the knees and lower the puppet to the seat; then finally straighten it up.

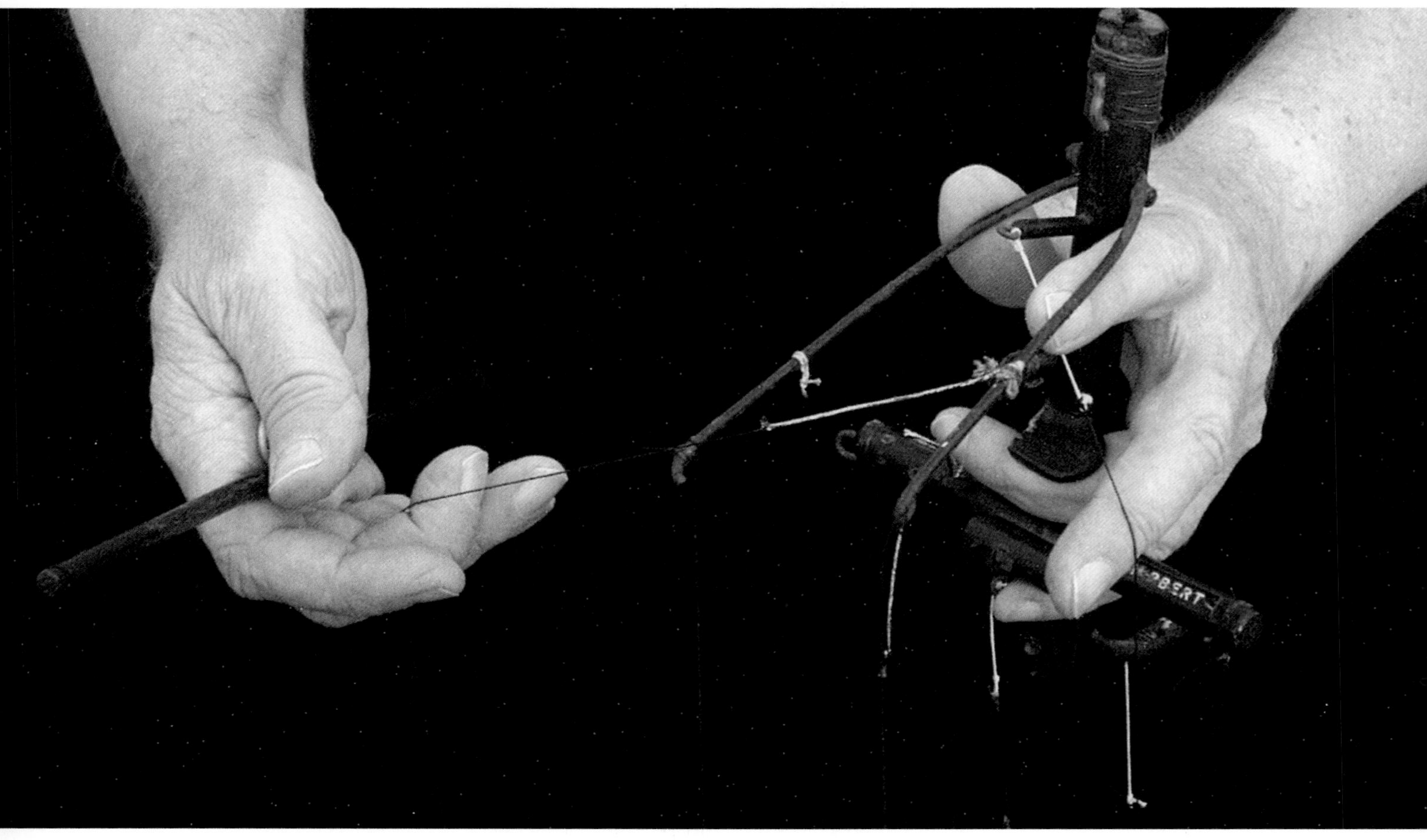

Operating mouth and eye strings with the fingers of the hand holding the control.

'walk' in a sitting position or floating in the air. Keep the puppet upright and the movements of the main control and the leg bar in harmony. Try to achieve a rhythm in the walking action; the rhythm of the legs is reflected in the rhythm of the main control. Note your own walking rhythm in a mirror; our bodies do not glide along at a constant level as our legs move. There is a slight rise and fall as we transfer the weight from one leg to another; it is not an excessive bounce, just a very slight spring in the step. Try to build this into the movement and let the natural swing of the legs assist you in walking the marionette.

Notice also how humans maintain their balance and control their movement as they sit down and stand up again. Try to copy the movement with the marionette rather than flopping it on to a chair. Tilt the control slightly forward, with a little tension on the back string if it has one. As the body leans forwards, bend the knees, lower the body to the chair, and then return the control to the vertical. When the marionette is to stand up, let the body lean forward and raise the control. Appropriate positioning of the feet and hands help to make the movement convincing.

To operate mouth or eye strings, either use the hand that holds the leg bar, or flick out one of the fingers holding the control. I prefer to use the latter method whenever possible, so the positioning of the attachments for these strings on the control is very significant, but ensure the control is held firmly by other fingers.

The Horizontal Control

Hold the main control bar in one hand and use the head bar to turn the head. Sometimes you need also to tilt the control very slightly forward to take the weight on the

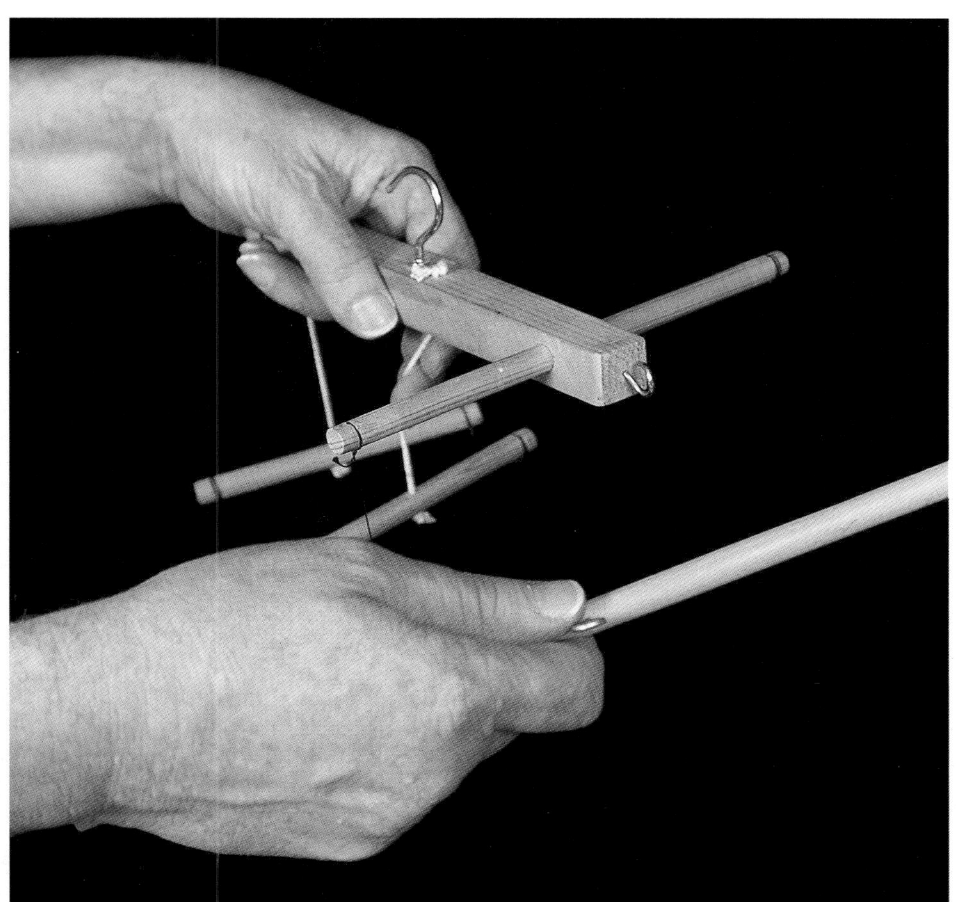

Operating the basic horizontal control.

shoulder strings while turning the head bar. You might be able to turn the head with your index finger and thumb of the same hand, especially if you have attached nails to the head bar to assist you (*see* page 80). Otherwise, operate the head bar with your other hand.

To incline the head to one side, tilt the head bar accordingly. To nod or bow the head, lift the shoulder bar to take the weight off the head bar. Try to do this with one of the fingers holding the control: move one finger and place the tip on the centre of the shoulder bar, drawing it up towards the control. If you cannot reach the shoulder bar, it might be sufficient to raise the string by which it is suspended. Alternatively, use your other hand but this prevents you performing any other operation with it. As you raise the shoulder bar, lower the control very slightly to keep the puppet standing firmly on the floor. To avoid bowing the body as well, keep the main control level.

To bow the body and the head, tilt the control

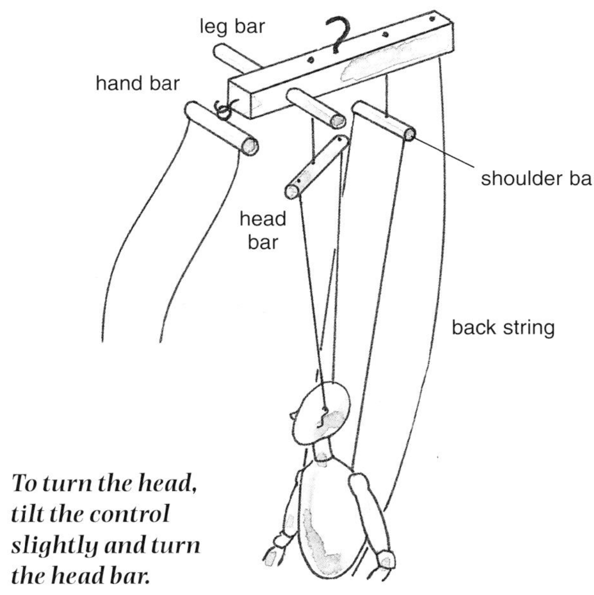

To turn the head, tilt the control slightly and turn the head bar.

forwards. To bow the body while keeping the head upright, tilt the control and lift the head bar.

To move the hands, either operate the hand bar with your free hand or use this hand to operate individual strings, as required by the actions to be performed.

To walk the puppet, rock the main control from side to side in a paddling motion. To lower it on to one knee, lift one leg string and draw it forward slightly while lowering the main control, also with a slight forward motion.

To make the puppet sit, tilt the control so that it leans forward, bend the knees, lower the puppet to the chair and straighten up.

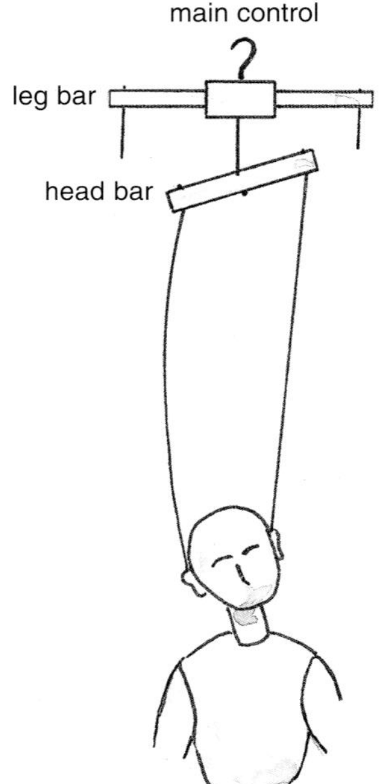

To incline the head, rock the head bar sideways.

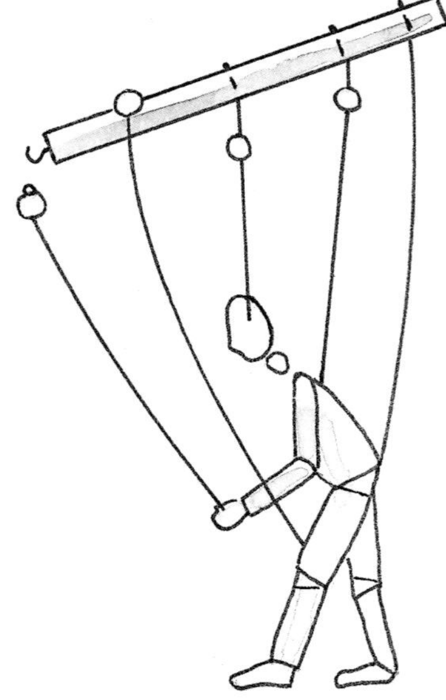

To bow the head and body, tilt the control.

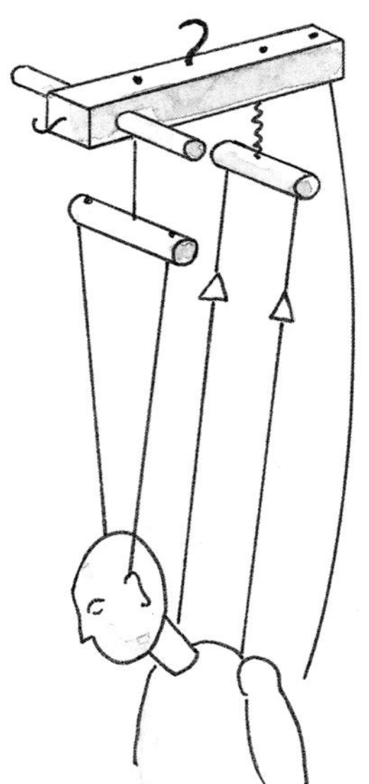

To nod or bow the head, raise the shoulder bar.

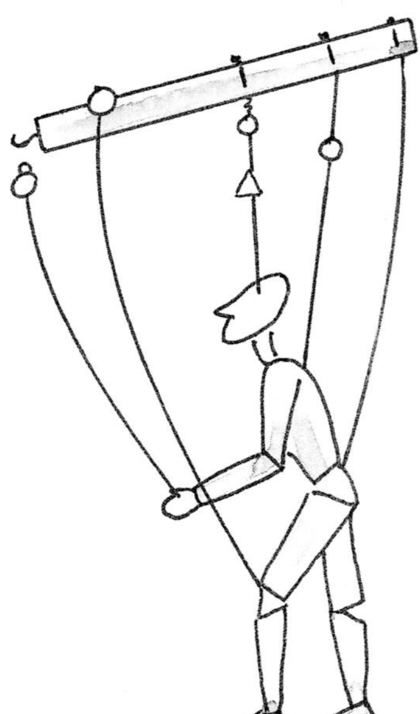

To bow the body but not the head, lift the head bar while tilting the control.

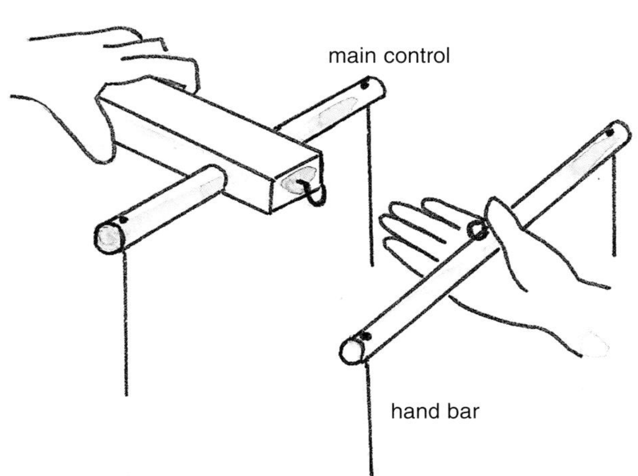

Operating the hands.

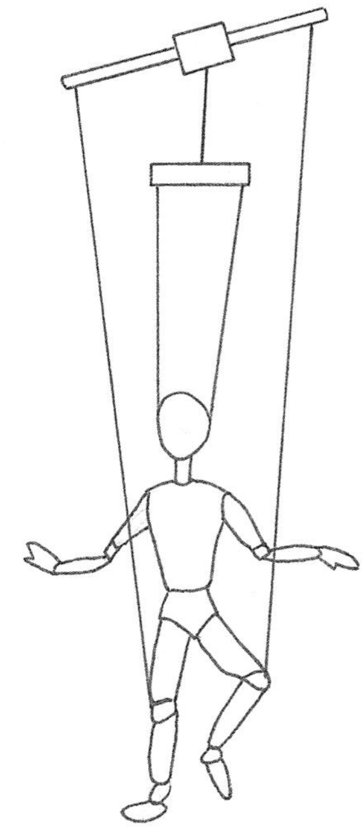

Paddle the control to walk the puppet.

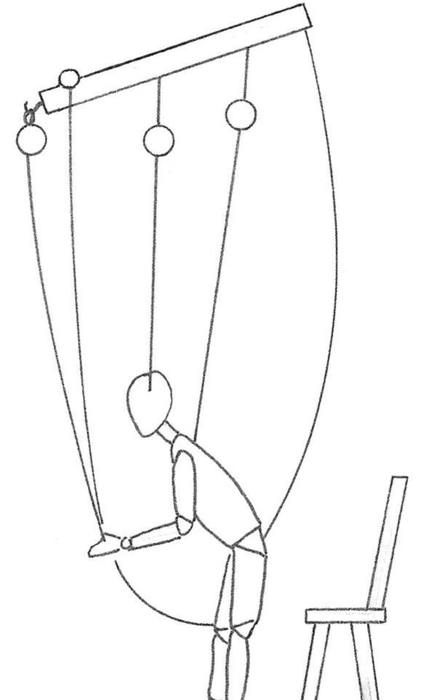

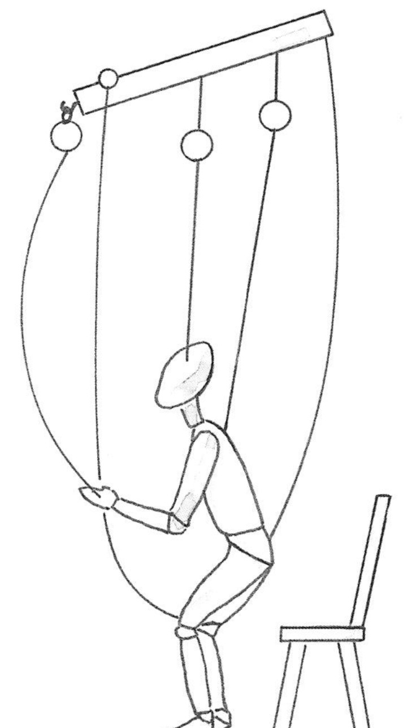

To seat the puppet, tilt the control, bend the knees and lower the control, then straighten up the puppet.

6 Animal Marionettes

General Principles

Animal marionettes may be made in a natural form or in a comic manner. The former may be created, like human figures, with some small modifications to proportion and will move in ways that suggest the natural movements of their live counterparts. Comic animals may be a caricature in both form and action or they may appear fairly natural but perform in unexpected ways.

When creating variety or circus-style acts with animals, consider whether, and how, a live act might translate effectively into a puppet act. We accept the idea of a puppet that counts or spells its name even though we know it is really the puppeteer who does the counting or spelling. Indeed, our suspension of disbelief and the special relationship between audience and performer applies to all of puppet theatre.

However, some people question whether an act such as a lion and lion tamer could work as it depends upon an element of real danger that simply does not exist with puppets. Nonetheless, puppets have performed such acts very successfully when the act has been well designed and executed. Its success may depend upon a clever piece of action, or elements such as danger may be replaced by humour, surprise, or perhaps the charm or elegance with which the essence of the live act has been captured.

While the creation of fantastic creatures such as dragons, unicorns and centaurs, and to some extent comic animals, allow the puppet maker freedom to depart from natural form, it is more difficult to achieve

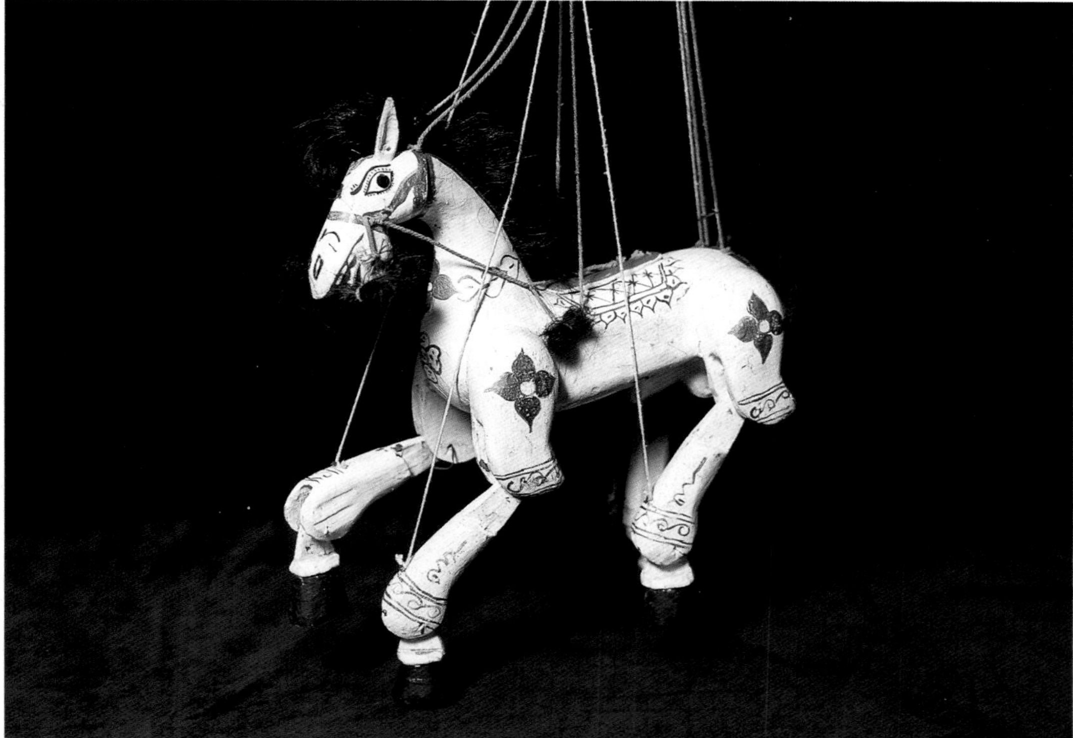

RIGHT: A Burmese horse: note the stylized structure of the legs with the unnatural front knee joints.

OPPOSITE: An elephant that performs tricks, including sucking up water from a bucket and spraying the audience, by Paul Doran, Shadowstring Theatre. The body is clad in fabric and the end of the trunk needs replacing every season.

A Burmese tiger, also with stylized leg joints.

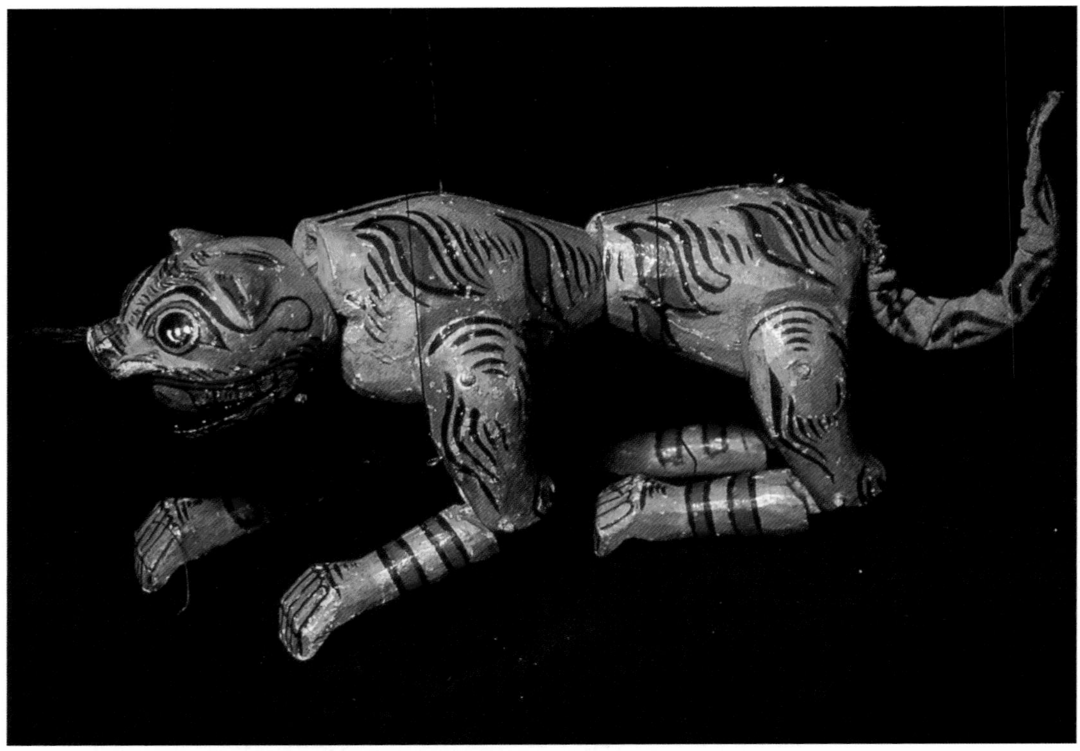

convincing animals than human figures. My first attempt at an animal marionette appeared more like a large dog with horns than the goat it was intended to be. This is largely because we are much more familiar with the human form and need to study animals in greater detail in order to achieve the appropriate shape, proportion and movement.

In many respects, movement has priority over accuracy of anatomical detail; if the marionette's design compromises its movement, it will not be very successful as a puppet. The Burmese animal marionettes illustrate how a stylized figure with stylized movement and a very basic control can provide as convincing a performance as any complex, natural figure.

Design

The general design features for various animals are set out below but the detail depends upon what the animal is to do, so it is wise to work out at least the broad outline of an act in order to create a design fit for the intended purpose. Useful additional information may be found in Chapters 7 and 8.

Animals that appear in plays are usually fairly straightforward in their design whilst those that appear in representations of circus or variety acts tend to perform many routines for which particular design features are required. In addition to the traditional circus animals – horses, elephants, bears, seals or sea lions, big cats, dogs, and members of the ape family – one may find storks, ostriches, flamingos, giraffes and camels. Variety acts that comprise all manner of amusing items may also include spiders, grasshoppers, bumble-bees, crocodiles and snakes – the possibilities are endless.

Animal marionettes may be made from a variety of materials and then covered with painted, dyed or fur fabric, provided the covering does not restrict movement. However, it is common for animal marionettes to be carved from wood or modelled over a base shape and then painted. Figures made in this way can be as convincing as, and sometimes more elegant than, those covered in fabric or fur.

Size and weight may be significant considerations affecting design and construction and there may be variations in relative scale between different animals or between animals and humans. If, for example, a horse, a

Scorpion, ***carved in jelutong by Gren Middleton, Movingstage Marionettes. Based on detailed drawings of a scorpion and with some abstraction required for the puppet, it is finished with a stained varnish. The figure is a character from*** **The Butterfly's (Evil) Spell** ***by Frederico Garcia Lorca, who was himself inspired by puppets.***

dog and a human figure were to appear together, it is likely that the size of the horse would be scaled down and that of the dog scaled up somewhat, and this would not appear unnatural on the puppet stage.

While larger animals should not be too heavy, smaller animals should not be too light; either extreme will make manipulation difficult. The bodies of larger figures therefore tend to be created over a light framework of cardboard, or on a base of balsa-wood or polystyrene. If wooden, they are hollowed out. Smaller figures need a relatively heavier weight to the body, legs and feet to anchor them firmly to the ground, prevent them swinging as they move, and generally facilitate manipulation.

Whatever the method of construction, ensure that there are strong fastenings for securing the head, neck and limbs to the body and for attaching the control strings. Blocks of wood and dowels glued in place provide good fixture points. Depending on the construction method, supporting strings may be attached direct to a body by drilling small holes at suitable points, by securing the string to a button inside or underneath a body, or by looping the end of the string and passing a length of galvanized wire through the body and the loop. Occasionally screw-eyes are glued and screwed in very securely if the body is capable of taking them. They should be sunk into holes so they are not visible.

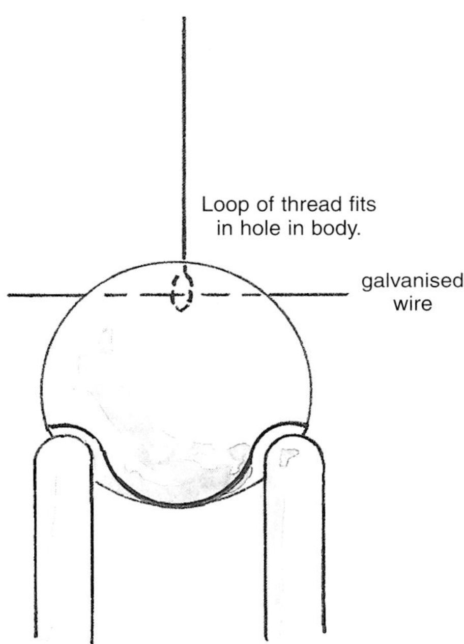

Securing a string to the body with galvanized wire.

Quadrupeds

The design for a horse provides a general structural framework for most quadrupeds. In the case of the horse, the outline around the body and legs tends to form a square, though these proportions will vary with different animals.

The limbs are restricted to moving forwards or backwards, unless it is a comic figure where they might splay in all directions. The leg joints are normally restricted to bend only as the animal would naturally, although the Burmese horse, with its front legs bending the wrong way, illustrates that exceptions are always

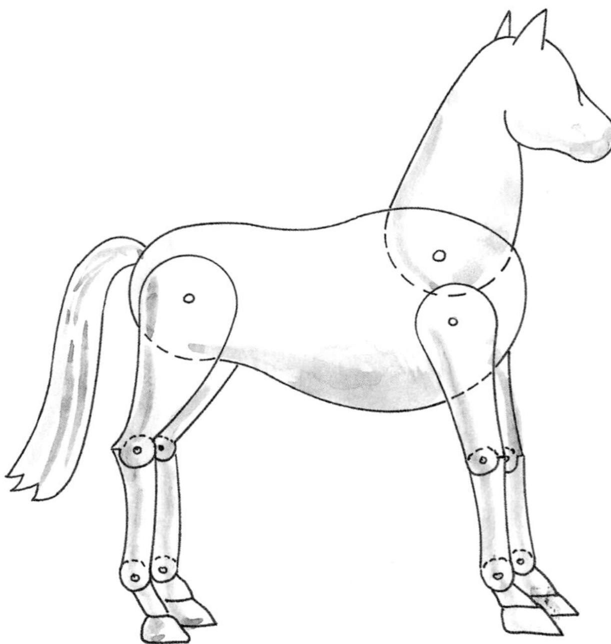

The structure of a marionette horse serves as a guide to most quadrupeds.

possible. The joint between hoof and leg requires some movement but with sufficient restriction for it to fall naturally into position as the horse walks.

Most neck movement of the horse is forward and, of course, the head will turn. Some puppet makers restrict the neck movement to one plane and pivot the head on the end of the neck. Others structure the horse and most other animals so that there is flexibility from the point that the neck joins the body as well as rotation between neck and head. The former method would normally be used for a carved marionette; either method could be used for a figure that is to be covered in fabric.

A horizontal control would be used for quadrupeds. If a human figure is to ride a horse, make its strings shorter than those of the horse so that when it is on horseback, the main control of each puppet can be held with one hand. You might even design the controls to clip together.

Apes and Monkeys

Apart from the shape of the head, apes differ from human figures in that they have little neck and the head is set close to the shoulders. The shoulders and back are somewhat rounded and the body may be made with or without a waist joint. The forearms are long but the legs are short, so when the figure is upright, the hands almost reach the ground. The legs remain partially bent most of the time and the feet have large great-toes that are rather like thumbs.

Such puppets are used to perform many of the acts also done by humans, so the upright or horizontal control previously described (*see* pages 74–84) may be used, depending on the needs of the act.

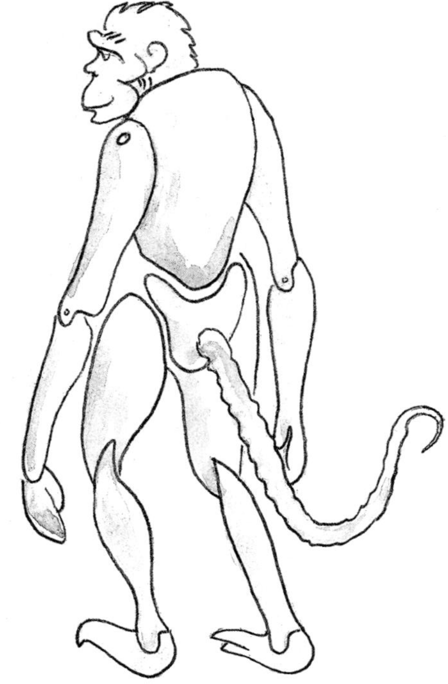

The basic structure of a marionette monkey.

Fish

Fish may be carved in low relief, modelled on a profile shape or on a framework of chicken wire, moulded in latex rubber, created with a fabric covering over a framework of chicken wire, or cut as flat shapes from either a rigid or a flexible material. They are painted or decorated as required.

A single, large fish may have a mouth or eyes that move like other animals. Fish in a shoal are usually very basic shapes suspended from a common control.

Other sea creatures can be constructed using the methods described later in this chapter (*see* pages 104–9).

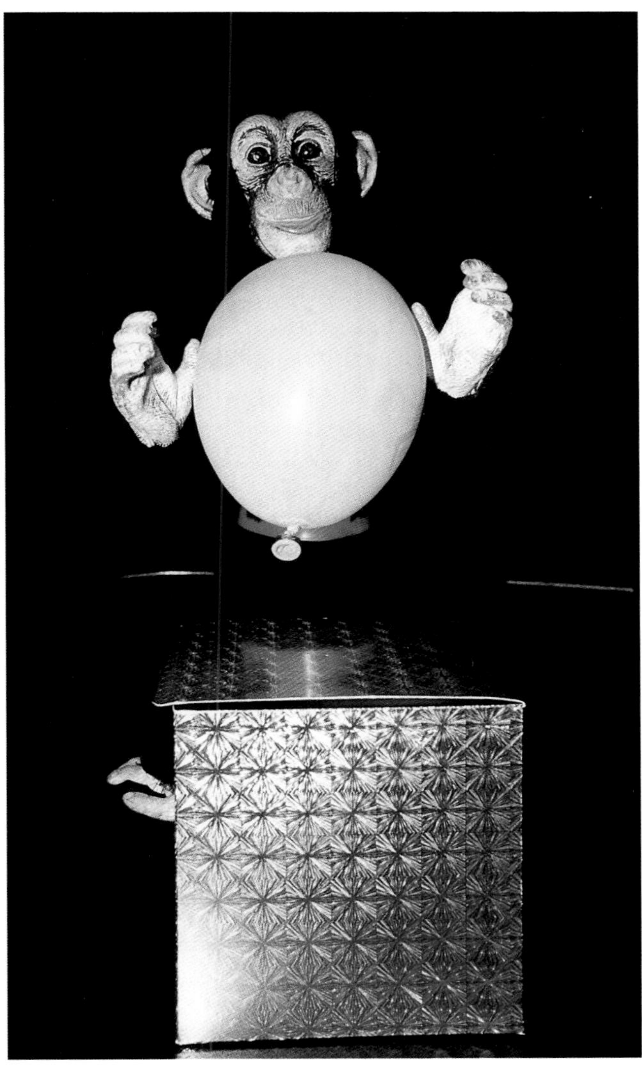

A monkey, formerly in the Harlequin Theatre troupe, is now in the repertoire of the Shadowstring Theatre.

Seals and Sea Lions

These puppets are designed typically to 'juggle' balls, balance on see-saws, manoeuvre over gently inclined ladders, and play tunes on horns or a keyboard with their noses.

They are usually quite simple in structure, comprising a covering of black, silky or velvet fabric filled with foam rubber, wadding and lead pellets, or suitable alternatives. The head covering may be given a stiff lining to help maintain its shape. Make the flippers from a flexible but reasonably firm material such as latex rubber or leather. Hinge them to the body by loops of galvanized wire shaped as square-cornered staples.

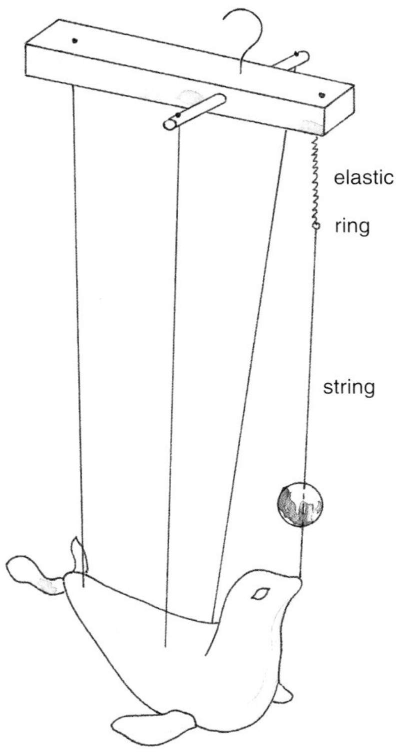

Design and control of a performing seal or sea lion.

Snakes

Snakes are often constructed with a modelled or carved head and a body that is made from shaped wooden segments.

They may also be made from balls or beads of varying diameter threaded on a strong central cord. If extra weight is required, include a few lead beads at selected intervals. The central cord is fixed securely to the head and the tail bead. Do not thread the beads too tightly; allow sufficient flexibility to permit the snake to coil and perform its other manoeuvres. Sometimes it is helpful to insert a very small bead between the segments or the larger beads to improve flexibility.

The body may be painted or covered with fabric, though any covering will almost certainly limit movement.

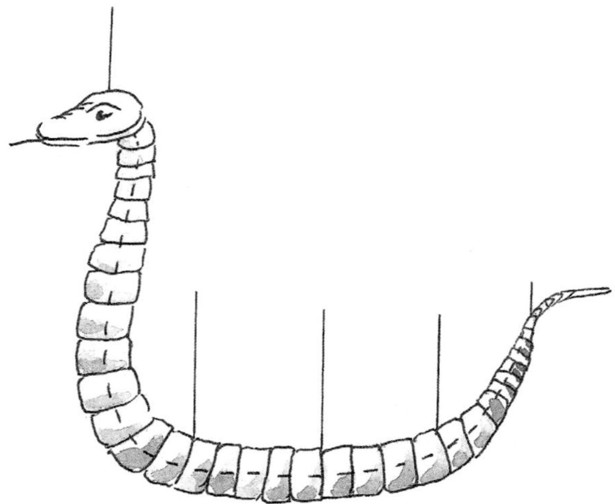

A marionette snake made from wooden segments or beads threaded on a central cord.

Insects

Insects need to be proportionally much larger than their live counterparts and techniques such as illumination from floor-mounted spotlights to cast large, dramatic shadows on a backcloth can create a menacing effect.

The head and body can be carved, modelled or cast in latex rubber. The legs are constructed from a core of twisted wire that is covered with fabric or a modelling material. Alternatively, they can be dipped in latex rubber. Wings are usually made from a slightly flexible, transparent material such as clear or coloured acetate. Colouring can be added to plain wings with translucent adhesive film or glass-painting colours. Markings such as veins can be painted on or drawn with permanent felt tip markers.

Butterflies can be made in several ways, ranging from a very simple design to that described above. They also can be large, elegant puppets using any of the techniques described in this book.

Birds

Small birds normally have a very simple structure. The head, body and tail may be carved, modelled or cast all in one piece with the wings hinged to permit them to flap. Many figures do not have legs; if they do, they usually dangle loosely from the body. This design is suitable for any bird that is required only to fly.

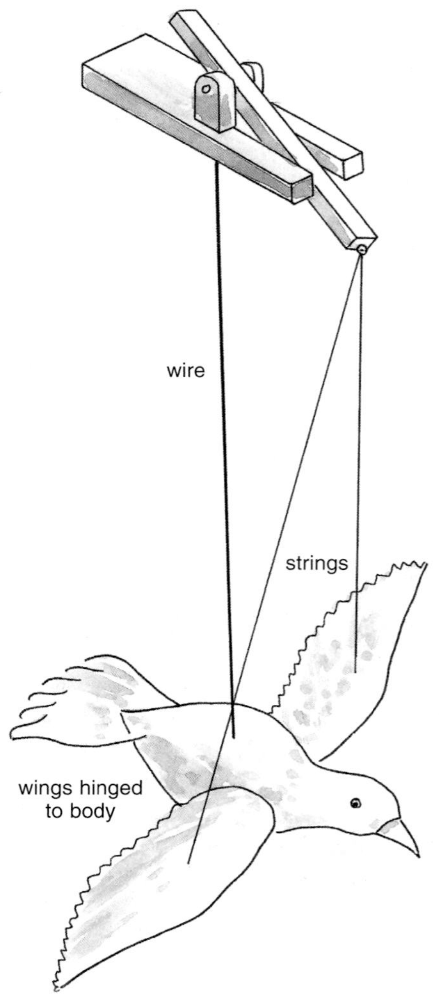

A bird with hinged wings operated by a lever on the control.

Articulated necks may be limited to simple up and down movement but they usually have two joints (head to neck, neck to body) with that to the body restricted to up and down movement and the head free to turn, as described for quadrupeds.

Larger birds are more complex in both structure and control even though they are usually walking rather than flying as puppets. Heads are made by any of the usual methods. Some bird puppets have jointed wooden necks while those with long necks, based on a central cord or rope covered with foam rubber tubing, have great flexibility.

Bird puppets frequently have a moving beak with the lower half of sufficient weight for it to open readily. If the beak were to be operated in the same manner as the mouth of a human figure, the size and weight of the moving part would probably require a fair amount of counterbalance for which the head provides little space. Therefore it is preferable to adopt an alternative design in which the lower part of the beak is not counterbalanced but is held closed by a control string (*see* page 115).

Legs are usually carved, modelled upon dowels, or possibly laminated in plywood, provided they are sturdy enough for strong joints to be effected. Fine joints effected with a strip of metal, such as aluminium, are very satisfactory. Comical figures sometimes have rope legs with the ends glued firmly into the feet.

Wings can be carved, modelled, or cast in rubber, and attached to the body with linen or leather hinges. The feathering of the wings can be carved in low relief or incorporated in the modelling, then painted. Alternatively, small feathers can be added or simulated from small, shaped pieces of fabric. If the wings are to open and the bird is to fly, the wings are made in two parts and pivoted (as illustrated below).

This ostrich by Gordon Staight is typical of the structure of larger birds.

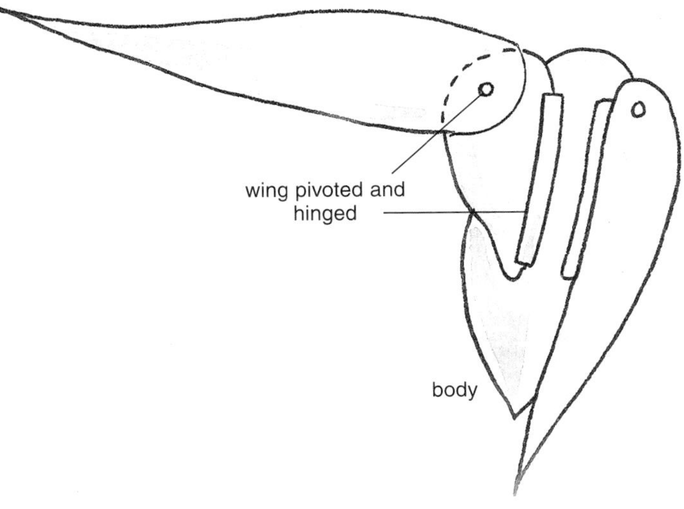

Hinged and pivoted wings for a large bird that is to fly.

Construction Techniques

Many of the methods and materials used in constructing animal heads and bodies are the same as those described previously for other marionettes. Significant features relating to animal marionettes are detailed below.

Heads and Necks

Animal heads may be carved, modelled or cast by any of the methods described for other marionettes and it is quite common for the head to have a moving mouth and/or eyes. Necks for animals may take a variety of forms, depending on the animal and the type of movement that is required. It may be painted or covered with fabric as appropriate. When a body is covered with fabric, it is common for this covering to be continued up the neck to the point where it meets the head, which would then be painted.

Necks may be made using any of the following methods.

- Model the neck and head together, with articulation only where the neck joins the body.
- Carve the neck from wood, cast it in latex rubber or model it upon a length of dowelling.
- Cut bevelled discs of wood and thread them on to a strong central cord. To improve flexibility, use small beads as spacers between the discs. Alternatively, use wooden balls throughout instead of the wooden discs.
- Join wooden segments with open mortise and tenon joints. Cut the joints to allow complete flexibility or to restrict movement as required. Cut the joints in line to restrict movement to one plane, or cut them horizontally at one end of a segment and vertically at the other to allow movement in two planes.
- A piece of suitable tubing or a spring may be used to form the neck.
- Cover strong cord with foam rubber tubing. Either leave the tubing intact or cut it into bevelled segments for increased flexibility.
- For an extending neck, use wooden discs joined at intervals by thread, as described for an extending puppet (*see* pages 154–5). The neck retracts into a hollow body (which I build around a large tin can) by means of a string that runs from the head-neck joint, down through the entire length of the neck, through to the end of the body and up to the control. Insert a piece of soft tubing into the body to carry the string and prevent fraying.

Most necks are joined to the head with cord to permit

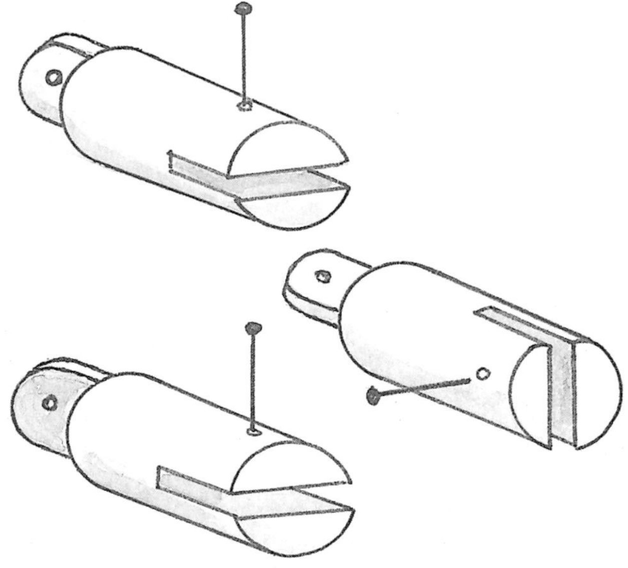

Open mortise and tenon joints with the tongues cut alternately horizontally and vertically allows for very flexible neck movement.

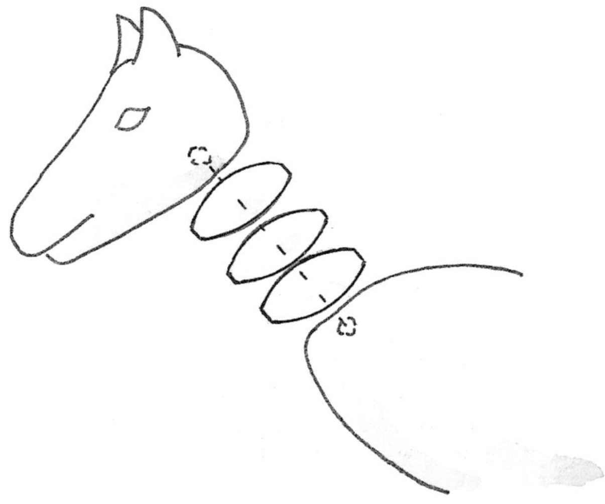

An animal neck made from bevelled segments of wood on a central cord.

the head to turn freely. To restrict movement, carve the head with a tongue protruding where it meets the neck or create the tongue from a piece of plywood or strip of metal built into the head. Use a nail to pivot the tongue in a slot cut into the top of the neck. Either of these methods is suitable for attaching the neck to the body.

Bodies

In the descriptions that follow, the body has a single central profile shape when the neck is secured to the body with cord. When the neck is restricted to up and down movement, there is a three-section profile core of plywood. The outer sections are identical in shape but the centre section is cut away to accommodate the wooden or metal tongue that protrudes from the base of the neck. The tongue pivots on a nail that is inserted through the two outer profile shapes. The head of the nail is secured with a spot of glue. If the three layers of plywood make the body too heavy, cut away some of the centre of the shapes with a jigsaw or a coping saw.

The dowelling attachments for legs may be replaced by galvanized wire or cord for alternative joints as described for legs (*see* pages 107-8).

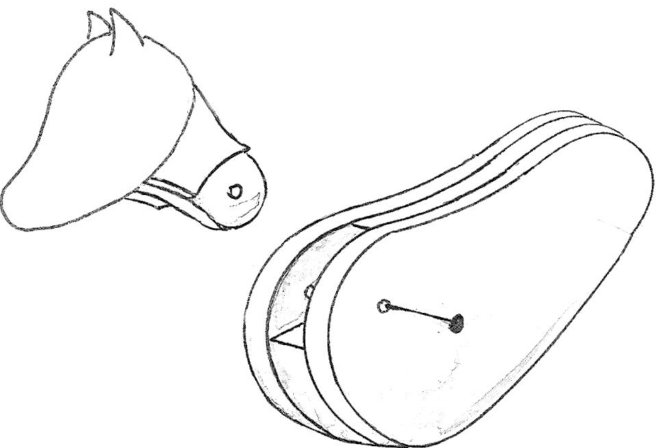

A laminated body shape with the centre section cut away to accommodate a plywood tongue at the base of the neck. The tongue pivots on a nail across the body.

A Cardboard Body

A cardboard body is made in the same way as a cardboard head, either as a base for modelling or for a direct covering of fabric (*see* pages 25–6).

Cut a profile shape from strong cardboard or thin plywood. Make a hole in the neck for a cord for the neck joint. Make holes in the profile shape to accommodate 18mm (¾in) dowels for attaching the legs. Glue the dowels into the holes. Glue 'ribs' and strengthening cross-struts to the profile shape then cover it with cardboard or strips of linen glued to the framework. Glue a circle cut from smooth cardboard over the end of each dowel to ensure free movement of the legs.

Cover the body with a modelling material, fabric, fur fabric, nylon 'hair' or fluffed up knitting wool.

Sometimes the profile and ribs are all cut from plywood, slotted and glued together. For large animals the weight is reduced by cutting away the centres of the rib sections.

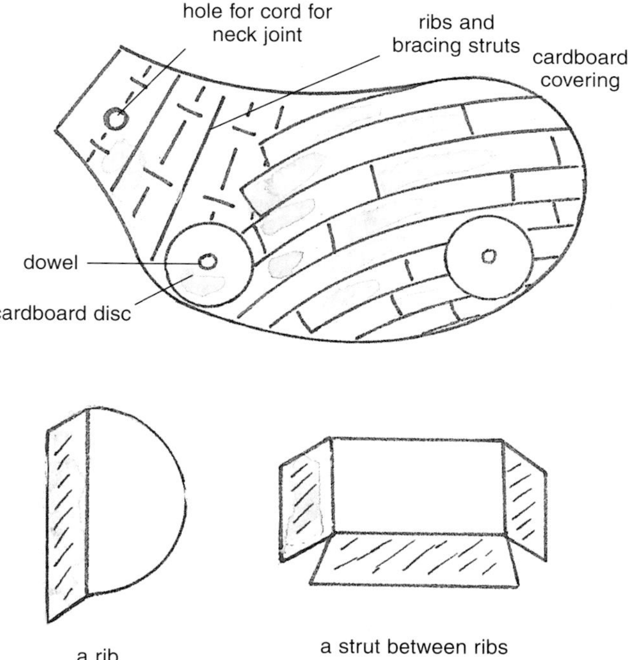

A cardboard body for an animal.

An alternative structure has solid blocks at each end of the body with strong cardboard strips joining them. Layers of strips are added crossways until a sufficiently strong body is achieved (*see* page 106).

A Modelled Body

Modelled like a head, over Plasticine, this body might well need a central profile shape of plywood, and perhaps also ribs and dowelling, to increase rigidity and facilitate the

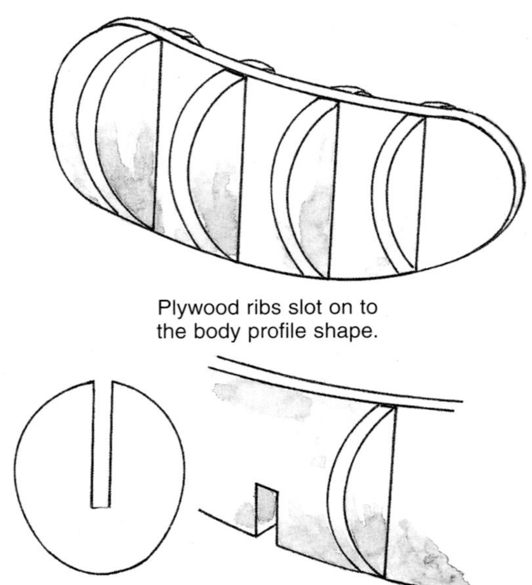

Profile and rib shapes cut in plywood.

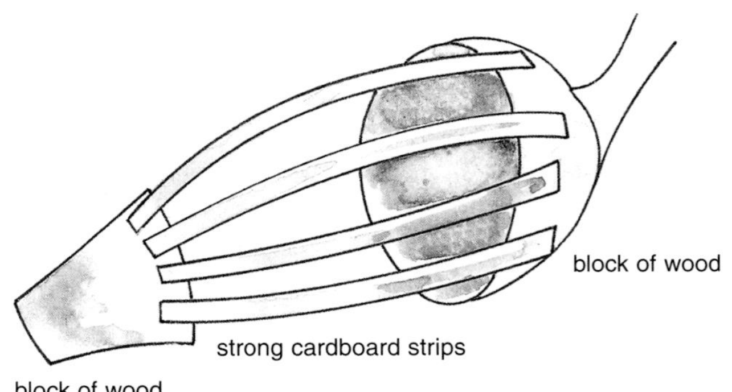

Solid wooden blocks at each end of the body joined by strips of strong cardboard. Further strips are added crossways to form a strong, hollow body.

attachment of the strings, neck and legs (*see* a cardboard body, page 105). Making a well-fitting insert after modelling is possible but you may find it easier to build the internal structure into the Plasticine model so that a perfect fit is achieved. Small nails tapped partially into the ends of the dowels will leave holes in the modelled body to mark the position for the later attachment of the legs.

Before modelling, cover the frame and the Plasticine with a separator to prevent the body shell sticking when you cut it open to remove the Plasticine. Glue the two hollow body shells back together over the plywood, noting the position of the internal dowels. Cover the joint with a little modelling material and finish with paint or fabric.

A Sculpted Body

Cut out a plywood body shape in profile with a coping saw or band saw. Drill a hole for attaching a cord to the neck. Glue blocks of balsa-wood, polystyrene or foam rubber to the plywood and shape the blocks appropriately. Drill holes through the body and glue dowels into them for attaching the legs (*see* page 107). Cover the body with material such as wool or fur fabric.

A body sculpted entirely in balsa-wood without the central plywood shape needs dowelling inserts glued securely in place to facilitate the attachment of the other parts of the animal. Supporting strings pass right through the body and are tied to buttons, or the looped ends of a length of galvanized wire, which are sunk into the underside of the body.

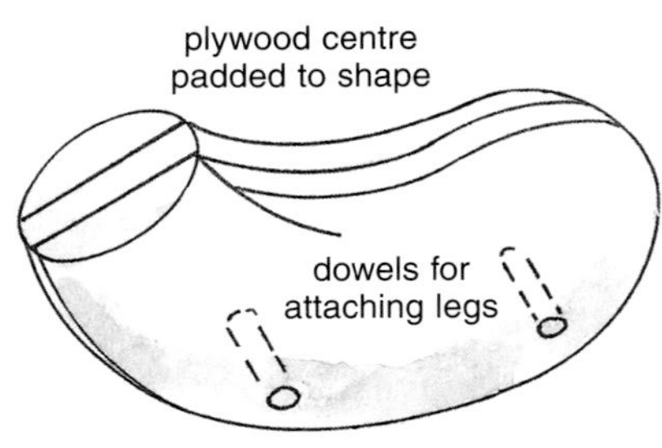

A body sculpted in balsa-wood, foam rubber or polystyrene on a plywood profile shape. Dowels are secured across the body for attaching the legs.

A Carved Body

Animal bodies may be carved in wood in the same way as heads. Use a lightweight wood and, to reduce weight further, cut the body open lengthwise, hollow it out and then rejoin it.

A Latex-Rubber Body

Bodies may be modelled in Plasticine, cast in plaster, and

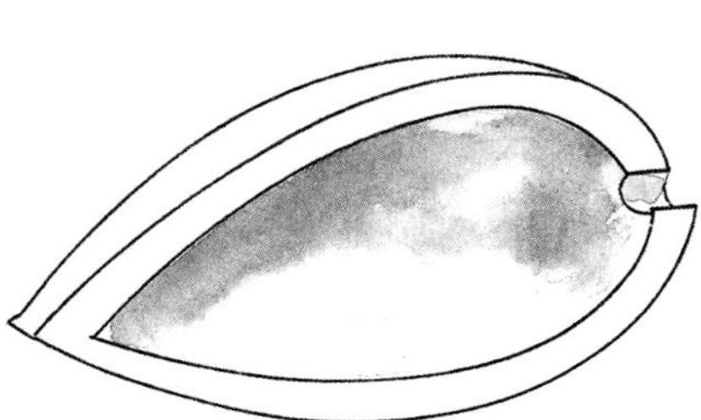

Carved animal bodies are usually cut open and hollowed out to reduce the weight.

then created in latex rubber, as described for heads (*see* pages 30–4). Larger bodies will need a plywood profile shape and some form of stuffing to help to retain the shape. The plywood also provides fixing points for control strings and fastenings for dowels if required for attaching the legs.

Legs

Legs may be carved from wood, modelled over lengths of dowelling (*see* illustration on page 64) or created from laminated plywood shapes, depending on the most suitable method for the size and style of the particular animal's leg. In most cases, they are given open mortise and tenon joints (*see* pages 60–3). The tongue and the groove for the joint may be carved, built into the design of laminated plywood shapes, or formed using a strip of metal such as aluminium for the tongue. The metal joint is both strong and neat for slim legs such as those of a large bird. The procedure is the same as that described for human legs (*see* pages 61–2).

It is not so common to create animal legs in latex rubber, though this may be suitable for comical figures or for long-legged birds.

There are several common methods for joining the legs to the body. In each case holes are drilled through the tops of the legs and the fastenings are countersunk to provide a flush finish.

- Screw the legs to the body or into the internal dowels, as appropriate. Ensure that the legs rotate freely on the screws.
- Thread cord through holes across the body and legs, then knot and glue the ends. To assist threading the cord through the body, make a large 'needle' of galvanized wire with one end looped. If these joints are made too loosely or too close to the bottom of the body, the legs may tend to swing in underneath it.
- Insert a length of galvanized wire through the front and rear of the body and suspend the legs on the wire. Place a small washer outside of each leg and bend the ends of the wire to form loops flush with the legs.

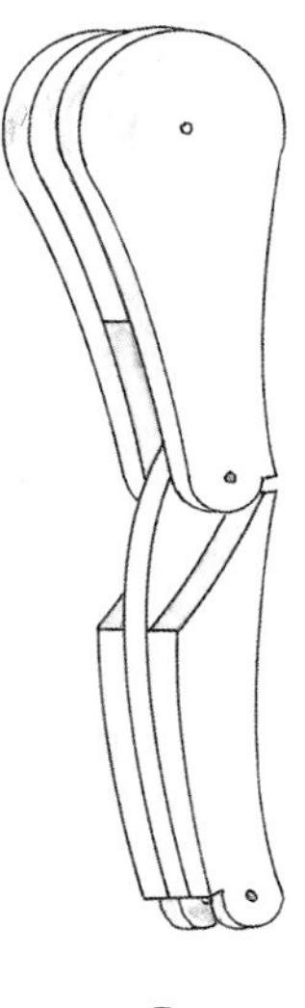

Animal legs made from laminated plywood shapes.

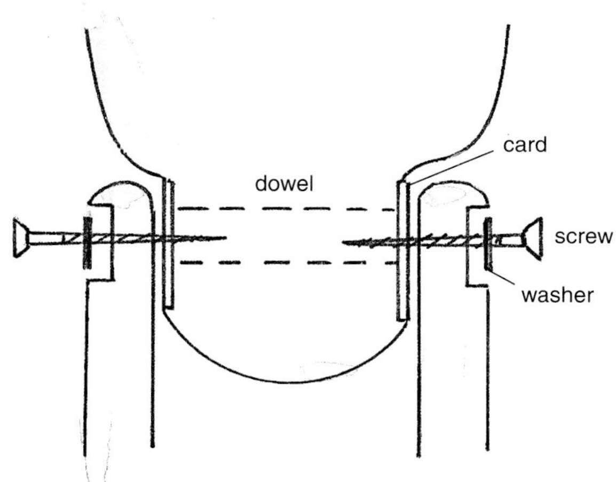

Joining the legs to an animal body.
Legs screwed to dowels inside the body.

- Suspend the legs on metal rods inserted through the body and secure them by soldering or brazing small metal discs to the ends of the rods.

Feet and Ankle Joints

For animal feet, follow the instructions for the feet of other puppets (*see* pages 67-8) or for hands modelled on a wire framework (*see* page 56). The joints described above for legs are also suitable for ankles, especially a metal or wooden tongue pivoted in a slot in the leg. As with human figures, some flexibility at the ankle is desirable but ensure that movement is sufficiently restricted to prevent the feet dragging as the animal walks.

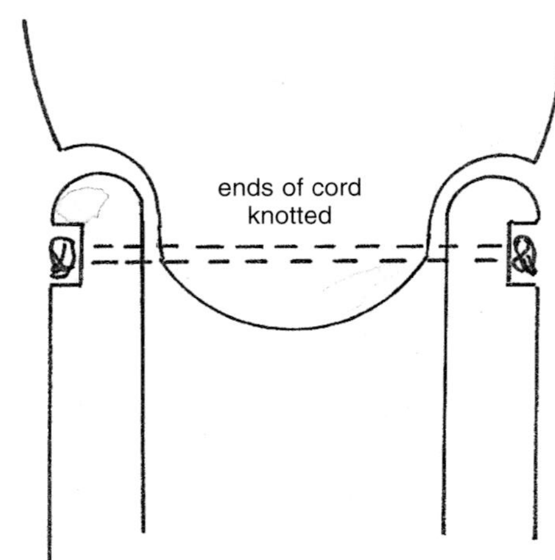

Joining the legs to an animal body.
Legs attached with cord.

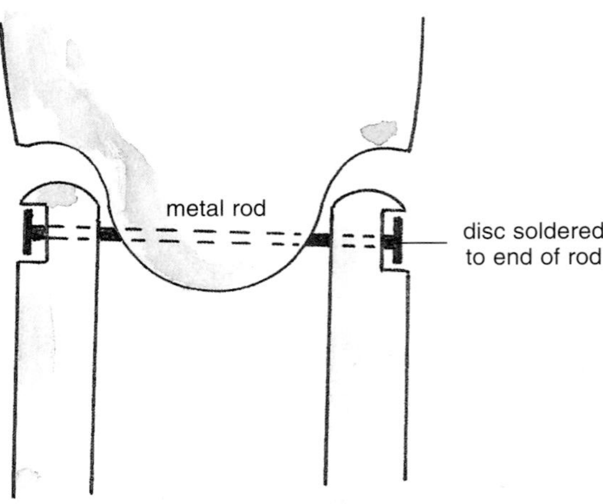

Joining the legs to an animal body.
Legs suspended on a metal rod with discs soldered to the ends.

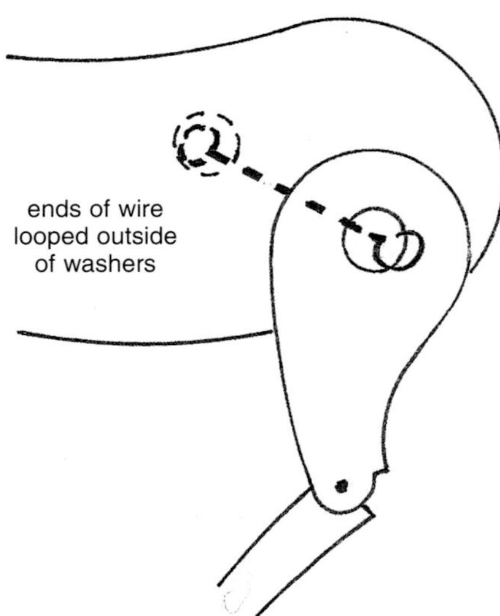

Joining the legs to an animal body.
Legs secured with galvanized wire.

An open mortise and tenon joint for an animal's ankle.

Tails

Tails can be made from artificial hairpieces, cut and bound tightly at one end. Use cord, string, strips of felt or leather, or any other material suitable for the type and style of animal. Glue the tail into a hole made in the rear of the animal. If a string is to be attached to the tail, it is a good idea to glue and pin the tail in place for extra security.

CONTROL AND MANIPULATION

In the past, animal controls have ranged from loops of string hung from the hand and forearm of the operator to complex structures that required considerable skill to operate.

Today, a horizontal control similar to that used for some human figures is the most common method, adapted as necessary for particular animals or for the acts they are to perform. Although animal marionettes do not have the range of bodily movement or gestures of the human figure, they can be surprisingly effective, even with a fairly simple control. Just a tilt of the head, or a leg raised and paused in the air or tapping the ground, can suggest various emotions or intentions to an audience (*see* Chapter 5 for general advice about stringing and care of the strings).

A Horizontal Control for Animals

The control is constructed from a main wooden bar about the same length as the puppet, and of 25mm (1in) square section, with dowel rods attached directly or suspended cross-wise.

Drill small holes down through the main bar for attaching the main supporting strings; these are secured to the body at the shoulder and rump.

Digby, by Gordon Staight, performs various tricks such as spelling his name and simple numerical calculations with the help of the children in the audience. It has a built-in, string-operated bark taken from a toy and its furry coat is cut from a fluffy dusting mop.

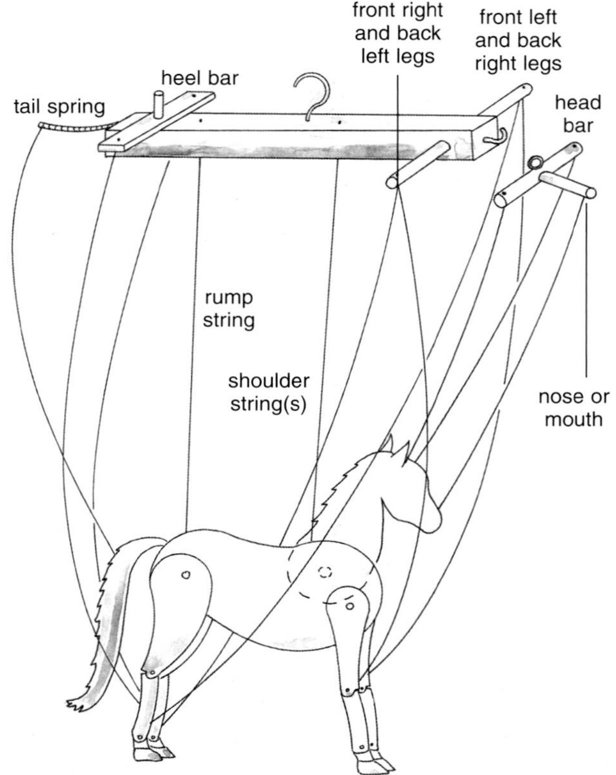

The basic control and stringing.

A 'T'-shaped head bar, a little wider than the animal's head, hangs from the front of the control by means of a hook in the control and a curtain ring tied to the head bar. To make the head bar, drill a hole in the centre of a 12–13mm (½in) diameter dowel and glue into it a 5–6mm (¼in) diameter dowel. Attach the main head strings to the ends of the larger dowel. A string to the nose or a string for a moving mouth or moving eyes is attached to the end of the smaller dowel.

If the animal has a moving mouth and moving eyes, a simple solution is to attach one control string to the end of the smaller dowel of the head bar. Arrange the other to run through a screw-eye in the end of the control and attach it to the centre of the larger head bar dowel. Rotate the head bar upwards to operate one feature; pull it away from the main control to operate the other. Perform both of these actions together to move mouth and eyes simultaneously.

A more satisfactory method, which does not require moving the head away from the body, uses a variation of the head control. The head control has a central bar that fits into a holder on the main control. The holder is made from a strip of aluminium, bent into a square-cornered, inverted 'U' shape, then glued and nailed to the control. A

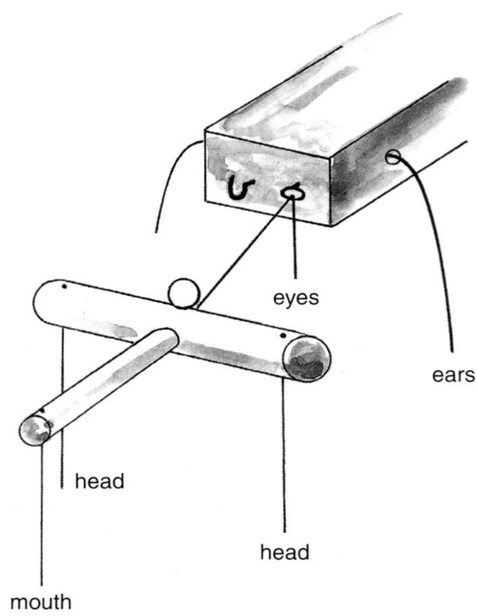

Mouth and eye strings attached to the head bar. Strings for the ears run through a hole across the main control bar.

dowelling crossbar carries the head strings; it is glued and screwed into a groove cut in the head control. A small dowel is glued into a hole in the front of the control for the mouth string. The eye string is attached to a wire lever with looped ends. The upper loop pivots on a nail in a slot cut in the head control. Rotate the control a little to move the mouth. Move the eye control wire with the fingers of the hand holding the control.

For the leg bar, glue a 10mm (⅜in) diameter dowel into a hole drilled across the main bar, near the front. For most quadrupeds, the opposing front and rear legs are attached to the same side of the leg bar so that front right and back left legs are raised together, and front left with back right. Connecting same-side legs to the control produces a rolling gait. Do check how a particular

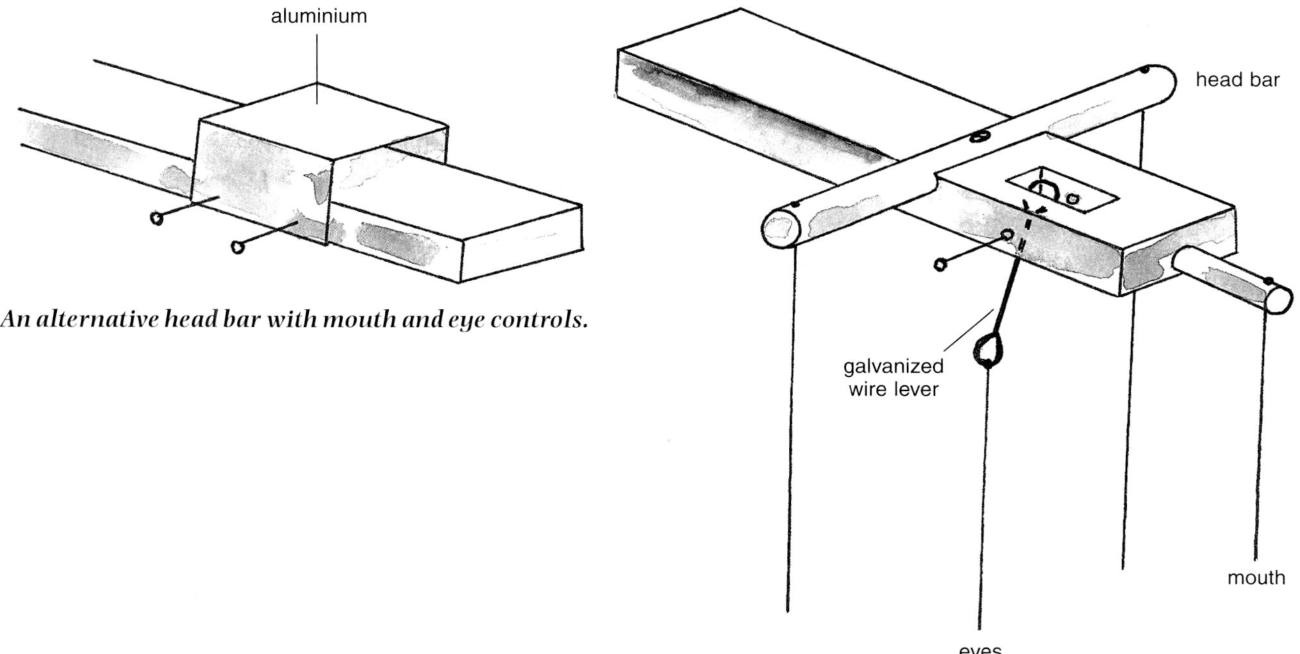

An alternative head bar with mouth and eye controls.

animal normally moves. Sometimes the leg strings might need to run through a small screw-eye or loop of wire in each side of the body to achieve the desired leg movement or to guide them without catching.

An additional leg bar may be added to raise the rear legs together for acrobatics or for a kicking action. Drill a hole through the centre of the leg bar; it sits on a vertical dowel peg glued into a hole drilled near the back of the main bar. The strings are attached to the back of the rear legs just above the feet/hooves.

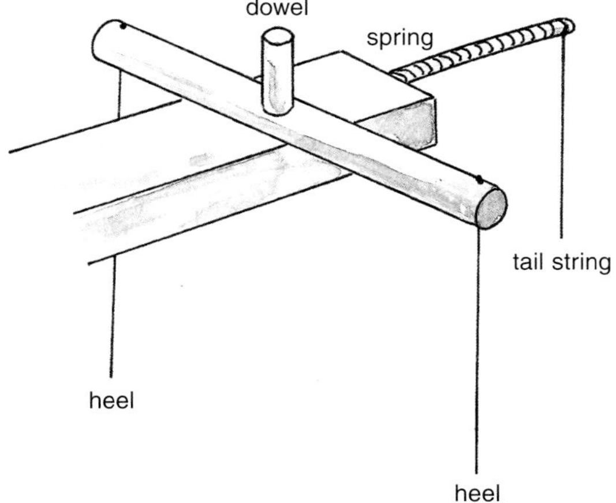

An additional leg bar for kicking rearwards and a tail spring.

To control a tail, glue a spring, such as a piece of curtain wire, into a hole drilled into the rear of the control. Attach the tail string to the end of the spring.

Add ear strings if required. Either attach them to the head bar or have a single 'run-through' string threaded through a screw-eye in the head bar or through a hole drilled across the front of the main control bar. If the strings are attached to the main bar, the ears will be raised whenever the head bar is unhooked and lowered. This same arrangement is possible with mouth or eye strings but is not generally very satisfactory.

Hold the control with one hand. To move the head, unhook the head bar and move it with your free hand. To effect movements of the body, tilt and turn the main control. To walk the puppet, rock the control from side to side.

A Control for One-Handed Operation

This control allows you, with practice, to manipulate the head, body and legs with a single hand. Although the range of movement of the head is somewhat limited, it is nevertheless quite effective. The basic control for supporting the body and operating the legs remains as a main bar with a dowelling leg bar securely attached. The

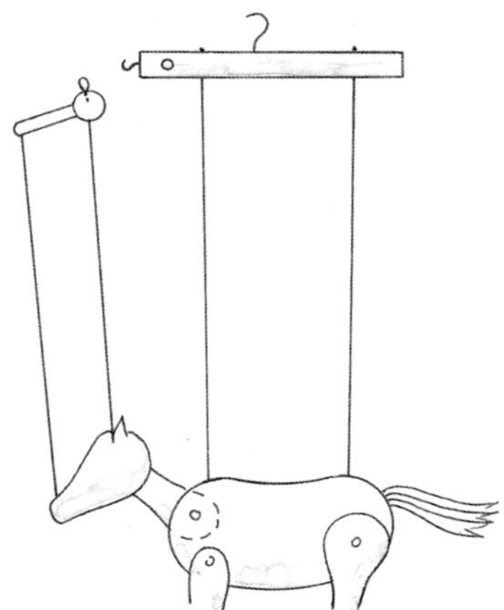

To lower the head, unhook and lower the head bar. To turn the head, turn the head bar.

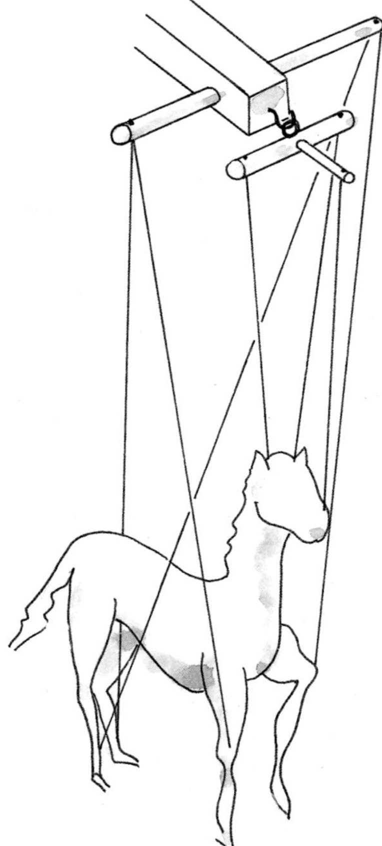

To walk the puppet, paddle the control.

head bar is very similar but with a shorter cross-dowel for attaching head strings. Suspend the head bar from the main bar with two lengths of cord threaded through vertical holes in each bar and knotted at the ends. Hold the main control in one hand, using your thumb and index finger to operate the head bar.

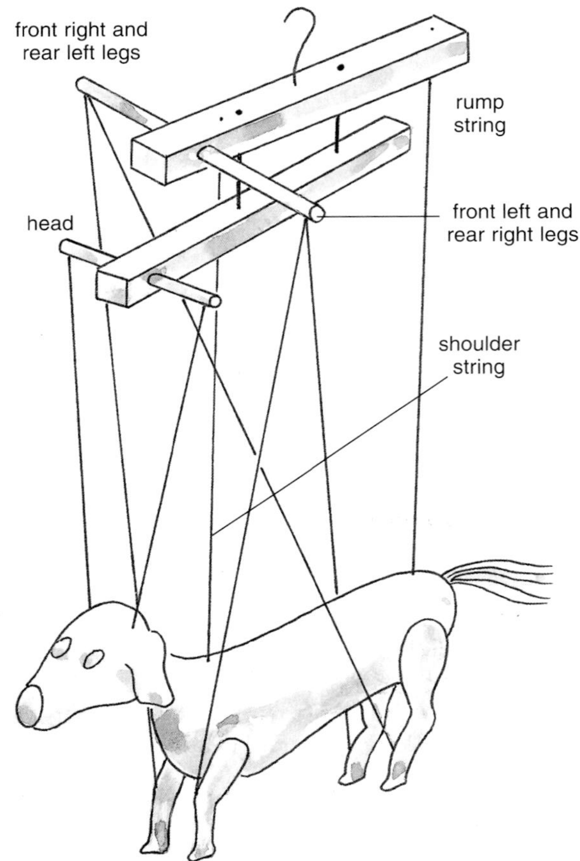

A control for one-handed operation.

Fish

Single fish with moving mouths or moving eyes have a simple, horizontal control, usually with two supporting strings plus other control strings as necessary.

Suspend fish in a shoal from a common control by one or two strings each: two strings keep them facing in the same direction while single strings allow them to turn. Alternatively, join groups of fish tail to head with loose fine thread, to permit movement but resist spinning. To avoid the fish hanging in a straight line, suspend them at different heights from horizontal dowels of different lengths joined to a main control bar.

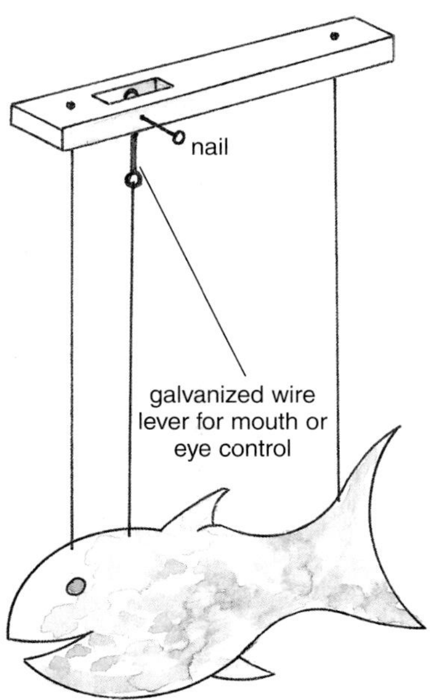

A simple control for a single fish.

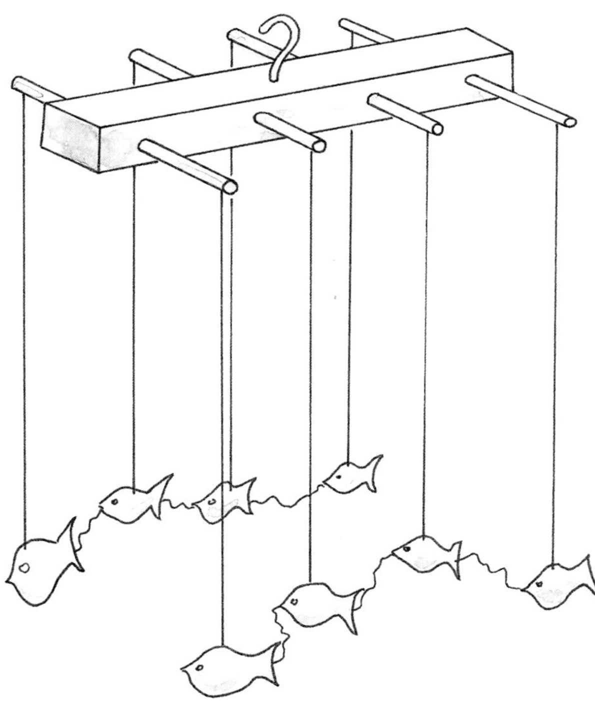

A control for a shoal of fish: the strings are of varied lengths and the fish on each side are joined loosely from tail to head to prevent them spinning.

Seals and Sea Lions

Strings to the head, 'shoulders' and tail are usually sufficient for general movement so only a very basic horizontal control bar is required. It has a main bar with a single, horizontal dowel glued into a hole drilled across the main bar (*see* illustration on page 101). Strings to the flippers may not be needed to assist the waddling action; if these are required, attach another horizontal dowel and attach the strings to the ends of it.

To juggle a single ball, thread it on a string to the nose. For a pair of seals to pass a ball between them, screw their controls to each end of a wooden bar so that they can be held and moved with one hand or rotated on the bar to face one another. Arrange the juggling strings in the same way as for a human figure juggling from hand to hand (*see* page 131).

Snakes

The control for a snake need be no more than a straight bar with strings fixed at appropriate points. Some performers use a length of fairly stiff but still flexible rope instead of a wooden bar, which assists in twisting and coiling movements. The head and tail strings on a wooden bar may be of the run-through type, attached to a curtain ring so that a pull on one of the rings can raise the head or the tail. A moving mouth would require an extra control string; raising only the head string would slacken the mouth string and automatically open the mouth if the mouth string were used to keep it closed rather than to open it (*see* pages 114–5).

One difficulty that sometimes arises is stopping the head swinging from side to side if it is heavy and there is only a single head string. Positioning the head string as far forward as balance permits and having another string on the body close to the head will help to prevent this. Alternatively, two strings, one to each side of the head, may be a helpful measure.

Bees and Insects

The method of control can vary from a single string or wire to the main horizontal control described above, modified as appropriate to the particular animal and what it is to do.

- Use a single string for puppets that are simply to flutter about. When a group is suspended from a single control, join the figures loosely with fine thread

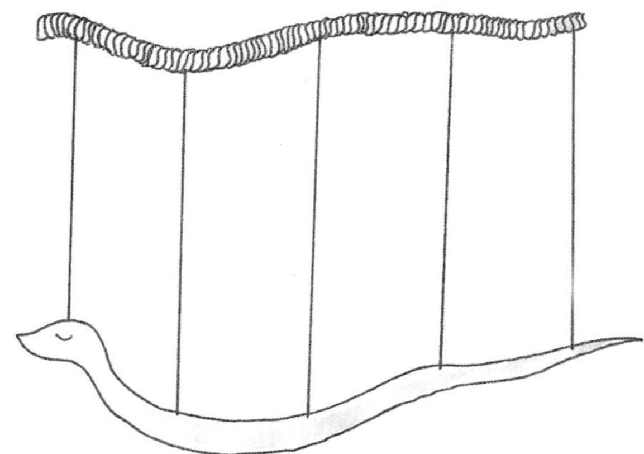

Controls for a snake.
A fairly stiff length of rope is sometimes used.

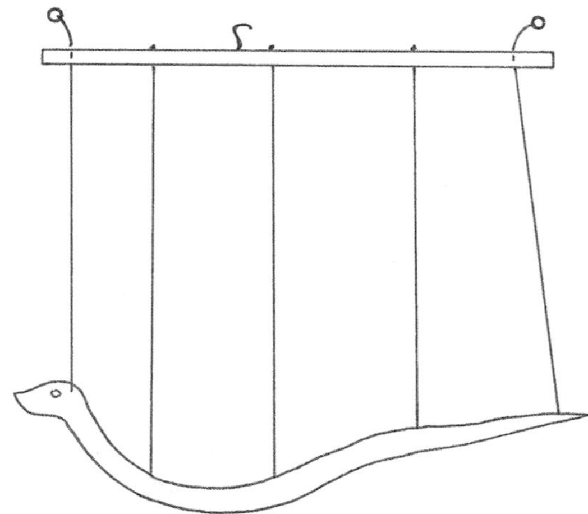

Controls for a snake.
A strip of wood with run-through strings attached to the head and the tail.

to prevent the strings tangling.

- Use a length of wire to control a single puppet for which direct control is necessary, for example if a bee is required to sting somebody or to burst a balloon (with a pin built into its tail).
- Adopt a more complex, horizontal control for figures that are themselves larger and more complex.

Birds

A simple bird control consists of a horizontal bar to which are attached either head and body strings, or a single string or wire attached to the body at a suitable point of balance. A wooden bar is attached as a lever to flap the wings (*see* illustration on page 102). An alternative to the lever is to attach three strings directly to the main bar, one to the body and one to each wing. Raising and lowering

ABOVE AND OPPOSITE: ***Gordon Staight's ostrich has a control string that holds the beak closed. In contrast to most puppets where the control string is usually lifted to open the mouth, relaxing the string allows it to open. Note also how the eye movements combine with beak movements in a very expressive manner.***

the central body string creates a smooth, graceful action of the wings as the bird flies.

The control for birds with articulated necks will require a separate head bar that may be detachable or suspended on strong elastic.

When the bird has an opening beak, one possibility is to arrange the stringing so the beak is normally open and the beak string is used to close rather than to open it. The beak string is attached to a 'T'-shaped head bar that may be held in a position that leaves the beak open and closes it by upward rotation of the head bar. Alternatively, it may be held in a position that keeps the beak closed and opens it by downward rotation of the head bar. These methods work surprisingly well.

A variation has a lever on a more substantial head control; the beak string is attached to the lever, which has elastic or a strong rubber band to keep it closed. Pressure on the lever lowers the string to open the mouth.

If the bird has moving eyes and a moving beak, either use a run-through string to control the additional moving feature (*see* illustration on page 110) or adopt the alternative control (*see* illustration on page 111).

Large, walking birds require a horizontal control much like other animals. The control has three strings to support the body, two to the 'shoulders' and one to the tail, and a fixed horizontal crossbar for the legs.

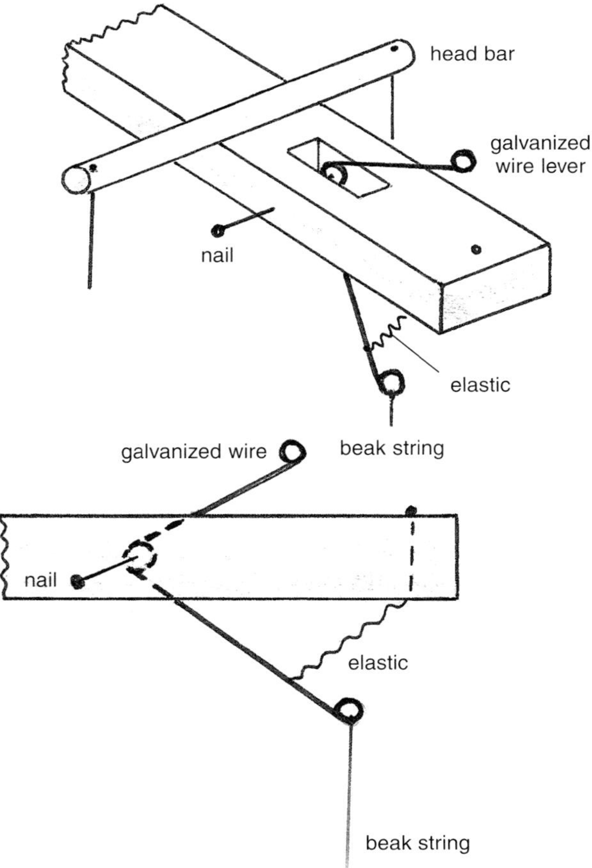

A lever mechanism for an opening mouth.

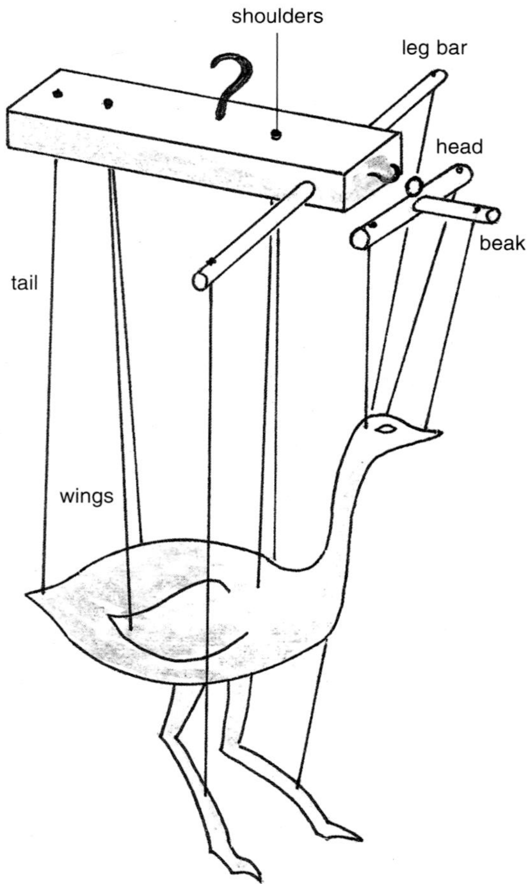

A horizontal control for large, walking birds.

Strings to the wings are attached at a suitable point on the horizontal bar so that they can be manipulated with the fingers of the hand that holds the control.

Some puppet makers add wire levers to move the wings but they are complicated to make and operate. They also require the use of your free hand, which you need to operate the head, so they are best avoided unless they are needed for a specific purpose.

A hook and a small ring are used to suspend a detachable head bar of dowelling from the front of the control. If the bird has an articulated beak, the string is attached to a 'T'-shaped head bar, as described above.

7 Specialized Stringing

General Principles

Special effects can sometimes be achieved just by adding a few carefully positioned strings. However, in some circumstances, a more complex approach may be required. This chapter describes stringing arrangements both for particular purposes and for the special effects that may be achieved with puppets constructed in the standard ways without any special design features. The principles outlined may be used for a variety of applications and puppet makers need to be creative in devising ways to achieve a new movement or trick for the puppet.

For the best results, keep the stringing as simple as possible and consider how you will replace a string when the need arises. The major supporting strings and those to the limbs are usually easy to replace but this is not necessarily the case with other strings, which may be secured easily during construction but not when the puppet is completed.

Some acts combine a number of specialized techniques such as juggling or playing an instrument while riding a unicycle or walking a tightrope and the marionettes will have a complex arrangement of strings to effect the different actions. Additional strings always need to be carefully positioned so that they can be found and operated quickly and easily during a performance – often in low light conditions. However, with practice, they will often be accessible without even a glance, provided they are suitably positioned.

Raising a Hand to the Mouth

It is possible to raise a hand to the mouth with no special stringing. However, when very direct and precise action is

Uncle Charlie by Gordon Staight. A run-through string is used to raise his hat, and a magnet, built into the tip of his index finger, removes a host of unlikely items from inside a piano after he attempts to play it.

Holding Run-Through Strings in Place

When a run-through string is raised and needs to be secured in this position, use either a small ring to hook it on to the control or cut a small slot in a suitable part of the control and knot the string so that you can slip it into the slot with the knot preventing it from dropping. Ensure that the ring or the knot will not be so low as to draw attention to itself.

required, additional stringing may be necessary. If the mouth does not open, drill a small hole between the lips. Attach a string to the hand or to an object held in the hand; thread the string through the mouth and out through a hole drilled in the top of the head. Particularly when the mouth is fixed, it is helpful to glue a suitable piece of tubing or a plastic drinking straw in the head for the string to run through and to facilitate replacement, but ensure that there are no sharp edges to fray the thread. Pull the string to raise the hand or object to the mouth.

Run-through strings can be used in several ways – to bring the hands together, through the nose for smelling a bunch of flowers, through the body for clutching the chest, or anywhere you need. As this is additional to the standard hand string, ensure that it is sufficiently long to permit the normal range of hand movements.

Eating

Eating is a simple extension of raising a hand to the mouth, using a run-through string with a moving mouth and a head sufficiently hollow to accommodate whatever is to be eaten. Instead of attaching the run-through string to the hand, it is attached to the object to be eaten, which must be held fairly securely in the hand so that the hand continues to hold the food when the run-through string is raised.

Gordon Staight's troupe 'Gordon's Puppets', featured a roller-skating puppet, which at one time peeled and

Willie, an extending puppet by the author. A run-through string is used to raise the clown's hand to his lips to blow up the balloon.

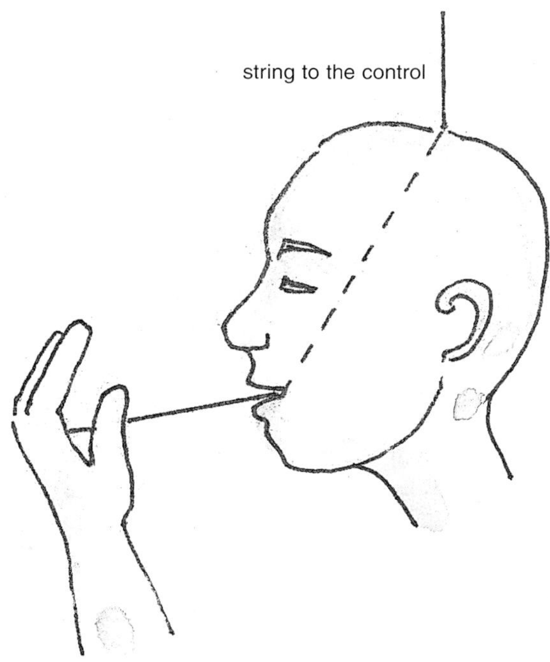

Stringing for raising a hand to the mouth.

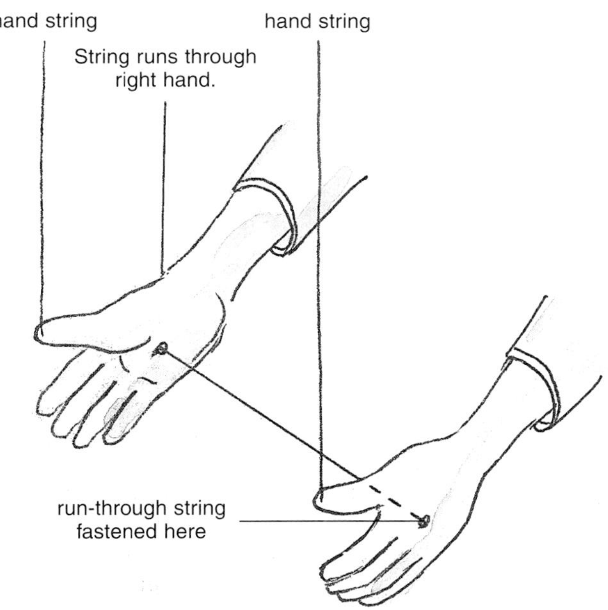

An extra run-through string used to bring the hands together.

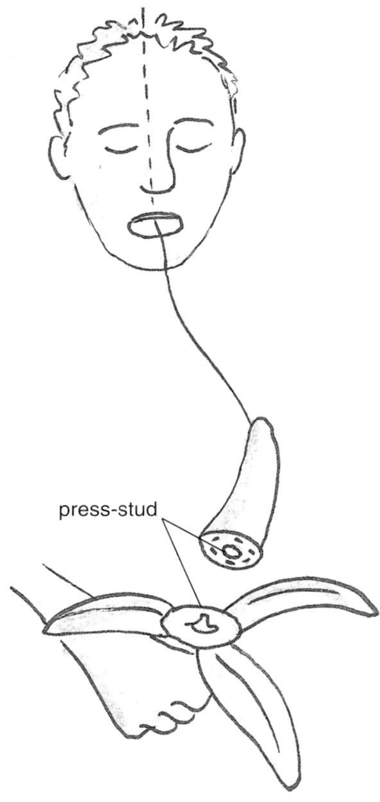

A puppet that 'eats' by means of a run-through string.
The banana is attached by a press-stud.

ate a banana; a later version ate an ice-cream. The banana was modelled and fixed securely in the hand by means of a press-stud. The strips of banana skin were hinged at the base with fabric and held in place, unpeeled, by a string from the base, which was wound around the top of the strips and held in a small slot in one piece. Raising the other hand to the banana and pulling this string to release the skin, created the effect of peeling it. A run-through string to the top of the edible part raised the banana to the mouth and a quick jerk of this string separated the press-stud and allowed the banana to disappear inside the head.

The ice-cream and cone were cast in fairly soft latex rubber and the cone was secured in the hand with a very small piece of Velcro. A run-through string, this time from the top of the cone, raised it to the mouth and a clean jerk on the string made it disappear inside the head. An additional touch was a topping of Crazy

A puppet that 'eats' by means of a run-through string.
The ice-cream is moulded in latex rubber.

Raising a hat with a run-through string.

Foam (a fun foam that wipes away cleanly), which made the ice-cream appear more realistic and some of which remained smeared all around the puppet's mouth.

Raising a Hat

Drill holes in the brim of the hat for the head strings to pass through. Ensure that the holes are spaced exactly the same distance apart as the head strings, which should be parallel, so that the hat has smooth vertical movement. Attach an extra string to one hand and thread it through another hole drilled in the brim where it meets the crown; drill the hole at an angle so that the thread passes inside the hat and out through another hole in the top. Pull the string to raise the hand to the hat; continue to pull it to lift the hat.

To adjust a hat, as opposed to raising it, make slots instead of holes in the brim so that it can move to and fro on the head. A run-through string can still be used but I prefer to use the puppet's thumb, or a small metal pin sticking out from the thumb. You need to ensure that the arm movement permits this action with ease.

Lifting an Object

Attach a string to the object. Thread the string through a hole in the hand and then attach it to the control. To pick up the object, rest the hand on it and pull the string taut. The hand will be lifted with the object. To replace the object, lower the run-through string and, when the object is in place, lift the hand string to remove the hand. To ensure that the hand remains firmly in contact with the object, particularly when putting it down, the hand should be a reasonable weight and you should bend the puppet as necessary for the hand to reach the required position.

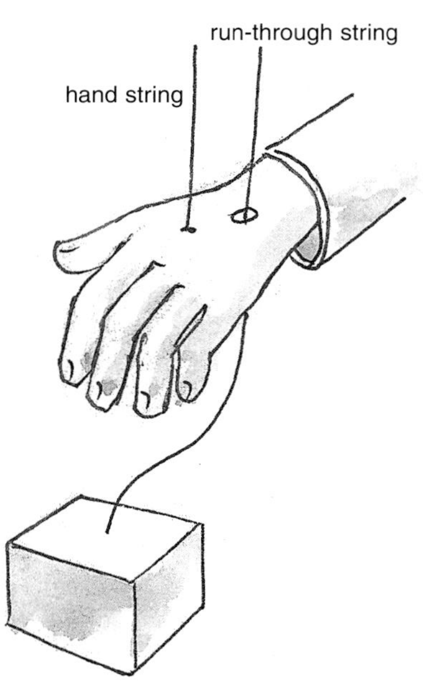

Using an extra string to pick up an object.

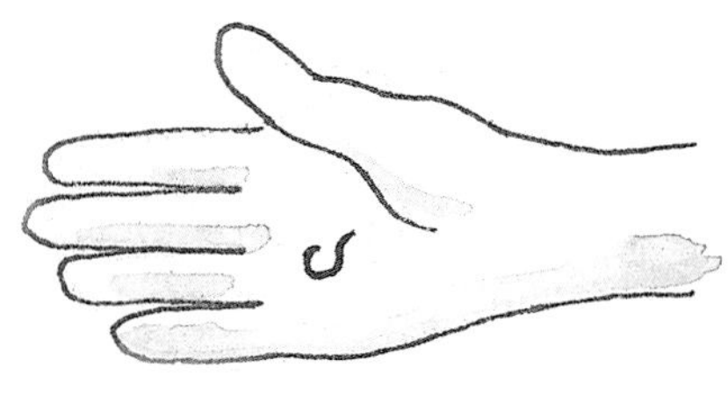

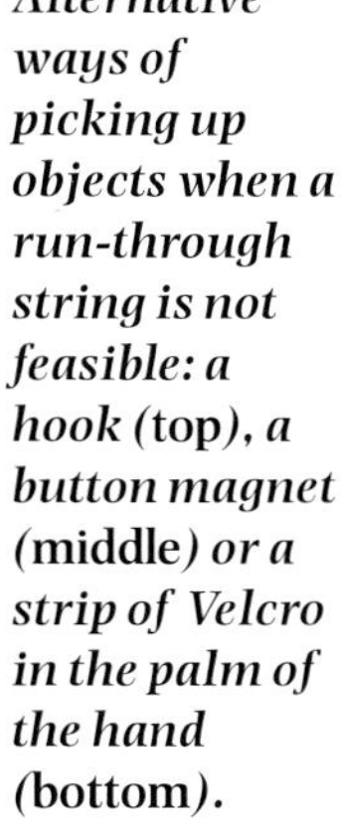

Alternative ways of picking up objects when a run-through string is not feasible: a hook (*top*), a button magnet (*middle*) or a strip of Velcro in the palm of the hand (*bottom*).

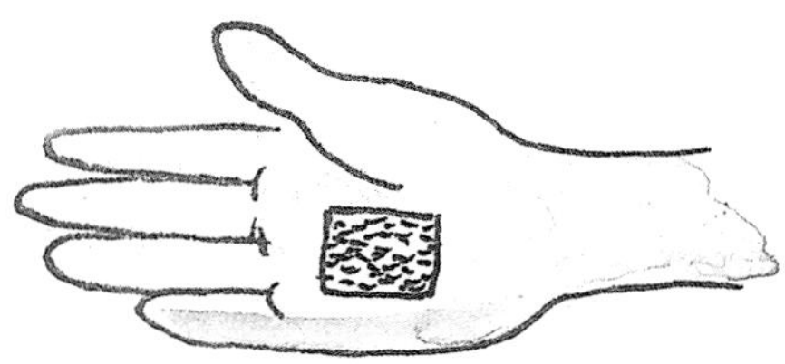

Alternative Ways to Lift an Object

If the puppet needs to move about the stage when not holding the object, any extra stringing would need to be very long and loose, which is not always practical. Alternatively, a small wire hook or a button-magnet may be built into the hand. If a magnet is used, a strip of tin needs to be glued to the surface of any non-attracted object to be picked up. If the object is to be put down on stage, a stronger magnet will be required on the surface on to which it is to be placed.

Velcro, glued to the hand and to the object is a possibility for objects that are not too heavy. They cling together when the hand is placed on the object, especially if the hand is of a suitable weight, but a good jerk of the hand string can separate the two. This can be problematic if unintended, or a helpful way to cast the object aside but it is certainly not a graceful way to replace an object.

Removing and Replacing an Object

There may be occasions when a puppet is required to remove an object from its pocket and then replace it, or to perform a similar operation. The compere and cowboy demonstrate two means by which such movements are effected.

The compere, with a handkerchief inside its jacket, illustrates how this is accomplished with run-through strings. Two run-through strings are attached to the

ABOVE AND ON PAGE 123: Mr Herbert by Gordon Staight. Run-through strings enable him to remove a handkerchief from an inside pocket and to replace it after blowing his nose and polishing his spectacles. All of Gordon's acts have nice touches of humour and, with Gordon in view of the audience, Mr Herbert attempts to demonstrate to the audience that he controls the puppeteer rather than the other way round. He shows how, when he raises his hand, the puppeteer raises his; when he lowers it, the puppeteer lowers his. Then he lifts both legs off the ground – and falls flat on his bottom! Time to reappraise his theory.

handkerchief; one runs through the body, out of the back and up to the control. The other passes in front of the body to the left hand, runs through a hole in the thumb and continues up to the control. Pulling this latter string taut draws the hand across the body to the edge of the jacket. To ensure the hand is drawn to the handkerchief and not vice versa, the handkerchief is lodged firmly in place between the jacket and the body. Continuing to pull the string lifts the handkerchief out and the puppet can blow its nose and polish its glasses. To replace the handkerchief, the hand is positioned by the edge of the jacket and pulling the other string through the back draws the handkerchief inside the jacket.

The cowboy illustrates how objects in the hand may be

Slim Tim Tex by Gordon Staight. ABOVE LEFT AND RIGHT: *The cowboy draws his gun.*

He shoots various items from a target. A smoking barrel effect is achieved with talcum powder in a bellows inside the body.

ABOVE AND TOP PAGE 126: *One string directly to the gun and another through the arm to the thumb on the butt of the gun provides the control required to draw and replace the gun in the holster. A tiny spike protruding from the left thumb enables the cowboy to adjust the angle of his hat.*

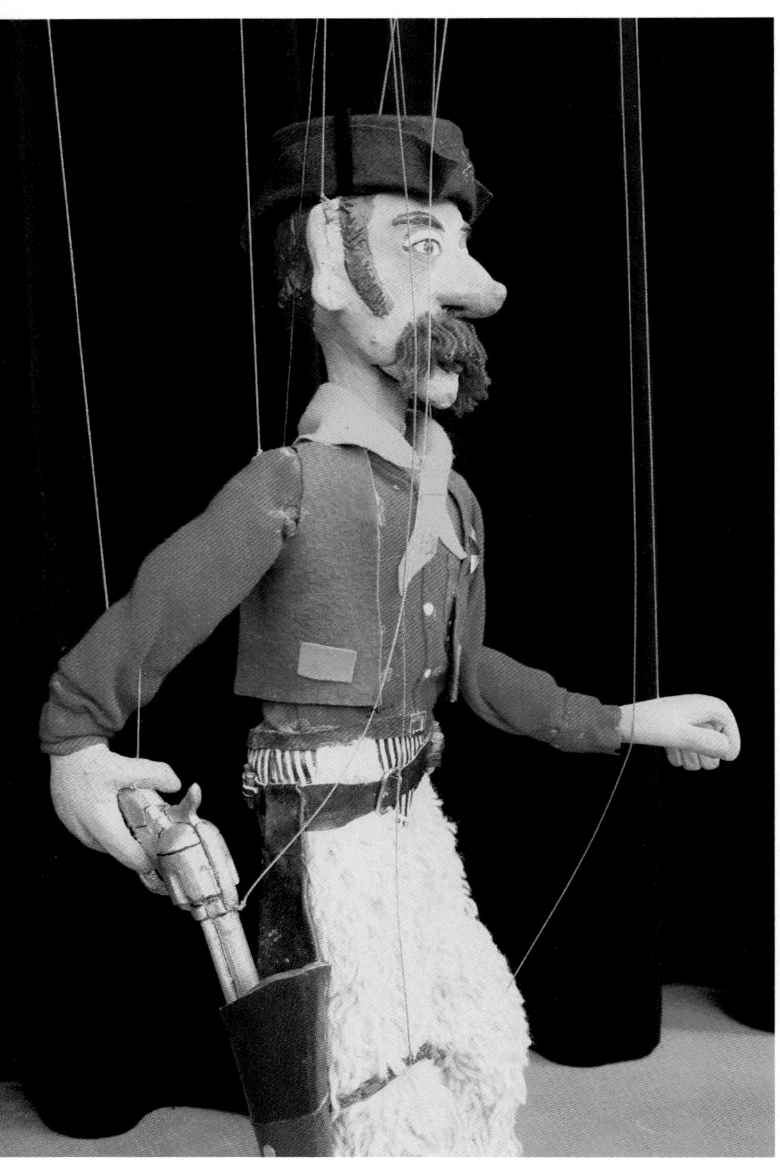

controlled by means of the relative tensions of two strings. A normal hand control wire is used for all the main operations of the gun hand. One string, attached to the wire, is secured to the gun where the barrel joins the bullet chamber: raising the hand wire draws the gun from its holster. An additional string is needed in order to replace the gun: this runs from the control down to the rear of the arm just above the elbow. It passes through a hole in the arm and is attached to the thumb where it touches the butt of the gun. Lifting this string while keeping tension on the main hand wire raises the elbow and positions the gun above the holster. The elbow string is now lowered and the gun, guided with the other string, is smoothly replaced in the holster.

When the gun is fired, sound effects of gunshots are accompanied by 'smoke' from the barrel, which is actually talcum powder blown from a bellows or rubber bulb as described in the following chapter (*see* page 154).

Opening Objects Without Special Stringing

When one needs a marionette to open a book, lift the lid of a piano or perform an equivalent movement, it is often sufficient to build a small projection on to the part to be lifted and to guide the hand under the projection and raise it. However, a little extra assistance

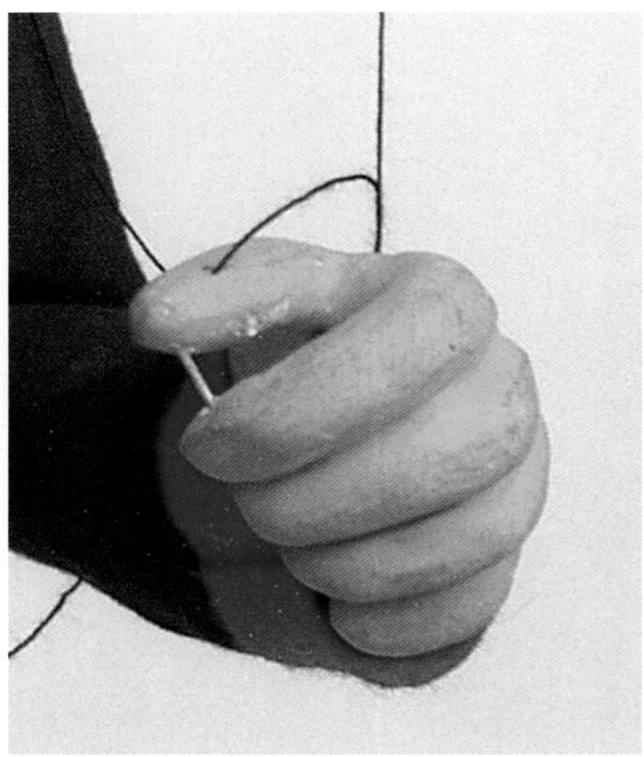

ABOVE AND RIGHT: ***Mr Herbert by Gordon Staight. A piece of galvanized wire fixed between the thumb and index finger helps to raise his glasses in a clean movement and without getting snagged.***

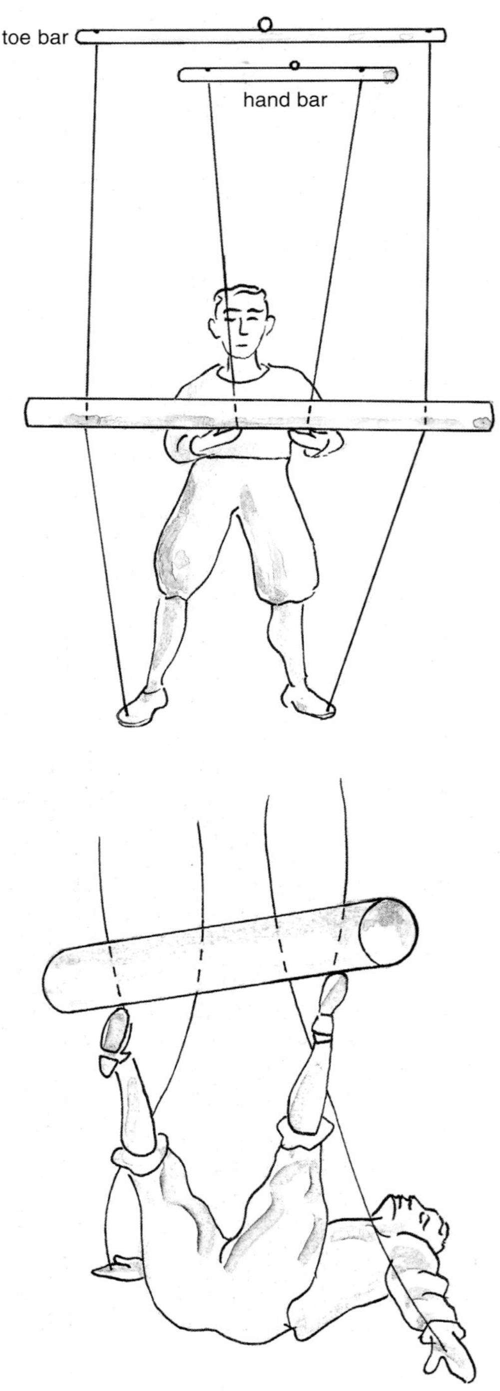

Stringing for a pole balancer, a traditional marionette act.

is sometimes required. The compere, for example, has a fine nail secured across the gap between the tips of the thumb and forefinger in order to help to raise the glasses in a clean movement. The cowboy has a small spike that protrudes from one of its thumbs; this is used to catch the brim of the hat and adjust its position on the head.

A Pole Balancer

The structure and most of the stringing of this traditional figure are standard. Strings from the hands and feet pass through holes drilled in a horizontal, brightly coloured pole. Moving the tension from one set of strings to the other allows the pole to be transferred between the hands and feet.

For the act to be convincing, the pole is thrown or bounced up and down by recoiling the relevant set of strings. You need to consider the position of the puppet for each transfer. It can enter carrying the pole, which it can

A simple version of a stilt walker.

throw and catch while standing. However, it cannot, for example, transfer the pole convincingly from the feet to the hands while upright: the puppet should be lying on the floor with its feet raised in the air.

A Stilt Walker

The stilt walker is a standard puppet, a simple version of which does not require the usual control. Movement is effected through the stilts, which are sufficiently long for the operator to hold. Secure the puppet's hands and feet to the stilts and support the head by strings attached high on the stilts. Hold the top of the stilts to walk the puppet. If the puppeteer is performing in sight of the audience, it is helpful to paint the top of the stilts a dark colour so that they do not draw attention to themselves.

Paul Doran of the Shadowstring Theatre (*see* page 188) has a more complex stilt walker that has shorter, hollow, metal stilts and a proper control. The figure walks on to the stage then leaps up on to the stilts and the act proceeds. In order to achieve this, the puppet has an extra string attached to each foot that runs through a hole a few inches above the ground in the stilt and continues up through to the control. These strings are jerked taut to make the puppet leap on to the stilts and are secured on the control in the raised position so that they remain in place until the puppeteer wishes to release them.

A stilt walker by Paul Doran, Shadowstring Theatre. The marionette walks on stage and jumps on to the stilts before proceeding with the act. This is achieved by using run-through strings from the feet to the hollow stilts.

A Simple Juggling Puppet

It is not essential to have elaborate stringing for a juggler. Skilfully done, the mere suggestion of juggling can be as effective as the real thing. Indian puppeteers have perfected such techniques to an amazing degree: a single loop of string is used with one end attached to each of the puppet's hands. A ball threaded on to each end of the string is bounced up and down by jerking the string. The balls can be thrown up alternately or together. When both balls are in the air, a sideways wiggling of the strings causes the balls to cross over and creates the illusion of juggling.

Instead of a loop of string, there can be separate strings to each hand. These strings are attached to a detachable hand bar, like a normal leg bar (*see* page 76). With this arrangement you might find it a little easier to throw the balls up but it will be more difficult to achieve the cross-over illusion.

One of the most effective methods of 'juggling' uses only a loop of string, on to which are threaded two balls. Bouncing the balls and jiggling the strings can create a convincing appearance of juggling.

When the operator is hidden, a nice touch is to have the ball thrown in the air but the operator catches it and there is a long pause before it is released. Meanwhile some humorous business takes place with the bewildered puppet wondering what has happened to the ball.

Separate strings attached to a hand bar used to juggle balls threaded on the strings.

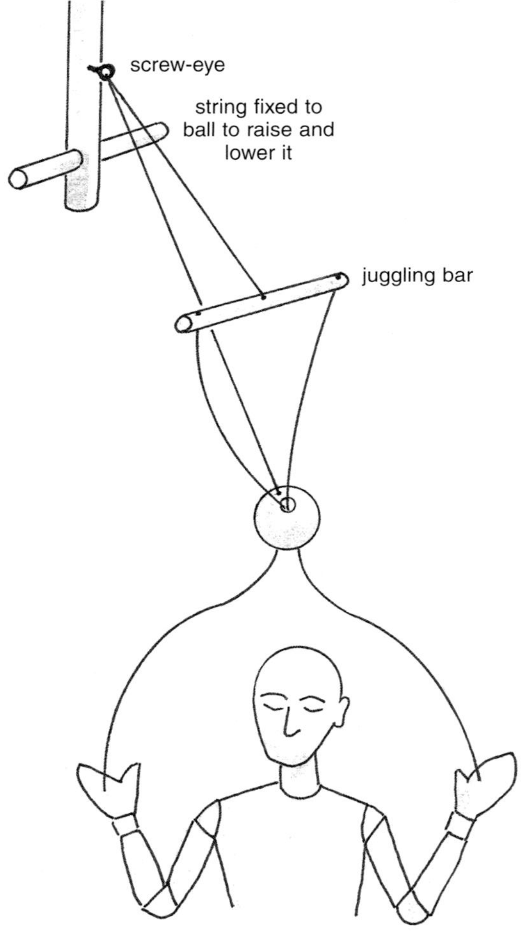

A string is used to raise and lower this single ball. Transferring the tension from one side of the hand bar to the other allows the ball to drop on to a different hand.

Throwing and Catching a Single Ball

Some performers juggle with just one ball. The hand strings pass through a hole drilled in the ball and are attached to a hand bar as described above. An additional string is attached to raise and lower the ball. It passes through a screw-eye in the main control and is then attached to the centre of the hand bar.

Pulling the hand bar forwards raises the ball. Tilting the hand bar to transfer the tension from one hand to the other allows the ball to drop back on to a different hand when the hand bar is moved back towards the control.

If the puppet is to walk while juggling, you will need a rocking bar to control the legs, leaving one of your hands free for the actual juggling.

More Complex Juggling

This juggling method requires an extra crossbar, the juggling bar, on the main control. Attach a string to each part of the body to be involved. Thread these strings through a hole in the ball or other object to be juggled and attach them to the juggling bar.

Take the tension on one string whilst leaving all the others slack. Now release this string and pull a different one taut to transfer the ball to another part of the body. Each of the strings must be long enough to let the ball bounce to any part of the puppet. You may find it works better if the puppet throws the ball up between the transfers. To do this, some performers attach a separate string directly to the ball while others simply bounce the ball on the hand or body part on which it is resting. It is essential to practise transferring the ball from one limb to another until the whole process is smooth rather than jerky.

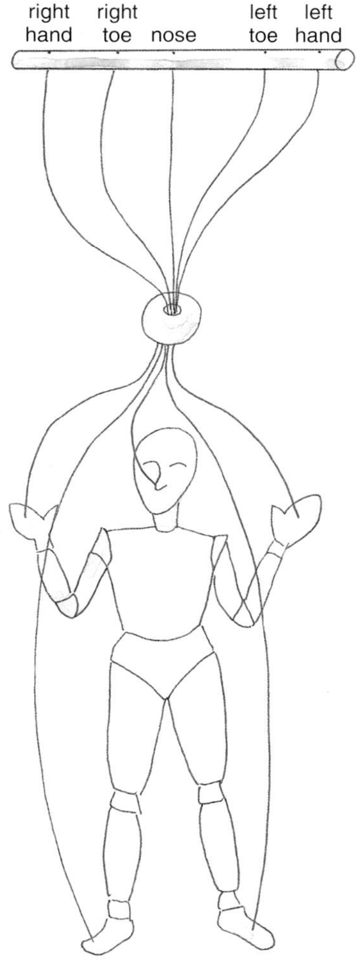

More complex juggling requires strings through the ball to different parts of the body. Bouncing the ball in the air, while pulling one string taut and leaving the others slack, transfers the ball from the nose or a limb to another part of the body.

An Acrobat on a Horizontal Bar

The horizontal bar offers a somewhat easier alternative to a trapeze. Two upright posts attached to a baseboard support the bar. The base should be secured to prevent toppling over; a simple method is to extend the base rearwards and stand on it during the act.

The puppet and control are of standard construction, though it may be helpful to have a hand bar rather than separate hand wires. Additions or amendments to the control may be made to achieve particular actions: a back string and heel strings are very useful. The puppet's hands are made with the fingers looped to enable them to grasp the horizontal bar.

You may invent your own act but some possibilities are as follows. The puppet enters and jumps up to grasp the bar; a back string helps it swing to and fro and it can raise itself with great effort to balance with its hips resting on the bar. By raising the heel strings, the puppet can do a handstand on the bar and then lower itself so that the head and body are on the other side of the bar, still with the hands gripping the bar.

ABOVE AND PAGE 133: A juggler performing with cups and saucers on a pole by Paul Doran, Shadowstring Theatre.

Having returned to the original hanging position, the puppet raises its knees between its hands and hooks its legs over the bar to achieve a sitting position. Slackening the hand strings releases the bar from the hands and the puppet can now hang backwards and swing from its knees. If there is a protruding heel or a small hook there, the puppet can slip further backwards and hang by its heels, again recovering to a hand-held position with considerable effort.

An acrobat on a horizontal bar.

A Trapeze Artist

The trapeze artist is sometimes attached to the trapeze so that it enters already swinging or it may be completely separate and actually jump on to the trapeze. These arrangements have different implications for stringing and for what the puppet can do. In each case the puppet is of a standard construction with the hands curved to fit over the bar. Some puppet makers use joints that restrict the limbs and waist to movement in one plane, rather than have them moving in all directions.

The exact positioning of strings on the body and the design of the control depends on what you want to achieve and some experimentation might be necessary.

Performers with suitable staging may have a traditional form of trapeze with a crossbar suspended by ropes fixed high on the stage or suspended from a form of 'gallows' attached to the stage.

An alternative trapeze consists of two horizontal dowel rods joined by two vertical dowels or rigid metal rods with the upper bar forming part of the control, as described below for the puppet permanently attached to the trapeze.

A Puppet Separated from the Trapeze

The marionette will have the normal stringing but may be assisted by a hand bar and additional strings to the toes or the front of the ankle. Many of its actions will be like those performed on the horizontal bar. The trapeze itself is suspended from a gallows attached to the stage.

The puppet can leap on to the trapeze and hook its hands over the bar. It can also hang from the trapeze and swing using only one hand, monkey-fashion. Swing the legs to build up the momentum ready for the acrobatics.

A trapeze artist by Paul Doran, Shadowstring Theatre. The puppet, separate from the trapeze, performs a succession of death-defying movements, including hanging by its turned-up toes.

Raise the knees between the arms and allow the feet to pass between the hands and over the horizontal bar so that the puppet is sitting and swinging on the crossbar. Loosen the hand strings to release the hands from the trapeze and let the puppet lean backwards until it is hanging upside down and swinging with its knees hooked over the bar. A small protrusion from the top of the heels would allow the puppet to slide back further and hang by its heels.

Instead of sitting on the crossbar, the puppet could raise its feet on to the bar, release its hands and swing in a standing position.

If the puppet is to hang by its toes, it will be achieved best if the toe strings pass under the crossbar and then back over it to the control. The puppeteer needs to skilfully manipulate a toe bar into this position without dropping it. As the puppet swings by its hands, the toe strings are raised to hook the feet over the crossbar. The hands are then released and the puppet is allowed to hang upside down. Turned-up toes assist in this.

A Puppet Permanently Attached to the Trapeze

This marionette is rather different in scope. It makes its entrance already swinging and can hang and swing from its hands or toes, raise itself waist high to the bar, alternately raising and lowering itself by the arms. It can also swing with its hands and feet on the bar and the whole trapeze can be spun around.

The control for this version of the acrobat is different from usual. To the ends of a main, vertical, central dowel are attached two horizontal dowel rods, the lower rod being the upper horizontal bar of the trapeze so that the puppeteer carries the puppet and trapeze together. The distance between the horizontal dowels is half the height of the puppet from toes to fingertips with its arms raised.

Hand strings are threaded through holes in the lower crossbar of the trapeze, a fair distance apart. Strings from the front of the feet near the toes are threaded through additional holes in the crossbar, between the hand strings. These hand and foot strings should be of equal length. The hand strings pass behind the upper crossbar of the trapeze and the foot strings pass in front of it. Both sets of strings are attached to the upper crossbar of the control.

Head strings are required but shoulder strings are not needed. The head strings pass behind the lower and upper crossbars of the trapeze and are attached to the upper crossbar of the control. They must be sufficiently long to permit the puppet to hang upside down from its toes.

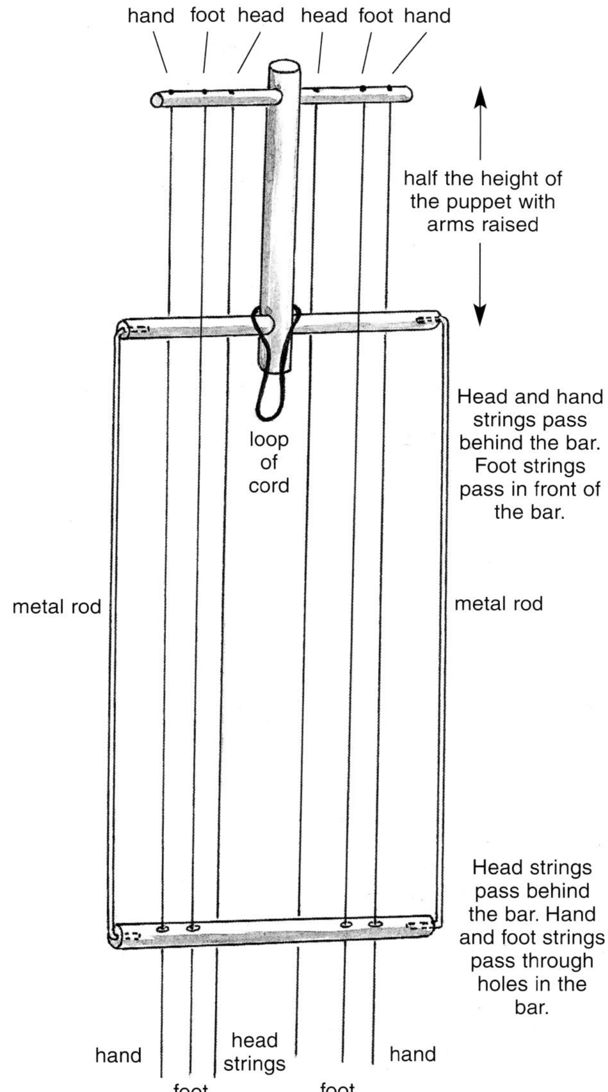

Stringing and control for a puppet that is permanently attached to the trapeze.

Because the head strings will be slack at some points in the acrobatics, it might help to use a neck joint that provides some restriction rather than having the head flop about.

A loop of cord attached to the control enables the whole trapeze and the puppet to be spun. Attaching the loop to the base of the control permits the trapeze to spin with the puppet hanging from either its hands or its toes.

When the control is held vertically, the hands and feet

Head strings omitted for clarity.

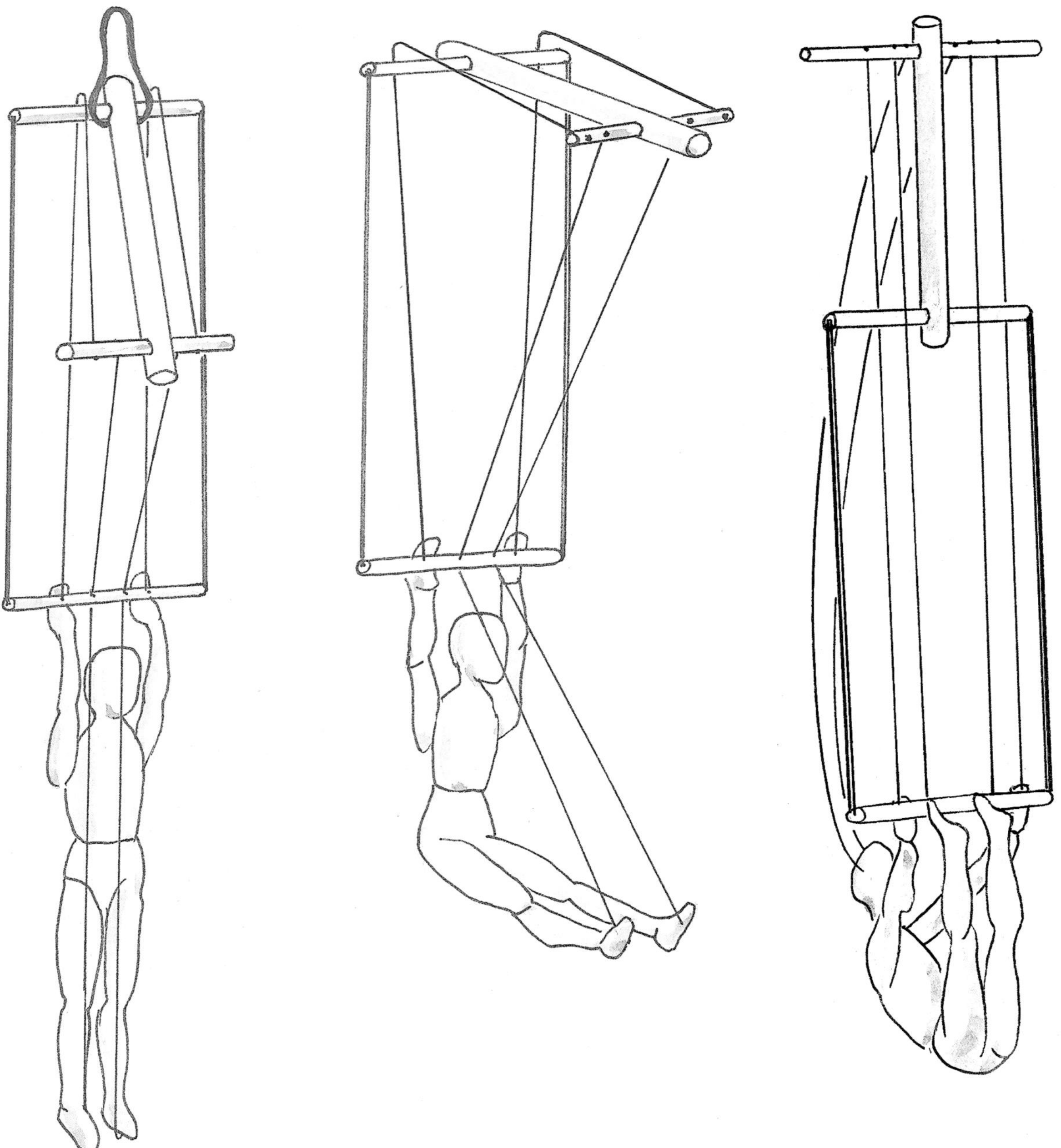

Tilt the control forward to raise the hands and release the feet.

Raise and lower the control slightly to swing the legs.

With the control upright, the hands and feet are on the trapeze.

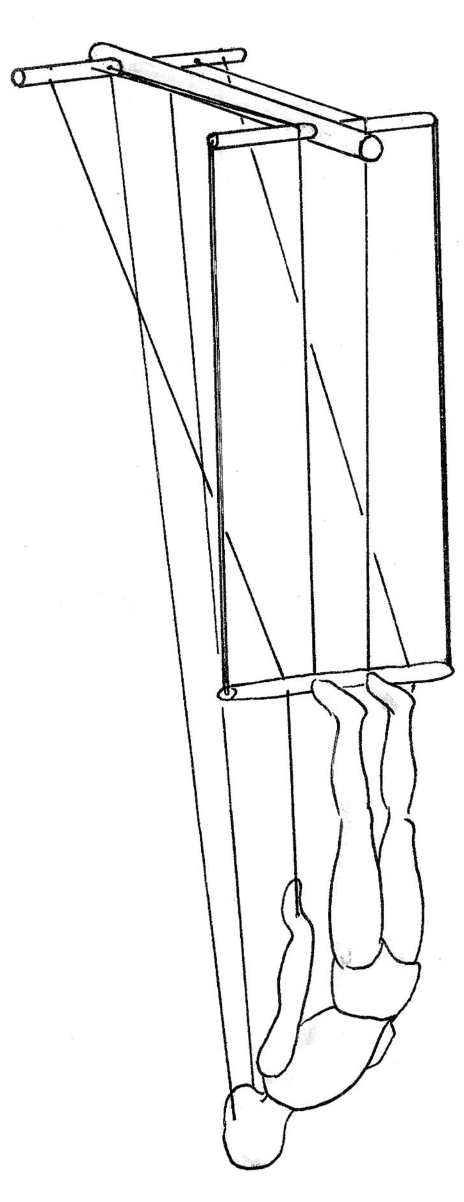

Tilt the control backward to raise the feet and lower the hands.

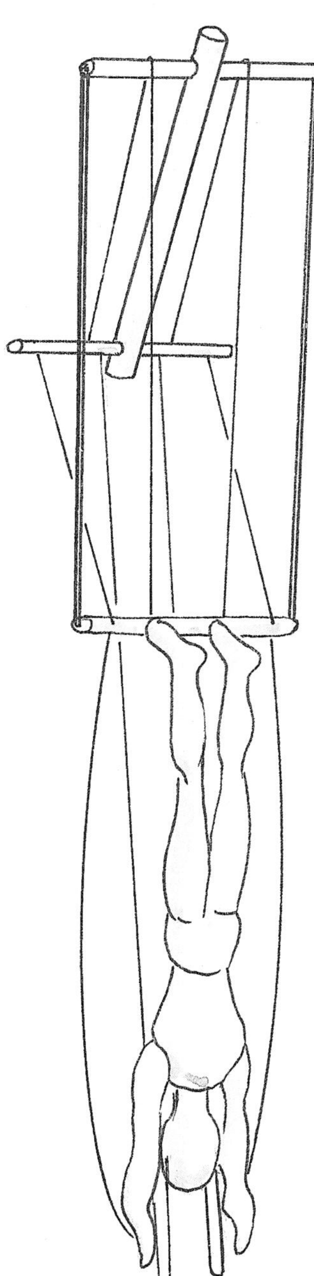

Tilt the control backwards to extend the arms fully.

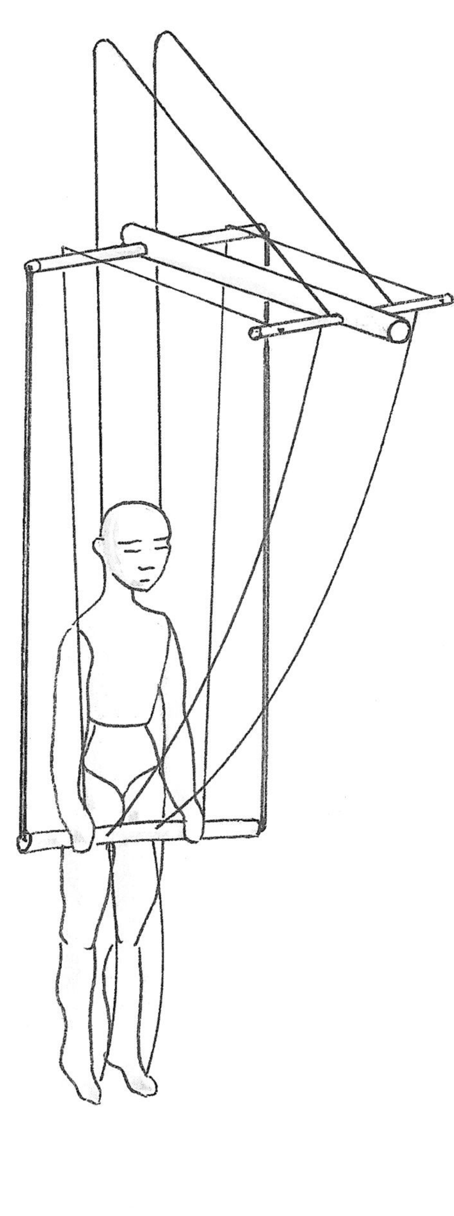

Tilt the control forward and raise the head string to raise the puppet to waist or hip height on the trapeze.

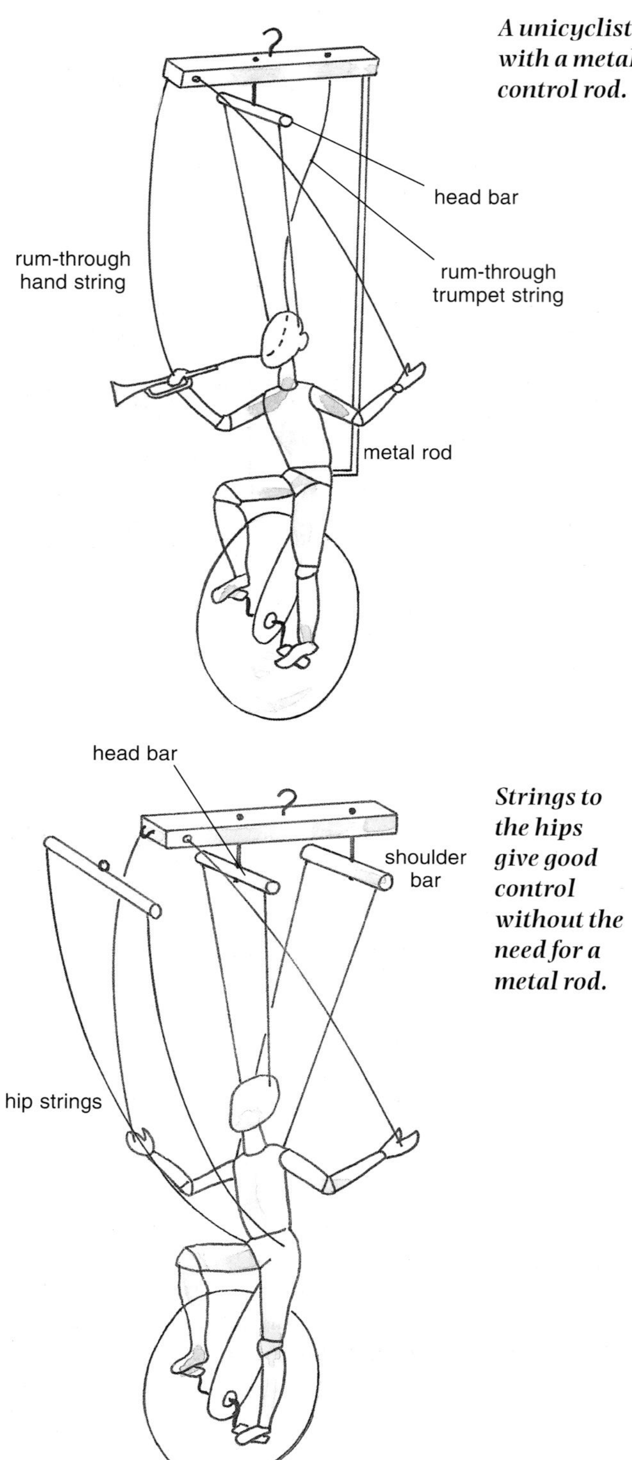

A unicyclist with a metal control rod.

Strings to the hips give good control without the need for a metal rod.

will be on the trapeze. Tilt the control forwards to lower the feet and hang by the hands; tilt it backwards to lower the hands and hang by the toes. Tilt the control and raise it repeatedly to build up momentum as the puppet swings. Tilt the control forwards and lift the head strings to raise the puppet to waist height on the trapeze. Continue to raise the head strings and slacken the ankle strings for the puppet to stand on the trapeze.

The act revolves around sequencing these actions smoothly and in a convincing way.

A Unicyclist

The unicyclist is a standard puppet but it is usually secured to the saddle of the cycle, and the feet are attached to the pedals on the wheel. Strings alone may control the puppet but, for more direct control, fast stopping and turning, many performers use a metal rod painted black to control the unicycle. The rod may run down through the puppet to the saddle but this restricts the puppet's movements. It is preferable to attach it to the saddle and run it up behind the puppet to the control. Strings to the control, allowing a little wobbly movement, can support the puppet's head and shoulders. The hands have a running string through the control. By contrast, Paul Doran achieves excellent control without the use of a metal rod by the addition of strings to the puppet's hips.

A Weightlifter

The weightlifter is made by a standard method, though joints have to be chosen carefully if the limbs are to be bare. This puppet often benefits from moving eyes and mouth so that appropriate grunts and gasps or rolling eyes can accompany the effort to lift the weights.

The hands are in a hooked position for lifting the weights. They may be attached with palms facing upwards or downwards, depending on the act. Hand strings are attached near the knuckles for the over-grip and at the heel of the hand, near the wrists, for the under-grip. The exact positioning depends on the weight of the hands and the length and curve of the fingers. You need to achieve a position that will look as natural as possible but will hold the weights securely when they are lifted. Remember that, in order for the hands to be hooked and unhooked, the thumbs will not curl around the bar as they would for a human; they will remain in line with the

Paul Doran's Shadowstring troupe includes a puppet on a 'break-away' bicycle (made by Steve and Chris Clarke of the Wychwood Puppets) that comes apart to become a unicycle.

fingers so they will not help to hold the weights in the hands. If the palms are facing upwards, the hand strings can help to control the weights if they start to roll out of the puppet's hands.

Usually the weights are placed on the floor in advance of the puppet's entrance. Some performers use a smaller puppet (of a child, for example) to enter and remove them with ease at the end of the act, after the weightlifter has apparently struggled to lift them.

If the weights are round they will need chocks to stop them rolling away or a suitable stand to hold them.

There is no trick to this puppet; the act revolves around a series of attempts to lift the weights or dumb-bells with eventual success. The weightlifter kneels behind the horizontal bar, hooks its hands over or under the bar and adopts a range of techniques to lift the weights – kneeling, standing, bending, even sitting or laying on the floor. Gordon Staight's weightlifter strains so hard that at first its legs rise up into the air instead of the weights! My own children's version concludes with the puppet achieving its goal but then falling through the stage floor by means of a trap door. This device has a catch released by a cord to a foot-operated lever.

A variation of the weightlifter uses strings that run through the horizontal bar of the weights to the hands. This enables the puppet to lift the weights securely but prevents it from moving far from the weights. Some people therefore have the puppet carry the weights on to the stage, but this rather defeats the point of the act! The weightlifter may also be arranged with the foot strings

ABOVE AND OPPOSITE: ***Gordonia, by Gordon Staight, struggles to lift the weights. At first his feet rise up instead of the weights but eventually he succeeds with much grunting, panting, and baring of teeth.***

Detail of the author's weightlifter: the upward-facing palms help to hold the weights securely when they are raised.

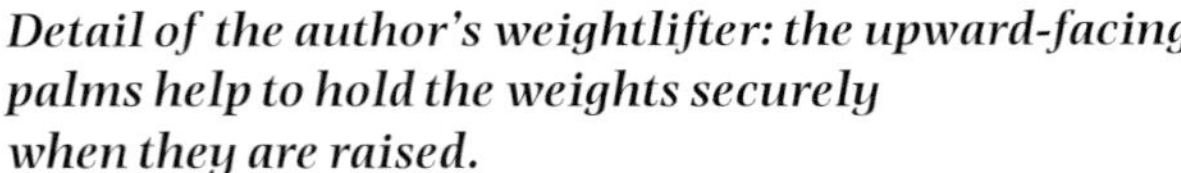

through the horizontal bar of the weights, so that the weights can be transferred from hands to feet, like the pole balancer.

A horizontal control is helpful as it allows the puppet to be walked simply by rocking the main control, leaving the puppeteer with a free hand to control the puppet's hands. The basic control follows the normal design with suspended head and shoulder bars, a back string attached directly to the control, and a leg bar attached near the front of the control. A horizontal hand bar that hangs from a hook on the front of the control operates the hands. The bar should be a little wider than the distance between the centres of the hands when lifting the weights.

It may also have heel strings and mouth and eye controls. An additional bar will be required if strings through the weights to the feet are to be included.

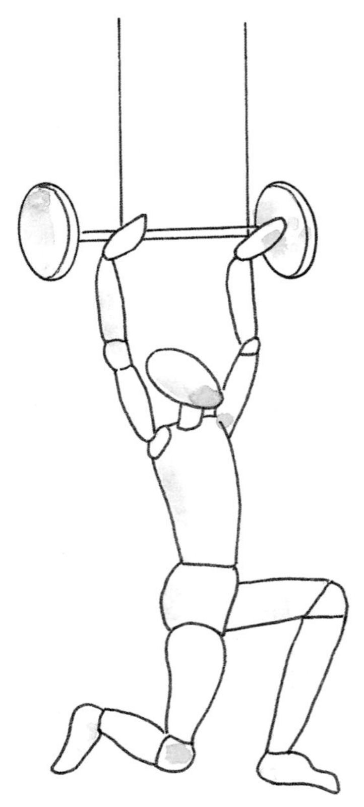

RIGHT: A weightlifter with run-through strings to lift the weights.

Musicians

The following examples demonstrate the general principles that may be applied to puppets with a variety of musical instruments.

A Pianist or Percussionist

Fasten a string to the back of each hand and another at the mid-point of each forearm. Make the hand control

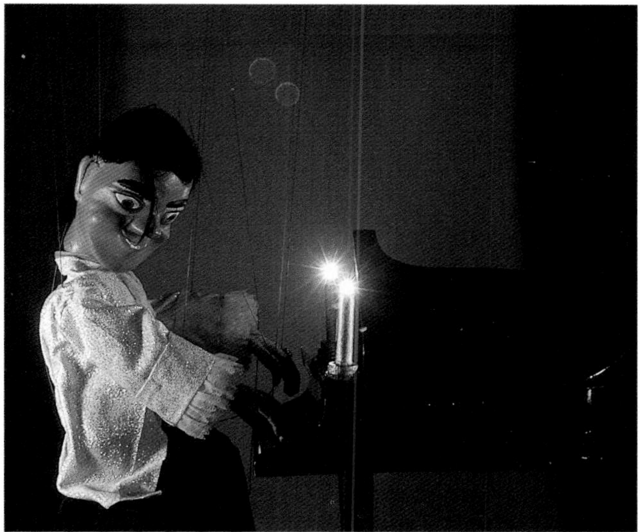

The control and stringing for a pianist's hands and forearms.

LEFT: Toski the pianist, an early puppet by the author, raises the piano lid, which causes the candelabra to illuminate. He raises the lid of the keyboard and proceeds to play, soon to be interrupted in various ways. The hands and the keyboard are moulded in latex rubber to prevent them clattering as he plays. The body of the piano has a plywood base and lid, with shaped aluminium for the sides and keyboard lid.

from three pieces of dowelling fixed in an 'H' shape. Attach the strings to the corners of the 'H'.

Rock and tilt the bar to produce a simulation of a pianist's hand action. Tie a small curtain ring to the centre of this control and hang it from a hook screwed into the main control.

The same arrangement would be appropriate for a percussionist but you might need to attach two of the strings to parts of the instruments instead of the hands, depending on the distribution of weight. A puppet with cymbals has run-through strings for bringing the hands together (*see* pages 118–9).

A Violinist

Although the puppet is standard, you will have to make a miniature version of a violin and a bow. Two strings support the violin: one runs from the main body of the violin, through a small screw-eye or loop of wire on the shoulder, and up to the main control. A small ring near the top of the string hooks onto the control and enables the violin to be raised and lowered. The other string runs from the puppet's left hand, on the neck of the violin, to a hand wire on the main control.

The bow is held against the strings by a small ring or a strong jewellery clasp (which allows the bow and violin to be separated for packing). A more complex arrangement has this ring or clasp attached to a string that runs through a loop on the violin. Allowing the string to slacken releases the bow from the violin, pulling it taut raises it to the violin for playing.

The bowing action is achieved by two strings attached to a separate dowel bar that hooks on to the main control. One string is attached to the bow-hand and the other to the end of the bow. The dowel bar is rocked to effect the playing movements.

The puppet's left hand may be fixed to the neck of the violin or closed around the neck but with freedom to move, which enhances the effect. Some performers have even hinged the fingers and devised ways of raising and lowering them on the neck of the violin, but this is visible only with a fairly intimate audience.

A Harpist

This puppet is included as an example of the use of a control that requires both hands to be free to manipulate specific strings. The figure may be of standard construction, though it is common for puppets that remain seated to have the part from hip to toe made in

The control and stringing for a violinist.

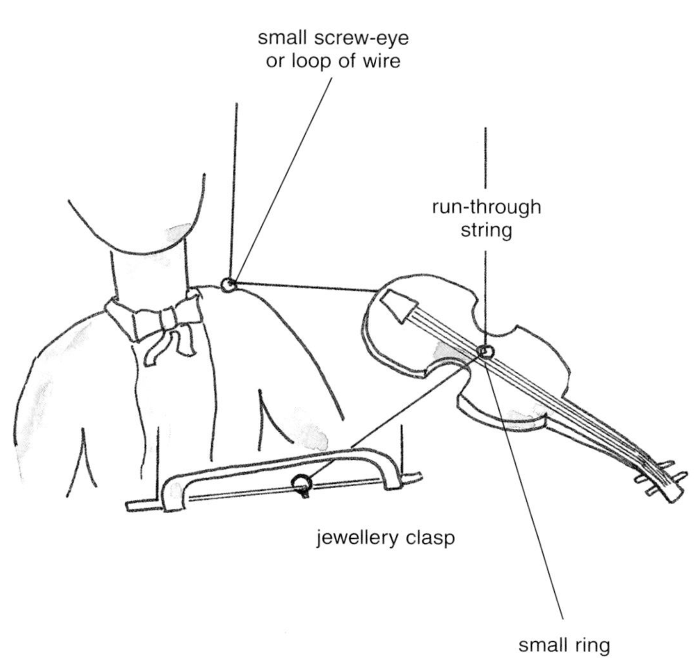

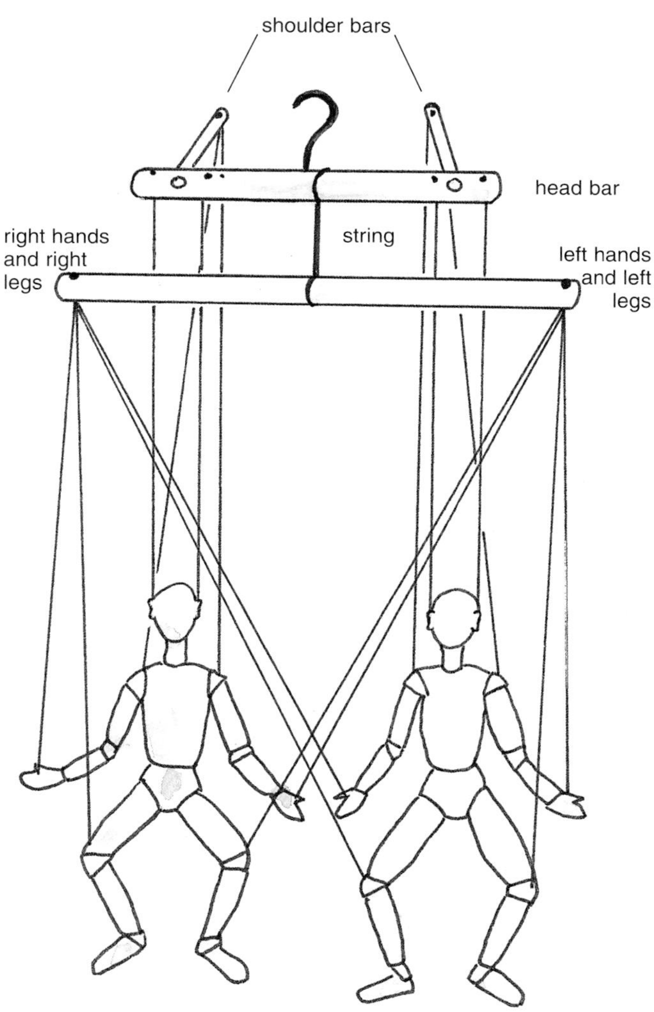

Stringing for dual control.

one unjointed piece and to be fixed permanently to a seat. The seat and the instrument would be attached securely to a baseboard.

The hand strings run through small screw-eyes or fine wire loops fixed to the harp. The ends of the strings are attached to dowel rods that are operated with a see-saw action. In order for a sole puppeteer to control the slight body movements and operate both hands, the main control may be hung from the puppeteer's wrist using a loop of webbing that is attached to the control. Hanging the control from a gallows on the stage is also possible but does not allow the puppet as much head or body movement.

A Trumpeter

Any wind instrument requires a run-through string to lift the object to the mouth and a further string placed on the instrument in order to support it. The supporting string is often attached to one of the hand wires, which is used to raise and lower the instrument as it is played.

Stringing for Dual Control

Dual control is used when two or more marionettes perform the same actions side by side.

Glue and nail the shoulder bar into a hole drilled in the head bar; this allows the heads to be tilted forward. Alternatively, attach the shoulder strings to the head bar on either side of the head strings. Join the head and leg bars with a length of string tied to the centre of each bar. Fix the right hand and right leg strings of both puppets together on the right-hand side of the leg bar and the left hand and left leg strings on to the left of the bar. Now the puppets will move or dance together.

Stringing for Tandem Control

Tandem control, when the puppets move one behind the other, is best effected with a long horizontal control that is really like two or more controls joined together. The range of movement is quite limited and such devices tend to be used for marching bands, soldiers, performing animals and the like.

For human figures, each puppet has a head bar and a shoulder bar suspended from the main control. What would normally be the leg bar is used to attach strings to the hands and knees: left leg and right hand on one side, right leg and left hand on the other, or same-side hands and legs, as required. The normal rocking action produces both leg movement and arm swinging.

It should be appreciated that such a control will not permit the heads to be nodded, as tilting the control will lower the front puppet. Further refinement will be necessary to achieve more complex movement.

For animals in tandem, the main control is once again an elongated horizontal bar that supports the rump and shoulder strings, and leg bars alternately lift opposing front and rear legs.

The head bars are not suspended in the usual way: they are pivoted on another long horizontal bar or rod that is itself suspended from the main control with strong elastic. The head bars are joined at the ends by string or galvanized wire so that turning either bar effects turning of both heads. The use of elastic to suspend the long bar permits a degree of natural head movement as the animal walks or trots and downward pressure on the bar lowers both heads together.

Paul Doran has a number of puppets that have tandem controls. For a set of four horses he has devised a control that leads them in single file and, as each section of the control may be swivelled and separated, the figures can perform both side by side and individually. This is a splendid example of the ingenuity of the puppeteer in devising ways to achieve variations on a familiar act.

For a pair of acrobats, he adopts the tandem control with the addition of strings that run from the feet of the rear character through small loops on the shoulders of the front character. This arrangement permits a number of acrobatic feats to be effected.

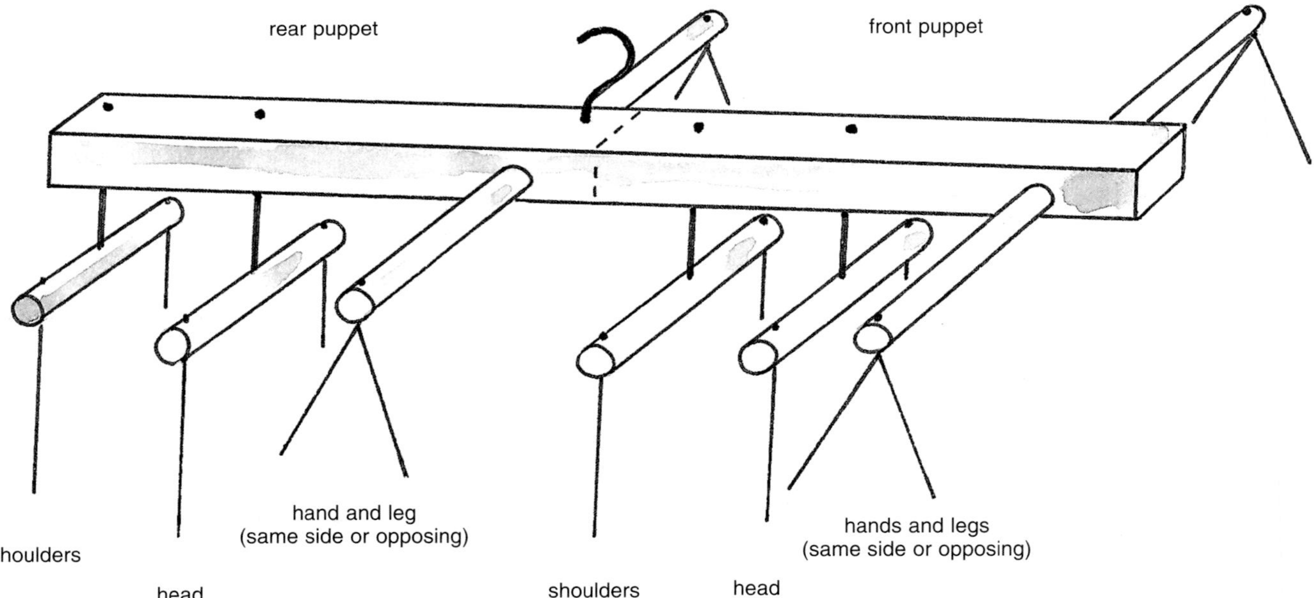

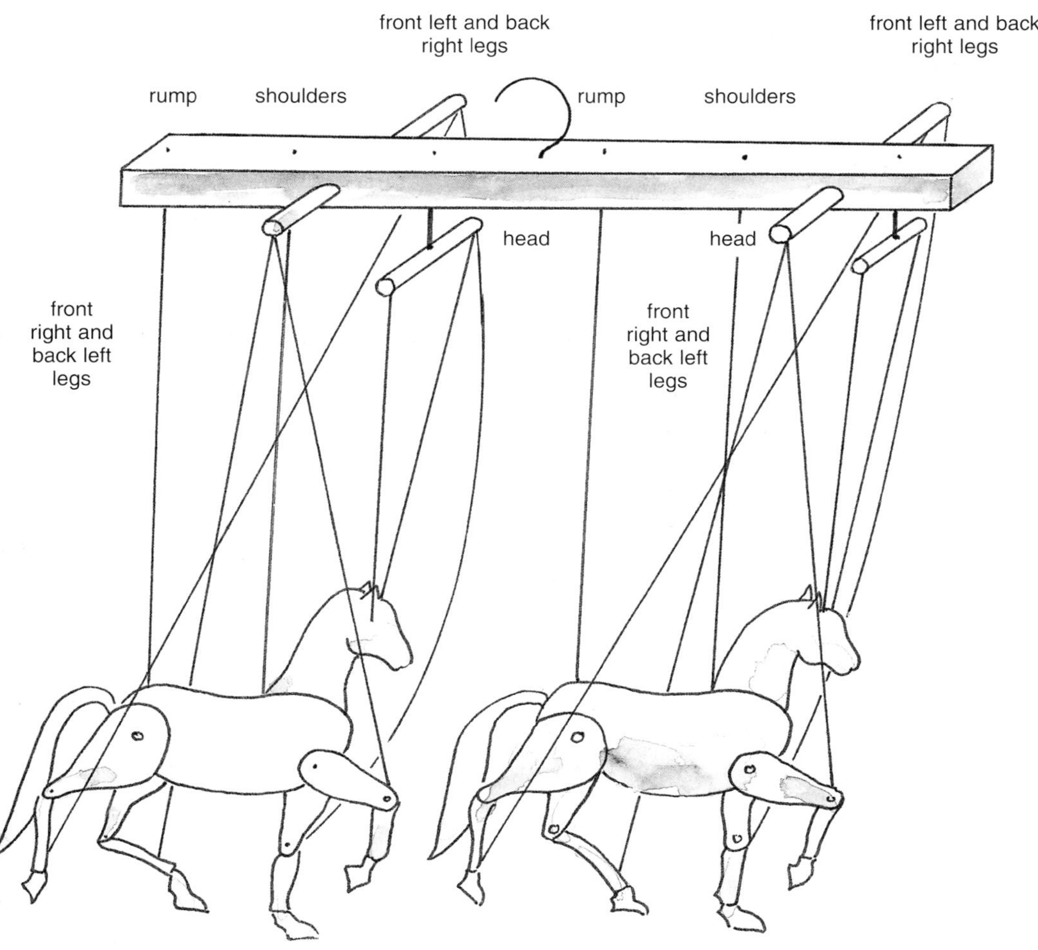

ABOVE: A tandem control for animals.

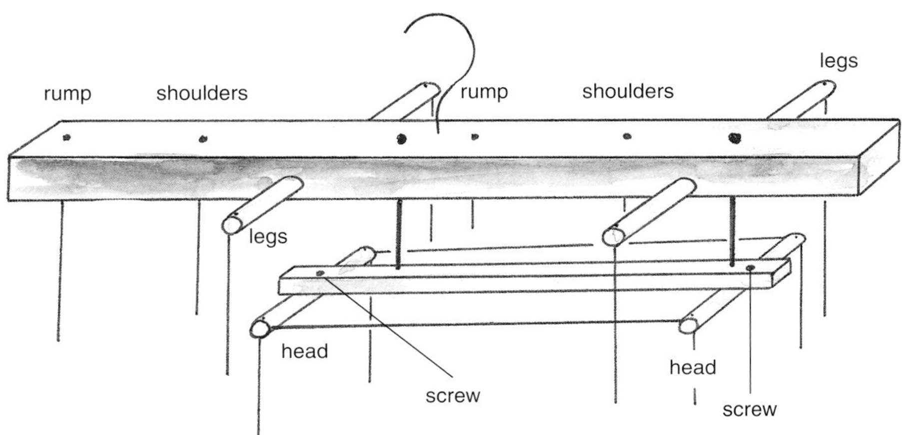

RIGHT: A variation on the animal tandem control to allow for nodding heads.

LEFT: A tandem control for human figures. The control may be detachable – see pantomime horse and reversible puppet.

OPPOSITE AND THIS PAGE: *Paul Doran operating a pair of acrobats with a tandem control. Additional run-through strings, from the feet of the puppet at the rear through loops on the shoulders of the front puppet, facilitate various acrobatic manoeuvres.*

A Puppet Puppeteer

The two puppets are made by any of the methods described earlier. Attach the head and shoulder strings of the large puppet to the upright control as usual and use a rocking bar for the leg control. This control has only one hand wire. The string attached to it is used to raise and lower the small control, held in the puppet's left hand.

In one end of the head bar fix a small hook and from it hang another dowel rod. This rod controls the small puppet's hand/leg bar that is held in the large puppet's right hand. Join the same-side hands and knees of the small puppet by a short cord, so that when a hand is raised the corresponding leg is raised too.

An interesting version of this act uses a puppet looking like the puppeteer to manipulate a scaled-down version of one of the main puppet characters. Of course, the point is apparent to the audience only if the puppeteer is performing open-stage and is therefore visible.

LEFT: A puppet puppeteer by Gordon Staight. Exceptionally, the main figure is modelled in a naturalistic manner as it is a likeness of Gordon Staight operating a miniature version of Mr Herbert, his puppet compere. A velcro patch on his jumper is used to attach a back-cloth when required.

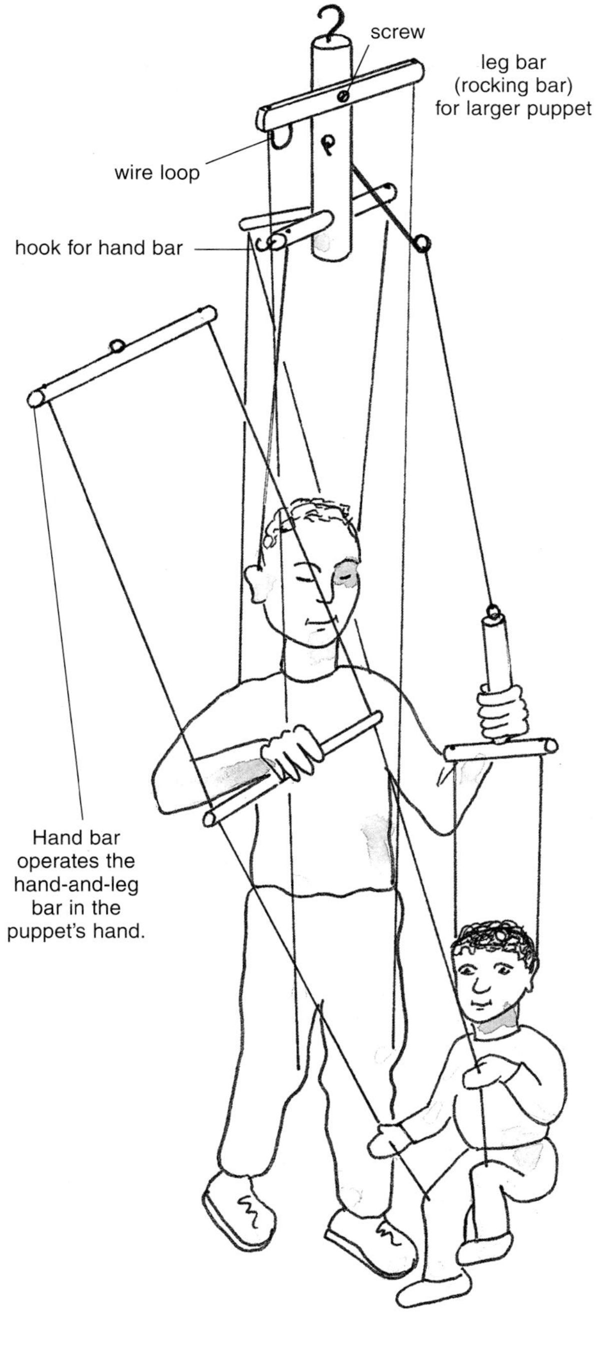

The control and stringing for a puppet puppeteer.

8 Specialized Designs

For many traditional marionette acts, specialized designs are just as important as the stringing arrangements but, as with stringing, the best results will be achieved if you keep the mechanisms and structure as simple as possible and allow for access to such mechanisms for adjustments or repairs.

Consider also whether an action by the puppet should be repeated. Sometimes repetition is unavoidable because it is in the nature of the act, but a clever piece of action that amuses or surprises the audience is often more effective if it is only performed once, just like a magician's trick. Although this means that 'trick' puppets will have comparatively brief acts, it does help to keep up the pace of the performance. Never draw out an act just to fill a certain period of time; if you have music, tailor the music to the act not the act to the music.

Willie the clown, by the author, becomes cross-eyed as he blows up a balloon.

Blowing, Bellows and Smoke

Some acts require the puppet to blow bubbles, to appear to blow up a balloon, or perform some equivalent action such as the elephant that squirts water over the audience. All are dependent upon rubber tubing that leads either to a mouthpiece through which the puppeteer blows, or to some form of pump or bellows that may be either a rubber bulb of the type used when measuring blood pressure or a specially constructed pump.

The bubble blower has a rubber tube running from its mouth, through the head, to a plastic mouthpiece (such as for a smoker's pipe) attached to the control.

The clown has a specially made holder for the balloon that fits inside its hand. The hand is made of latex rubber so that it can be manipulated over the nozzle when the balloon is attached. The balloon holder contains a small metal pipe to which is attached the rubber tubing that runs up the arm, down the body inside the costume, then trails along the floor to a foot pump behind the backcloth. In this case, as the puppet blows up the balloon it grows taller and becomes cross-eyed.

Make the foot pump from latex rubber (*see* pages 30–4). It is wedge-shaped with a small hole in the deeper edge and a larger hole in the top. Into the smaller hole insert a piece of metal tubing for attaching the rubber tube; it should be a tight fit and may be further secured with adhesive. Into the larger hole glue a non-return valve. To make the valve, drill a substantial hole down through the centre of a short piece of dowelling and cover the base of the dowelling with a circular piece of thin and fairly flexible rubber. Partially glue this rubber flap to the dowel but leave between half and two-thirds of the circumference unattached. When the pump is depressed, the pressure of air inside closes the flap and prevents air escaping so that it is forced down the rubber tubing to the puppet. When the foot is removed, the flap allows air to enter the pump through the hole in the dowel. The narrow gauge of the rubber

Bubbles by Paul Doran, Shadowstring Theatre. A rubber tube to a mouthpiece attached to the control enables this puppet to blow bubbles through a pipe. It also creates bubbles with the ringed end of the wand held in its left hand.

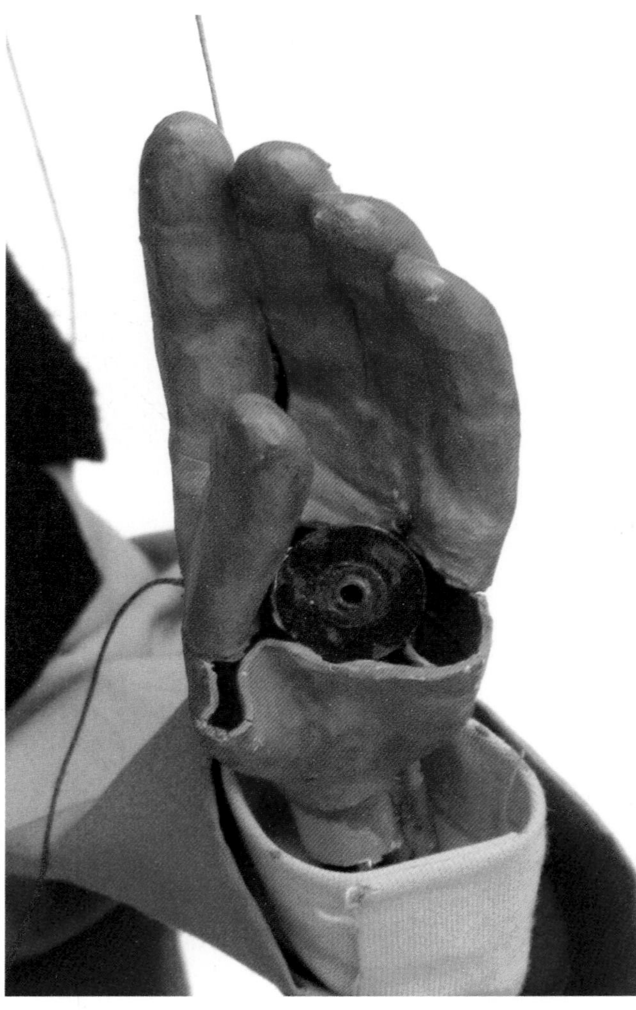

The balloon is attached to a metal holder to which is fixed a length of rubber tubing. The tubing is threaded through the arm and body and along the stage to a foot pump.

tubing and metal pipe helps to prevent the air drifting back into the pump from the balloon. There might be slight seepage but this will be countered by further pumping or by keeping the pump depressed when the desired size of balloon has been achieved.

The cowboy described in the previous chapter (*see* pages 124–6) has a gun that smokes when it is fired. In the distant past, the smoke would have been produced by the puppeteer smoking and blowing the smoke down a tube to the gun. Nowadays, the smoke is generally replaced by talcum powder held in a small bellows inside the body or in a rubber bulb attached to the control. A fine rubber tube runs through the arm and hand into the gun and along the barrel. The bellows is operated by a string attached to a lever on the control, while the bulb is simply squeezed by the puppeteer.

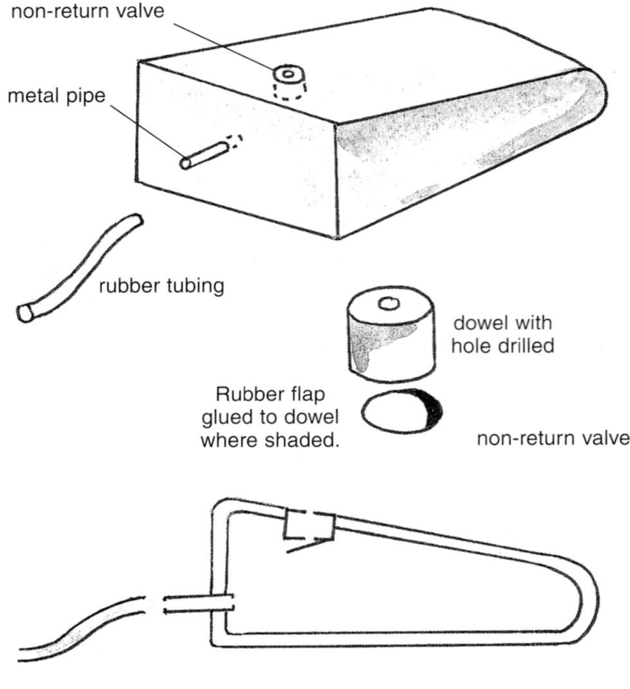

A purpose-built foot pump moulded in latex rubber and with an improvised non-return valve.

A Collapsible or Extending Puppet

The body consists of three pieces of plywood or hardboard joined at the front, rear and sides by strong thread, such as that used for stringing the puppet. Shape the top of the shoulders with balsa-wood or foam rubber glued on to the top section. Make the legs from a series of wooden discs cut from plywood or a large dowel rod. Join them in the same way as the body.

Drill small, aligned holes on each side of the legs and body pieces. The strings that raise and lower the legs and body pass through these holes. The strings run freely through the whole puppet, being attached only to the feet and to the control.

The stringing arrangements for an extending or a collapsible puppet are illustrated [below right]. For an extending puppet, the legs and body are contracted when normal; to lower them, tilt the control forwards. For a collapsible puppet, when the control is held upright, the legs and body are at their maximum length; to raise them, tilt the control upwards, raising the bottom section and therefore the strings that run through to the feet.

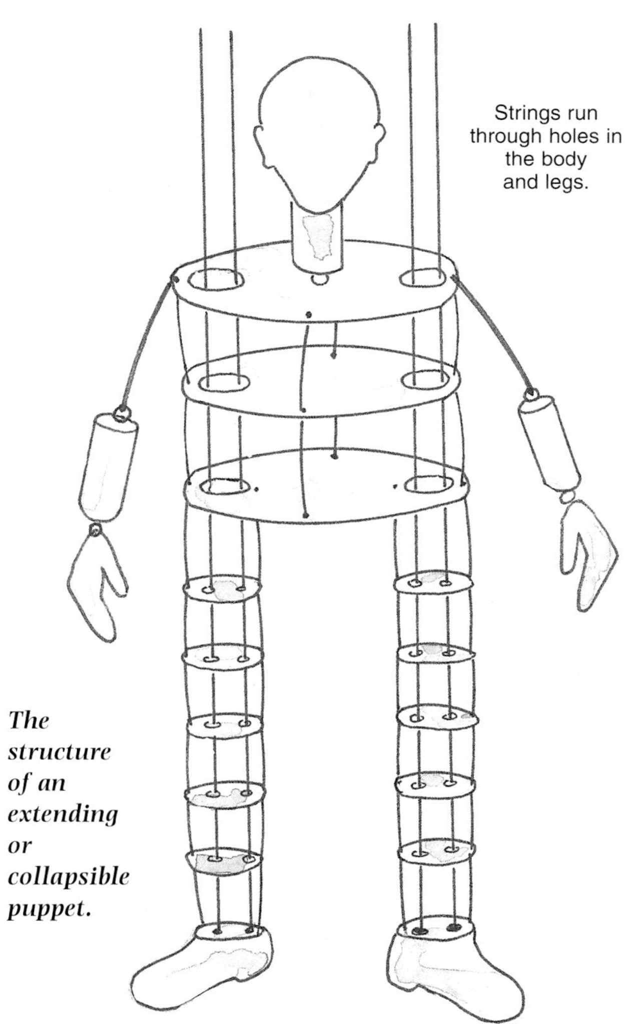

The structure of an extending or collapsible puppet.

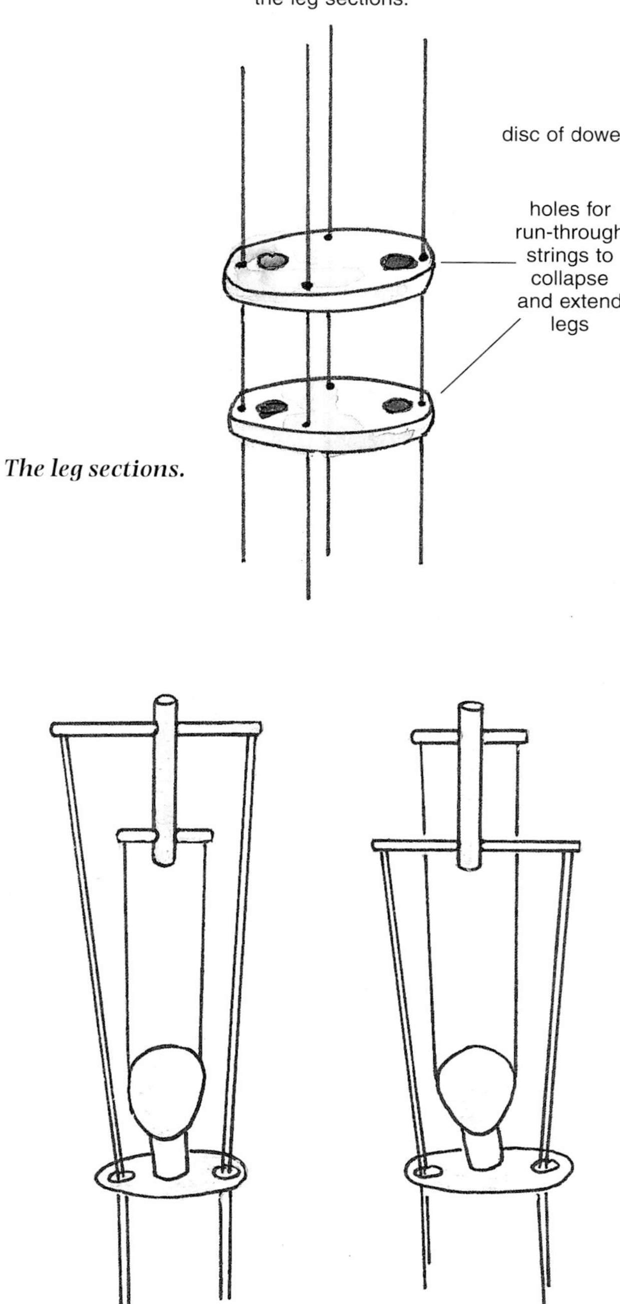

The leg sections.

The control for an extending puppet.

The control for a collapsible puppet.

Willie the clown is also an extending puppet.

SCARAMOUCHE

There are several versions of this traditional puppet. One has a number of heads hidden in a hollow body that emerge one above the other. Another has hollow heads that fit inside each other.

The act itself is very simple but can be most effective when performed with careful timing. With the former version, the neck starts to grow, the head weaves from side to side, forwards and backwards in a humorous fashion, and then the second head appears. And so it continues with another head, then another until the puppet is fully extended. The version with the hollow heads can proceed in a similar fashion but also enables you to replace a head inside the body and to raise instead a larger head in which it sits. A good deal of business can proceed around re-inserting and revealing the nested heads.

Two versions of the traditional Scaramouch. One has heads inside the body while the other has heads nested inside each other.

A Tumbler Puppet

This is a traditional transformation but the principle can be applied to a variety of purposes. The puppet has two heads and two bodies joined together at the waist. Each body has arms and hands but no legs. The lower body is hidden by a voluminous skirt, which may need to be weighted around the hem. Make the skirt from a reversible material that looks attractive when turned inside out or use two pieces of material joined at waist and hem.

Raising the strings attached to the lower head whilst releasing the tension of the upper head strings will make the puppet 'tumble', or turn over, and reveal the hidden puppet. The skirt drops to cover the other puppet.

The two heads must face in opposite directions, so that when it tumbles, the hidden puppet will rise facing the same way as the other.

A traditional tumbler puppet.

A Reversible, Two-Headed Puppet

Two-headed, reversible puppets are sometimes required and there are three basic versions.

The first, which is more of a comic figure, has a single body with two fronts and a single set of limbs but a two-faced head. The limbs normally have sideways movement so the figure tends to be used for song and dance purposes. An upright control with just a head bar and a rocking bar attached to the limbs would be adequate for this puppet. The strings to the hands are secured and then continue down to the legs so that the same-side hand and leg move together. Sometimes a single wire is used to the head instead of two strings so that the puppet can be spun around.

The act sometimes has a pair of such puppets, identically dressed with costumes of contrasting colours (especially black and white) on each side of the puppet. At one moment they are both showing black costumes, then they both show white, then one shows black and the other shows white, all of which is based around a simple dance routine.

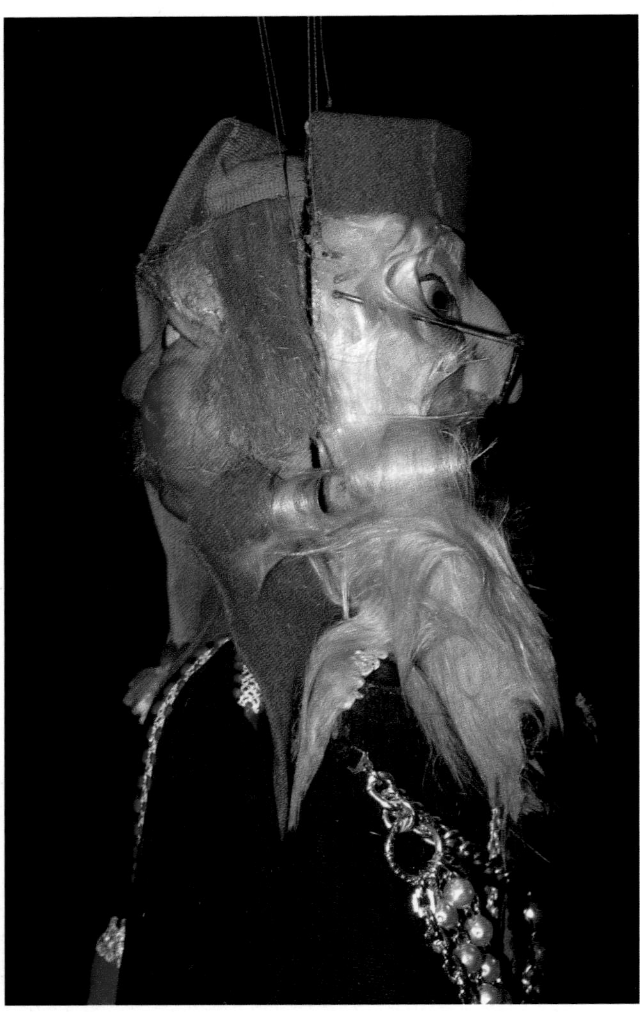

ABOVE AND OPPOSITE: **A reversible, split-headed puppet by the author.** ***The wizard and his apprentice are back to back and cannot find each other.***

A second, more versatile, version is made with two faces and a body with two fronts and two sets of limbs. Such a figure needs to be kept fairly square to the audience if the figure on the reverse is not to show before you intend it to. It could be used, for example, for a transformation or for two aspects of a character's personality. A reversible horizontal control with limb controls at each end is used here. The hand strings are the run-through type and the leg bars are suspended from each end of the control by cord. If they were fixed to the control in the usual way, both puppets' legs would be walked when either one were manipulated.

After a good deal of amusing business, they are separated and can appear side by side.

The third version is like the previous one but the head and body are split down the centre, dividing the two figures completely, so that they have half heads and bodies but whole limbs. Once split apart, they can appear together on stage. They are held together by a simple mechanism. A small strip of metal, bent into an L-shape and with a hole in it, is fixed in the back of one head, the strip with the hole protruding. The other figure has a corresponding slot in the back of the head, inside which is secured a slotted block of wood. A galvanized wire pin runs down through this head and through a hole drilled in the wooden block. The metal plate fits into the slot and is secured by the pin through the hole in the plate. The top of the galvanized wire is looped for attaching the release-string and a small notch is soldered on to prevent it coming too far out of the head.

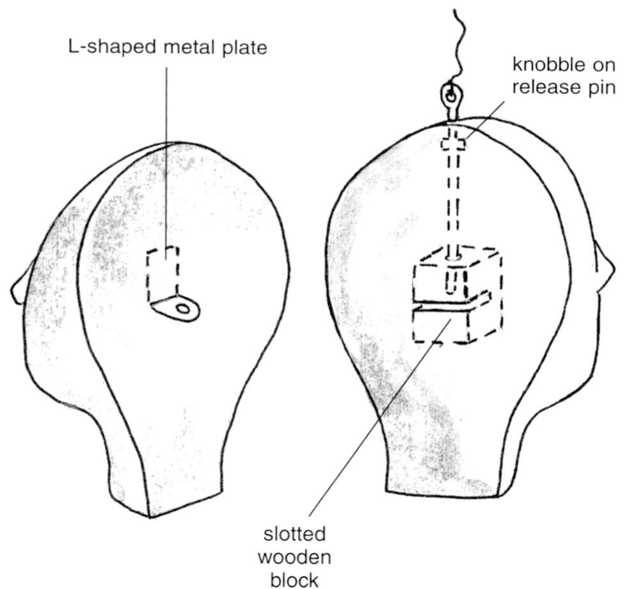

The securing and release mechanism for a split-headed puppet.

The control consists of two separate horizontal controls attached back to back: two screws in the top of one fit into keyhole slots in the other. Ensure that the slots fit cleanly and fairly tightly on the screws so that they do not separate unintentionally. The string for the release pin is attached to the control of the puppet with the pin in its head.

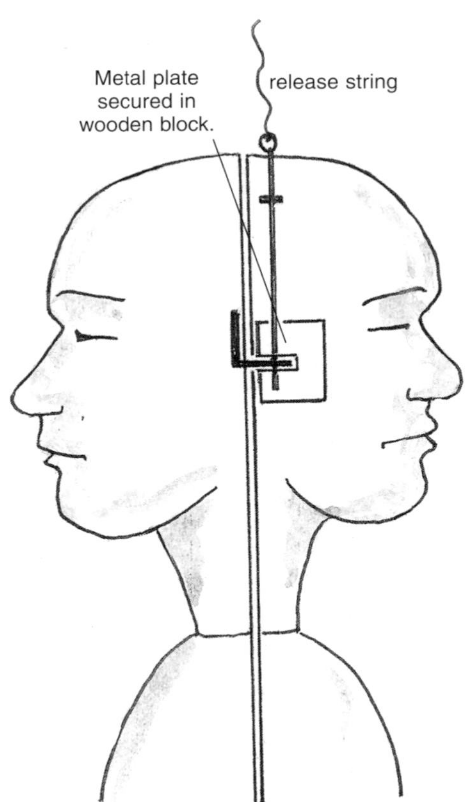

The two heads locked together.

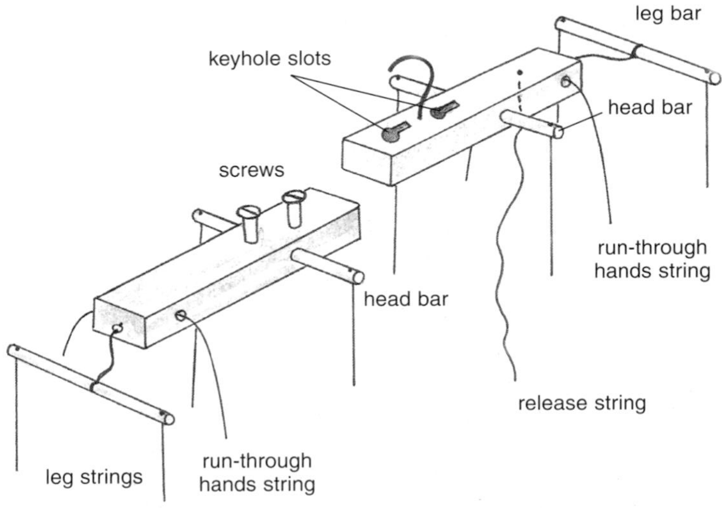

The controls are joined by screws in keyhole slots.

A Chinese Bell Dancer

This is a traditional act for which the puppet may be constructed in the usual way. The illustration on page 161 demonstrates the original method and shows the angle at which the arms and legs are joined to the body to produce the characteristic 'dancing' movements as the bells are rung. The legs are attached to a rocking bar on the control to leave the puppeteer's hand free to operate a hand bar to which strings from the bells are attached.

Alternatively, the leg strings can be attached to the puppet's wrists so that the legs and arms move together. While this may appear quite comical, it does limit the puppet's movements more than one might wish. With practice it is possible to produce a recognizable tune with the bells.

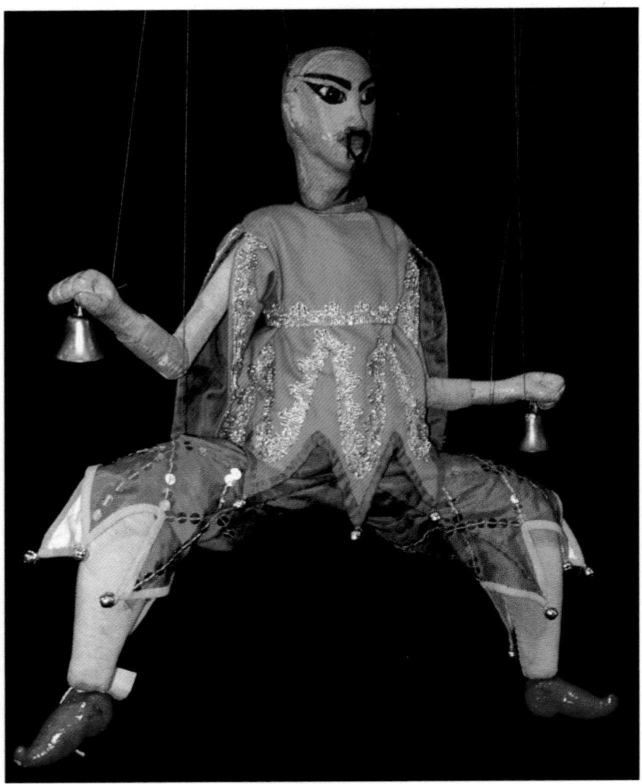

A Chinese bell-dancer, a traditional, fantoccini-*style figure from the turn of the last century, performed by Dédé in the 1920s in the Gardens of the Palais de Justice, Marseilles. Now in the Hogarth Collection of the Puppet Centre collection.*

Laying an Egg

Another old favourite is a bird that lays an egg; sometimes the egg also opens to reveal a smaller bird inside. Part of the bird's body is hollow to accommodate the egg, which has a small loop of string or fine wire that is secured in the body by a release pin.

Make the pin from galvanized wire and loop one end to attach the release string. Thread the string up through a small hole in the body and attach the end to the control at a point where it can easily be found in low light.

An alternative method used by Gordon Staight for the ostrich secures the egg in the body by a shallow, curved 'cup' the shape of the end of the egg. The cup is sprung to hold it firmly against the egg. A release string runs through the body and is attached to the cup; pulling the string retracts the cup and allows the egg to drop.

Flaps made of fabric-covered latex rubber cover the hole in the base of the body, which hold in shape but flex open under the weight of the egg, from which a newly hatched ostrich emerges. The egg is in two sections with overlapping edges; they press together securely but come apart when bounced on the floor by the string to reveal the puppet inside.

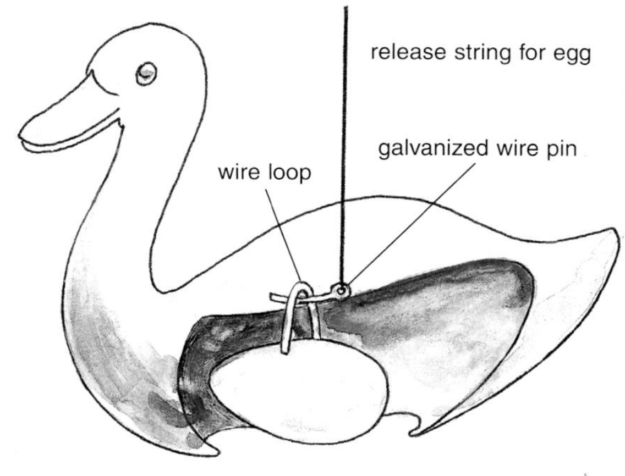

An egg secured with a galvanized wire pin through a loop of strong thread or fine wire.

The structure of a bell-dancer.

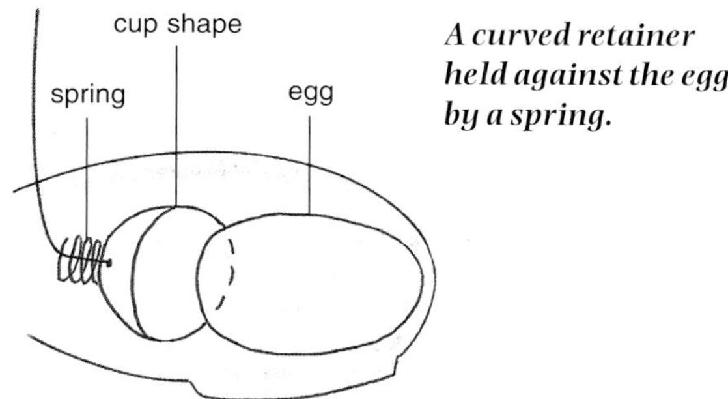

A curved retainer held against the egg by a spring.

A Tightrope Walker

This puppet has only one special feature, a slot cut along each foot to fit over the tightrope. Do ensure that the legs, particularly the hip joints, have sufficient flexibility to allow the legs to cross over one another. Occasionally the feet might slide a little along the rope but this is acceptable: humans do this too. Sometimes the puppet just seems to find the rope and slot on to it; sometimes it takes a little longer to get it right but you can make this part of the act with the puppet shaking, appearing to tumble, regaining its balance, losing confidence half-way along, perhaps having exchanges with the audience – 'Is it further to go on or further to go back?' he asks. 'Come on, you can do it!' the audience shout, and so on.

A tightrope walker by Paul Doran, Shadowstring Theatre. The marionette has a removable mask that reveals a different expression; the mask is held in place by run-through strings.

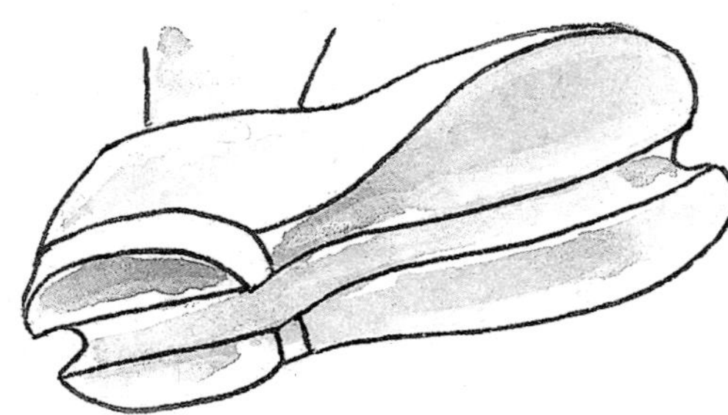

The tightrope walker's feet are grooved to grip the rope.

To make a simple tightrope, screw two pieces of wood at right angles to the bottom of two uprights, such as dowelling, to make bases. Cut a slot in the top of each upright to accommodate the tightrope.

Either attach the bases to a long board that is wide enough to prevent the prop from toppling over or fasten metal angle brackets to the bases and fit them into slots in the stage. To help to hold the brackets securely, screw blocks of wood under the stage on each side of the slots.

Fasten the tightrope between the upright posts. Secure the ends to screw-eyes in the bases. To maintain the tension of the cord, attach a strong rubber band between one end of the cord and the screw-eye.

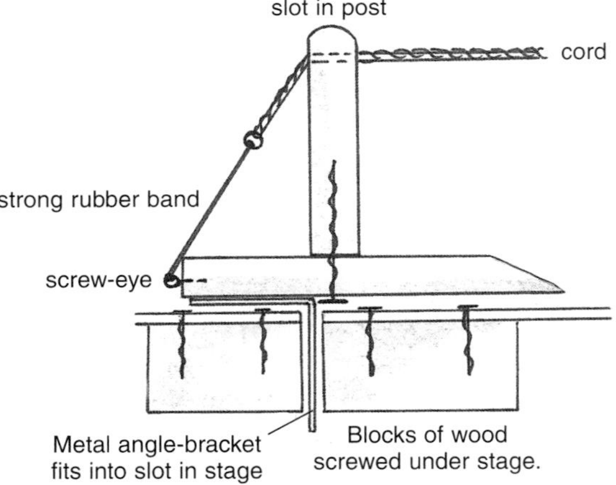

A simple structure for supporting a tightrope.

If you wish to make a more complex tightrope structure, you should first consider how you will dismantle it for packing, transport it and set it up in a short space of time.

A Pantomime Horse

This comic, pantomime horse attempts all manner of feats before coming apart on stage, revealing the two characters inside. One version of the act starts with a finely made horse performing, followed by the pantomime horse mimicking its act with hilarious results.

The pantomime horse consists of two puppets with separate, horizontal controls joined together using screws and keyhole slots. Both characters inside the horse are made as figures bending from the waist, the one at the rear bending rather more than the one at the front. The head, shoulders and hands of each character are made protruding through the front of their costumes.

The front character is hidden by the false horse's head and neck, which is secured by a small, galvanized wire pin through a wire loop on the horse's shoulders. The seat of its trousers is visible through the front half of the horse's body when the puppet comes apart.

The head of the character at the rear fits inside the front half of the horse and is secured in place by a galvanized wire pin through a small wire loop in the top of its head and another in the rear of the front section. The body covering of the rear section fits just inside that of the front section so it should be of slightly smaller diameter. The joint between the two bodies is covered by a horse blanket.

A pantomime horse.

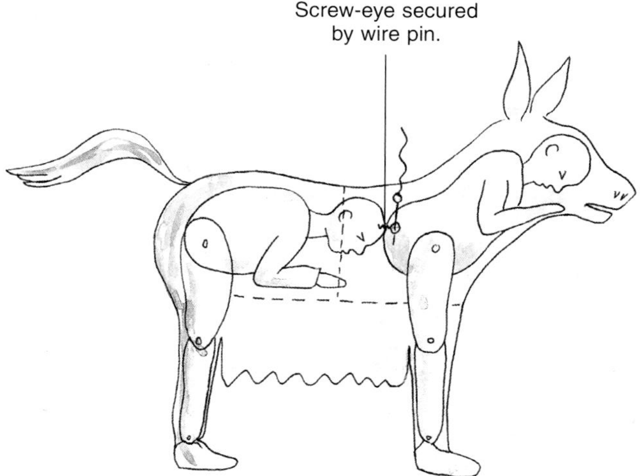

The internal structure of the pantomime horse.

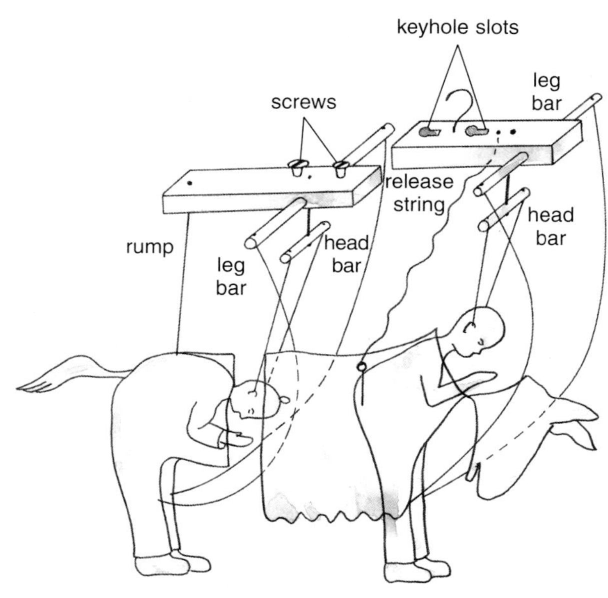

The control of the pantomime horse and the characters revealed.

The controls each have suspended dowel rods for the head and shoulder/rump strings and fixed dowel rods for the leg bars so that rocking the controls produces the walking action. If the leg strings are fixed to the same side of each control, when the controls are joined and walked together, the same-side legs will be raised with a comic, rolling gait rather than the normal opposing front and rear legs.

The wire pins that hold the pantomime horse together are looped at the top for securing release strings that are attached to each control between the head and shoulder/rump strings. When the other comic business is complete and the revelation is due, one of the release strings is pulled, dropping the horse's head. Then the second release string is pulled and the controls are separated, completing the revelation, and the two characters chase one another off the stage.

A Trick Rocking Horse

This is an example of the use of a standard puppet with a trick figure that some might consider a puppet but others would regard as a prop. The clown is a standard marionette but the rocking horse is double headed. It appears to be a normal rocking horse but, when the clown has gone through the business of working out how to mount it and which way to face, and started rocking, the head drops to form a tail and the tail at the other end rises to form the head. Confusion ensues and when the clown manages to reposition itself the correct way round, the heads and tails switch again.

Before proceeding to make the horse, it is a good idea to work out in cardboard the head and body shapes and the positions of the pivots, slots and nails.

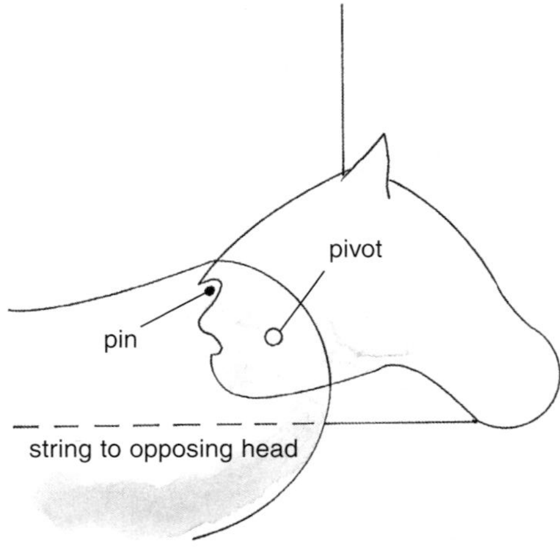

The head mechanism of the two-headed rocking horse.

The horse's body is made of two plywood shapes with blocks between to separate them. The heads are cut from plywood and pivoted between the body shapes on a nail. The head shapes and the position of the pivot are arranged so that the head drops down into the space in the body leaving only the mane visible to form a tail.

In order to hold the raised head in place, the base of the head is slotted and the slot clicks over a second, carefully positioned nail. Another groove is cut slightly below the slot so that the head does not snag on the nail when it drops down. Each head is attached in this way and a small screw-eye is inserted under each jaw. A fine thread that runs through the centre of the body joins the screw-eyes; the thread should be taut when one head is fully down and the other is fully raised.

Two strings, one to the top of each head, control the horse. They are attached to opposite ends of a horizontal dowel rod. When a head is to be raised from the tail position, the head string is pulled up. As the head rises, it pulls the thread attached to the opposing horse's jaw. This releases the other head from the raised position by uncoupling the slot from the retaining nail and the head drops to form a tail.

A Contortionist

This marionette, another traditional figure, is both a contortionist and a hand-balancer. The figure is constructed with a body in three sections that were traditionally joined by strips of leather or webbing to provide greater flexibility. All major joints are restricted to prevent too much sideways movement. The feet and hands might need to be weighted with lead, depending on the construction materials used. Ensure that the costume is sufficiently soft and loose to facilitate the intended movements.

Usually, the puppet has strings to the head, back, and soles or insteps of the feet. Some versions have strings to the hands while others have them to the arms instead. Knee strings enable the puppet to walk on to the stage but are not used thereafter so some performers dispense with these and the puppet enters with a series of leaps.

The control has a main vertical dowel rod with

***OPPOSITE:* Spotty the clown and Rocky by Gordon Staight. The rocking horse is part-puppet and part-prop with two heads which ensure that, whatever the clown does, he is always facing the wrong way.**

crossbars near the top and bottom. The top crossbar is fixed while the lower one, which is wider, hooks on to the rear of the control.

The head strings are attached to the top crossbar. If control of the knees is required, they have a single string, one end attached to each knee, which runs through screw-eyes inserted in the top crossbar. Moving the string from side to side effects the knee movements.

The strings to the feet are attached to the lower crossbar (the foot bar); the back string, on the lowest section of the body, is tied to a screw-eye in the base of the control. An additional string to the chest may be attached to the front of the central body section to enable the puppet to bend backwards too. Attach it to any convenient point on the control: a short horizontal dowel glued into a hole drilled in the control is a useful method. Ensure that the string is sufficiently slack to permit all the required movements.

Cut a slot in the control to accommodate a single hand wire that is looped at each end. Insert one loop in the slot and pivot it on a nail through the dowelling. The loop at the other end carries a run-through string, the ends of which are attached to the backs of the hands or the forearms.

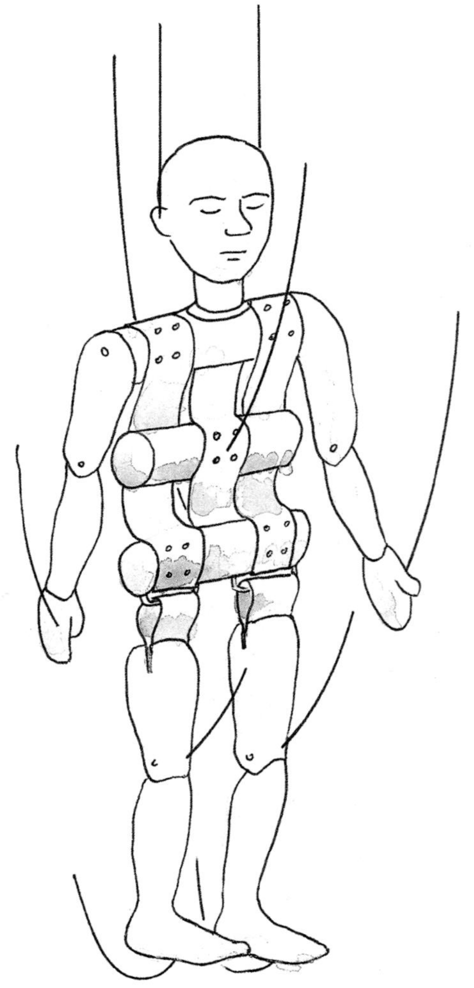

The structure of the puppet.

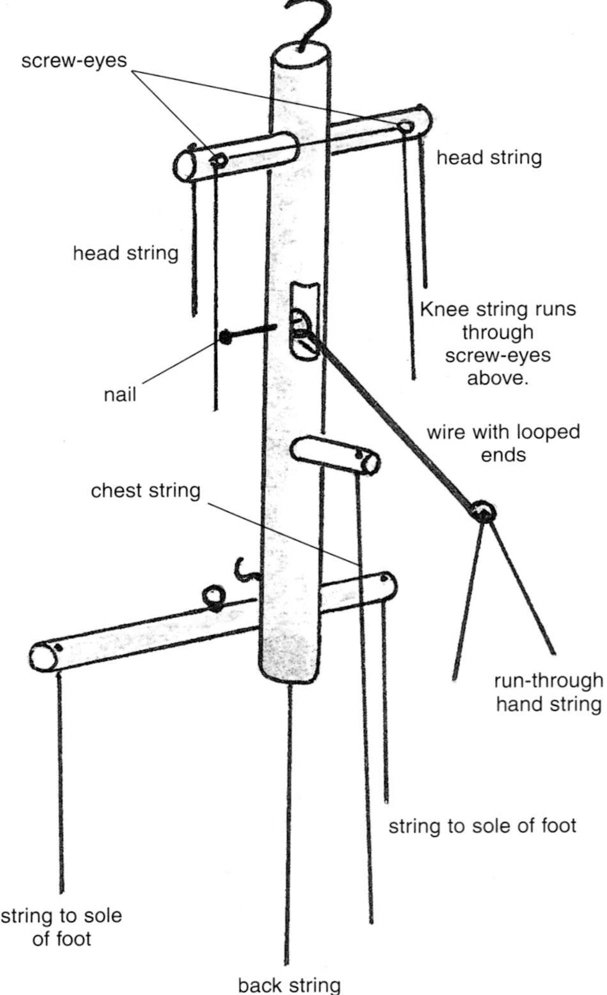

The control.

Tilt the control forwards to bow the puppet. Tilt it further and move the hand wire forwards with your index finger to place its hands on the floor. Unhook and raise the leg bar to its full extent for a handstand. Manipulate the hand string for the puppet to walk on its hands. Bring the foot bar over the top of the control and lower it in front of the control for the puppet to lower its feet on either side of its head. Depending on its dimensions and flexibility, the puppet should be able to reach the ground with its feet and move around the stage in this position.

A sequence of these main elements can be interspersed with such movements as raising and lowering the control to achieve press-ups with the legs in the air, kicking the legs and bouncing on the hands, swinging the feet alternately over the head, raising and lowering the knees while handstanding, and single-hand balancing.

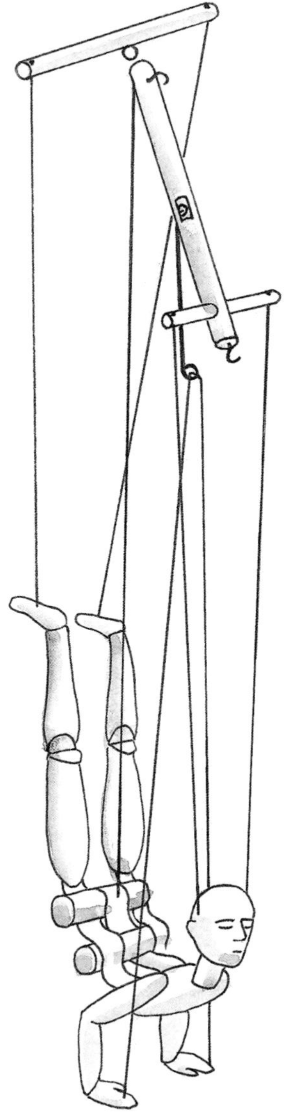

Hand-balancing.

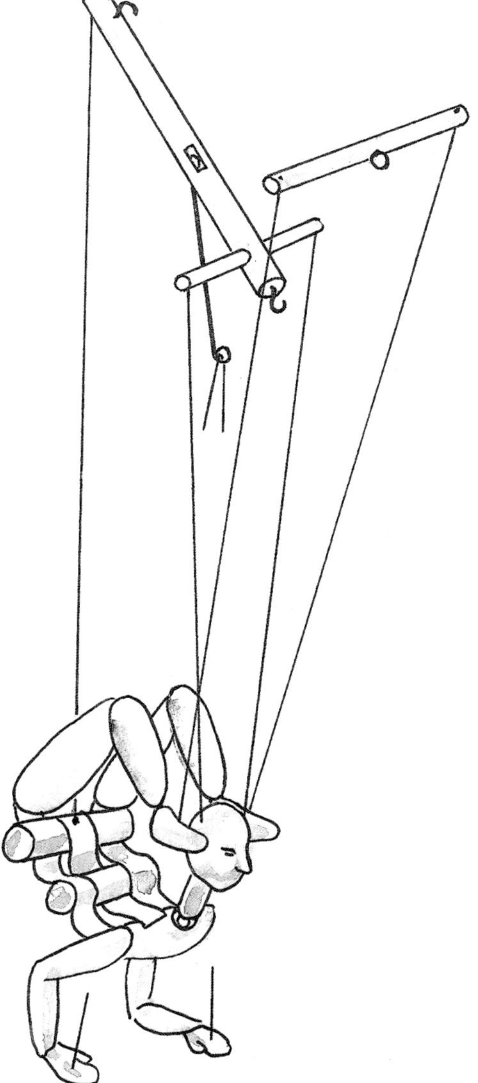

Lowering the legs in front of the hands.

The Grand Turk

Often used as the grand finale of a puppet variety show, this is a single puppet that transforms into six different characters. However, the means by which this is achieved is comparatively simple, despite the length of the description that follows.

The characters may vary of course; it need not be the Turk but the very full, baggy costume and turban is ideal for containing the six puppets. This particular Turk transforms into the four wives, which emerge from his limbs; a mother-in-law, which is inside the body; and a Grand Wizard hidden in the turban.

The puppet consists of three full-sized heads, four somewhat smaller heads for the wives, a wooden shoulder block and the Turk's own hands and feet, made by any of the standard methods.

I cast all the parts in latex rubber, creating the heads with necks attached. Three different casts were used for the three larger heads but only one for the wives. The casts used for the large heads were used also for other puppets; significant variations in painting and finishing altered their appearance and the resemblance has never been noticed.

Two of the wives' heads are attached a little above the wrists of the Turk's hands and two just above the ankles. There needs to be some flexibility at the ankles so that the feet dip and allow the costume to hang down when the wives are revealed.

The head of the mother-in-law is attached securely to the underside of the shoulder block: a dowel is secured in the head and neck, and a screw-eye in the base of the dowel is attached to the shoulder block with strong cord.

The head of the wizard is attached directly above the Turk's head. A single dowel rod the same diameter as the neck runs from the base of the Turk's neck, out through the top of the head and then up through the wizard's neck to the top of his head.

The Turk's head is attached to the shoulder block in one of three ways. The first is the most secure and is the method used for my own Grand Turk. The other methods require little or no metalworking.

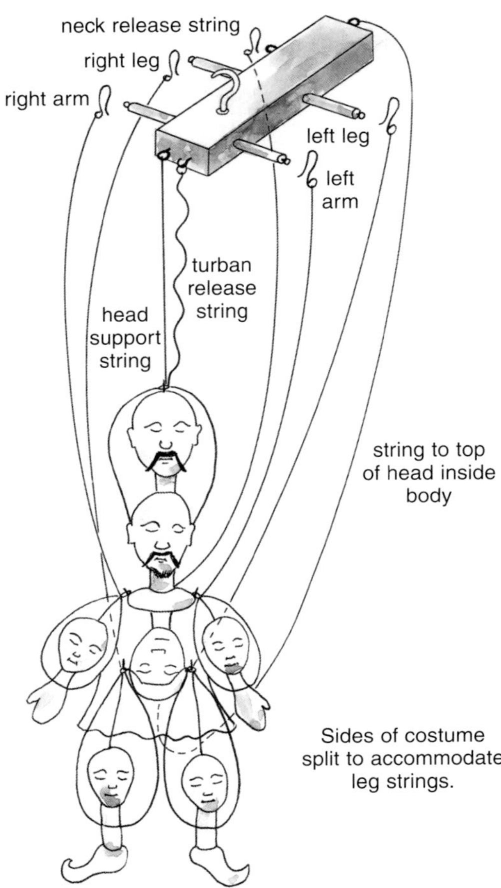

The Turk with six concealed puppets.

- A specially constructed mechanism is used. It consists of a strip of metal, bent to form a square-cornered, inverted 'U' shape with two flanges with holes drilled to screw it to the shoulder block. A second strip of metal, soldered half-way up the inverted 'U', acts as a guide to keep the release pin appropriately aligned. A hole is drilled through the centre of both horizontal plates to carry this pin, which has a looped top for attaching the string, and a knobble on the shaft to prevent it coming out of the mechanism.

  A keyhole-shaped metal plate with two holes drilled in it is screwed to the base of the neck with the rectangular part facing rearwards to fit into the mechanism. The pin is depressed to engage the hole in the plate and lock the head to the shoulder block. A slight pull on the release string raises the pin and separates the head from the body.

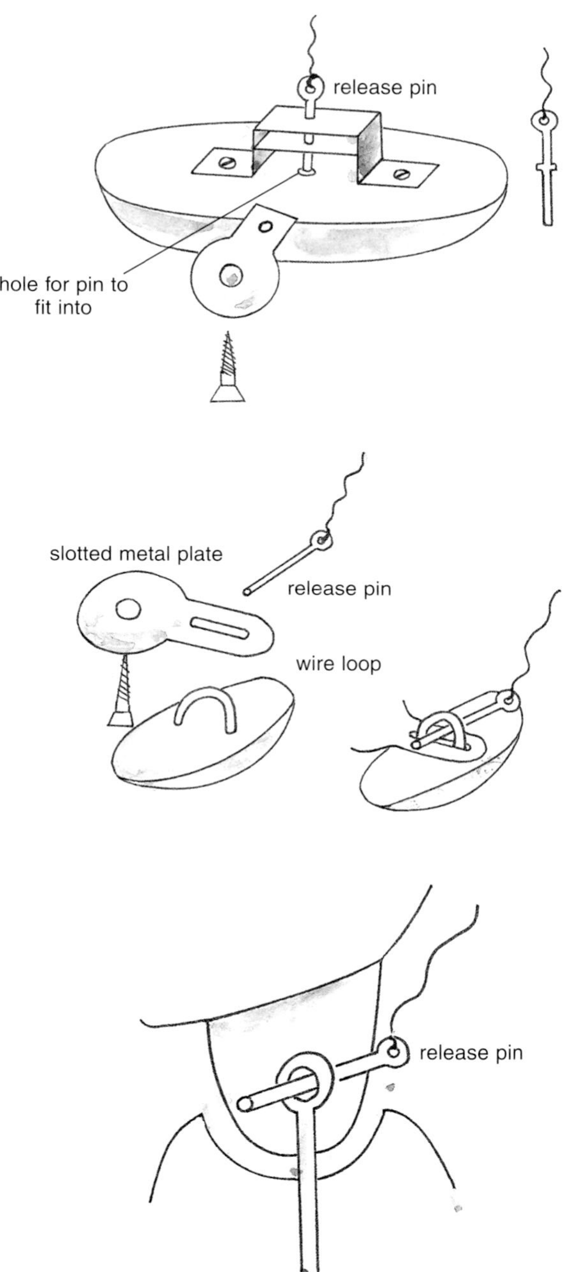

Three types of release mechanism for the head.
Top: ***A keyhole-shaped plate held in a purpose-built mechanism.***
Middle: ***A keyhole-shaped plate secured by a release pin.***
Bottom: ***A strong, looped wire secured by a release pin.***

- A keyhole-shaped piece of metal is screwed to the base of the neck. The rectangular part, which extends rearwards, is slotted. A wire loop fixed in the shoulder block protrudes through the slot and a piece of galvanized wire is inserted to lock the head to the shoulders. One end of this wire pin is looped to attach a string; pulling this string allows the head and body to be separated but take care not to pull it by mistake and release it too soon.

- Strong galvanized wire is secured in the shoulder block with a looped end protruding. The loop fits into a hole in the base of the neck and is secured by a release pin inserted through a hole in the back of the neck.

A small 'spike' of galvanized wire is glued into a hole drilled in each end of the shoulder block for attaching the arms and another piece of galvanized wire is inserted across the mother-in-law's head with the ends bent over to create spikes behind her ears. These spikes should point downwards on her head, upwards when the head is inverted inside the Turk's body. A further galvanized wire spike is glued into a hole drilled through the top of the wizard's head, down into the dowelling inside it. You need to leave enough of the spike protruding to hold the turban; at this stage, leave it long and cut it to the required length later.

The wizard, the mother-in-law and the wives each have a single supporting string from the top of the head to the control. Attach the string to the head with a small screw-eye that can be covered by hair. This may make them liable to spin around once they have been revealed but the costumes touching the floor help to control this.

These characters have no bodies but full gowns that are gathered at the neck and hang freely. You can add arms and hands to each figure but they should not be bulky and could be made of fabric. Just inside the hems of the gowns are sewn a series of small loops or curtain rings. These are gathered up so that the gown encloses the head. The rings are slipped over the spikes on the shoulder block and on the mother-in-law's head, as appropriate. This has now created the Turk's arms and legs.

The mother-in-law has a string from the top of her head to the control. Her gown is attached to the shoulder block and hangs over the tops of the legs when she is inverted. Ensure that both sides of the shoulder block are covered so that the costume, not the wooden block, is visible both before and after the transformation. If her costume is reversible, it will serve as the costume for the Turk as well. Alternatively, two different fabrics may be used, preferably joined at the hem.

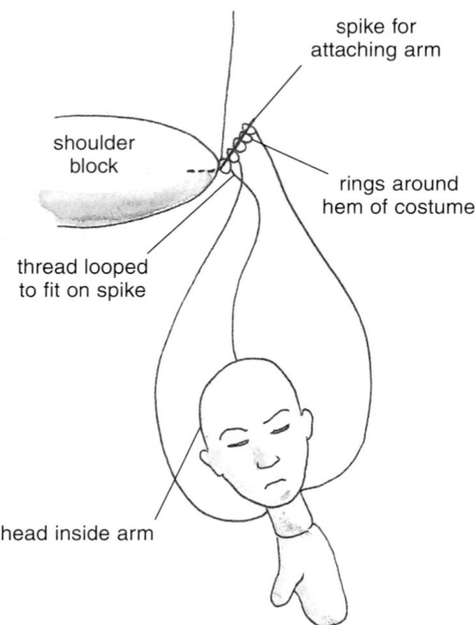

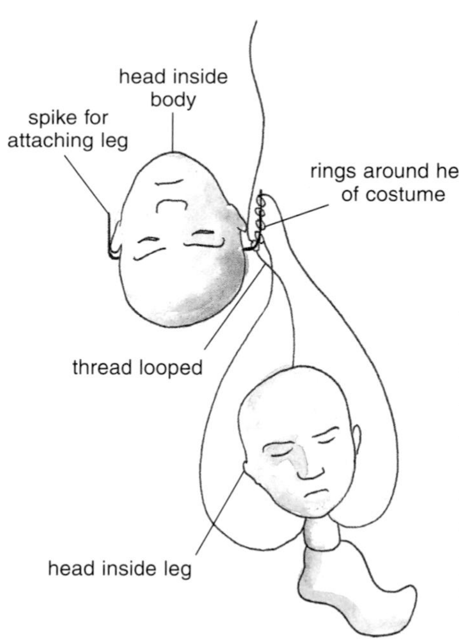

Attaching the arms and legs to the body: if used, the looped head string must go over the spike before the rings around the hem of the costume.

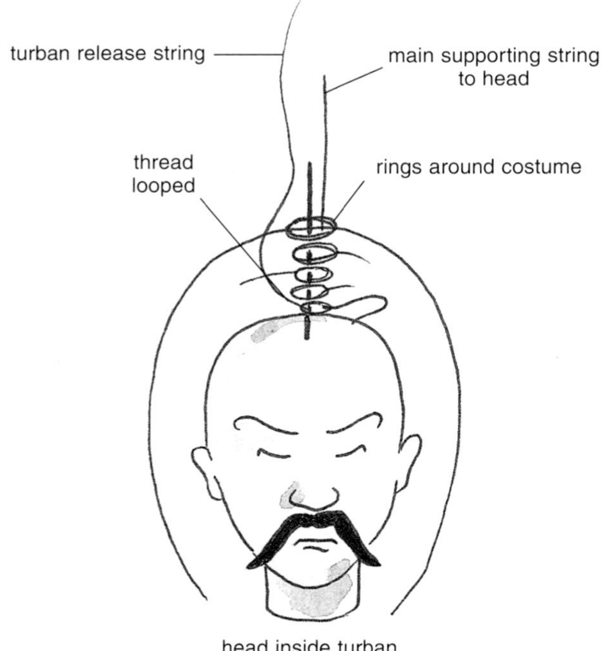

Securing the turban: first, the turban release string goes around the spike, followed by the rings inside the wizard's costume.

The turban fabric is glued to the Turk's head and must be long enough to form a robe for the wizard when they transform. Small rings are sewn inside the gown at a suitable point and the fabric is gathered up, covering the wizard's head. A good deal of fabric will need to be turned in when the rings are placed over the spike on top of the head.

The wizard has two strings attached to the top of his head – the supporting string and another to release the turban for the final reveal. The release string is knotted to form a small loop a short distance above the head. This loop is slipped over the spike before the rings so that, when it is pulled, it will lift the rings off the spike and allow the costume to drop down. Once released, this string hangs to the back of the wizard's head so that the loop is hidden.

Two Variations

Some puppeteers knot the head string of each wife to form a small loop like that described for the wizard. This loop is slipped over the spike before the rings to take the weight of the figure rather than having the weight taken by the rings on the costume. The position of the loop on the string should allow for the length of the arms and legs. The idea of this is to help keep the fullness in the baggy pants and sleeves, but the loop may not come off as cleanly as the rings and, once the figure is revealed, it can draw undue attention to itself, appearing like a little fly above each head.

The second variation is to attach the legs to the Turk's costume rather than to the mother-in-law's head. A ring of galvanized wire is inserted into the hem of the costume with two spikes protruding upwards to accommodate the leg rings. Although a loose flap made from additional costume material can hide the attachment, it spreads the legs quite far apart and the wire loop can interfere with the smooth dropping of the costume when the mother-in-law is revealed.

The Control

The puppet has a simple horizontal control that consists of a main bar with two dowel rods glued into holes drilled across it. Small screw-eyes are fixed to the ends of the dowels for attaching the arm and leg strings (the wives). Three more small screw-eyes are attached directly to the main bar, one at the back bar for the mother-in-law's support string, one on the side for the body/mother-in-law's release string, and one on the front for the turban release string.

A hook is screwed into the front of the main bar to hold a ring on the end of the wizard's support string, which supports the entire puppet. All strings other than this one are slack and are tied on to small galvanized wire hooks for attaching to the screw-eyes. This allows them to be unhooked and the character danced around the stage as it is revealed, then hooked back on the control ready for the next transformation. The string to the mother-in-law should be sufficiently long to allow the Turk's costume to hang unhindered.

The Grand Turk is now ready for action. Clearly he will be able only to shuffle along but gentle swaying of the control with a little rhythm in the action can make it more convincing. After some little business the transformation takes place. Raising each of the wives' head strings in turn lifts the rings off the spikes and allows them to float away from the body, the costumes falling to cover the hands and feet.

With the head and body floating in the air, a pull on the

The puppets inside the Grand Turk are revealed.

neck pin separates the head from the body and allows the costume to fall, revealing the mother-in-law now that her head string takes the weight.

Now only the head and turban are floating. Finally the string on top of the turban is raised, lifting the turban rings. The costume falls to hide the Turk's head and reveal the Grand Wizard. The transformation is complete.

Sometimes the release strings for the mother-in-law and the turban are pulled simultaneously so that both transformations happen in one grand operation. If you have an assistant, instead of replacing the strings on the control after each transformation, you might pass them across to be hooked on to a separate bar and danced separately from the Turk.

A Dissecting Puppet

This is a marionette that comes apart and goes back together again with very simple manipulation of the control. The act is most often performed with a skeleton, sometimes coated in fluorescent paint and used with ultra-violet lighting. Other versions of the act exist, a traditional one being a come-apart clown that also juggles balls and finally appears to juggle its own limbs.

Whichever version of the act is adopted, the principle is the same: the puppet's head body and limbs are made as usual but with no fixed joints at the neck, shoulders or hips. Instead, run-through strings are used to hold the elements together and permit them to come apart when these strings are slackened. A description of the skeleton follows as its construction is unusual but the stringing arrangements apply to any dissecting puppet.

The head is modelled or carved as normal. Fasten a dowel across the head with strong glue. Insert a screw-eye into each end of the dowel, through the sides of the head.

Make the ribs, breastbone, shoulder blades and pelvis from plywood or a modelling material over a cardboard shape. If necessary to help adhesion, smear the cardboard with UHU glue or an equivalent clear adhesive. You may find that it is best to have only eight ribs to avoid the body appearing too long and thin. The first five ribs are made as a closed loop and the bottom three open in the front to join on to the breastbone which is glued on to the top five ribs. File, or carve, grooves in small pieces of dowelling for the vertebrae.

The body is assembled on a length of strong galvanized wire that is glued to the pelvis and runs through the whole backbone. When all the parts are glued together, cover and strengthen the joints with a modelling material.

A come-apart, juggling clown.

Carve the hands and feet or model them on pipe-cleaners (*see* page 56). Carve the arms and legs or create a general shape with dowelling and build up details with a modelling material.

The wrist, elbow, knee and ankle joints are open mortise and tenon joints (*see* pages 58–64). The tongue is a strip of aluminium, glued and nailed in one part, and pivoted on a nail in the other part.

The head, arms and legs are joined to the body by strings that form part of the method of control (*see* page 174). To attach the string to an arm or leg, drill a small hole down through the knobbly protrusion and make a small countersunk hole in the underside. Thread the string down through the hole and knot it.

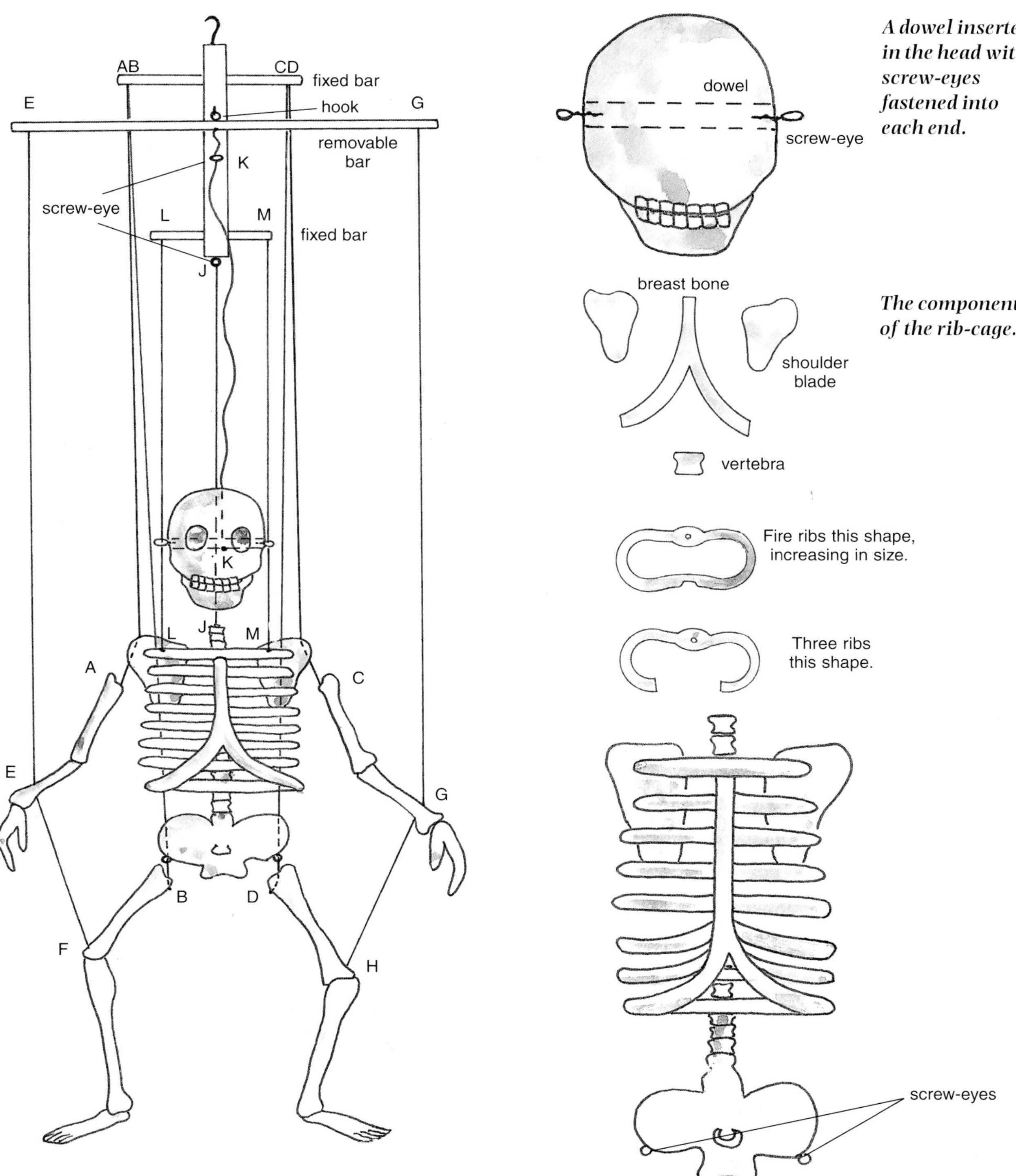

A dowel inserted in the head with screw-eyes fastened into each end.

The components of the rib-cage.

The control and stringing.

The assembled body.

Press the knot into the countersunk hole and smear it with clear glue.

The control consists of a vertical dowel with two narrower, horizontal dowels glued into holes near the top and bottom. Another, the arm-and-leg bar, is suspended from a hook on the control.

String the puppet so that when the control is held upright with the leg bar hooked on to it, the parts are all close together and not dissected.

The puppet is supported by the body strings, L and M, and the centre string J. Attach strings L and M to each side of the top pair of ribs; they run through the screw-eyes in the head to the control's lower cross-bar and must be parallel. Attach J to the top of the neck; thread the other end through a hole in the dowel fixed in the head, and through the top of the skull to a screw-eye in the bottom of the control.

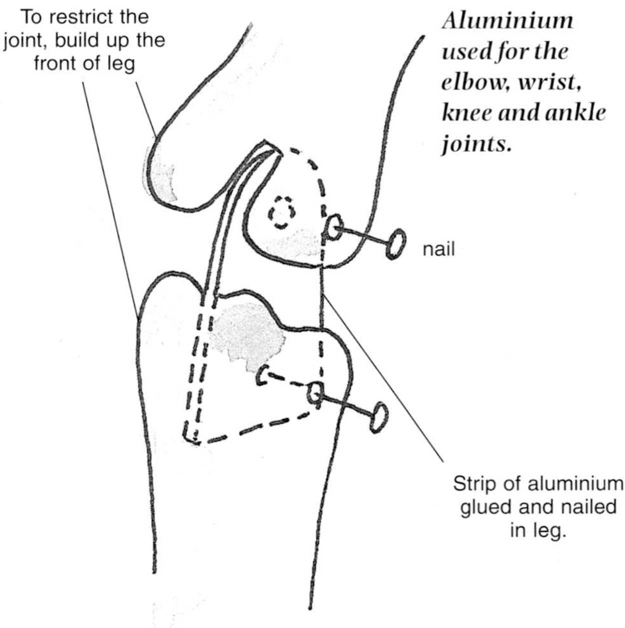

Aluminium used for the elbow, wrist, knee and ankle joints.

Fasten another string, K, to the dowel in the head; this runs through a screw-eye in the centre of the control to the centre of the arm-and-leg bar. Pull this bar forward to raise the head. The head returns to its normal position when the bar is replaced.

Attach the hand strings, E and G, to the arm-and-leg bar. F and H join the wrists to the knees. By paddling the bar the arms and legs are moved together.

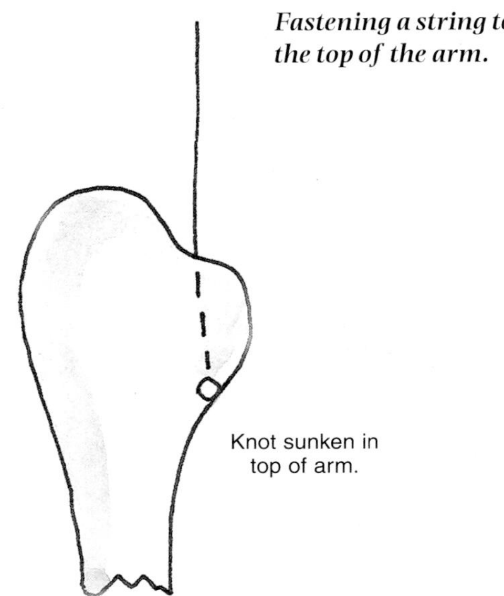

Fastening a string to the top of the arm.

Fasten the strings, A and C, which support the arms, and B and D, which support the legs, to the top crossbar of the control. A and C run through the shoulder blades; B and D run through screw-eyes on each side of the pelvis, up through the rib cage and through a hole in the top rib. The arms and legs are detached from the body by tilting the control forwards.

Skeleton in Disguise

Gordon Staight created an amusing act around the dissecting skeleton that is contained within a costume with an attached mask. The skeleton enters the stage in the guise of a football supporter but, when he hears that his team has won the cup, he is so surprised that he jumps out of his skin and dances around the stage, coming apart and rejoining as he does so.

The costume has weighted feet attached but no hands: the ends of the sleeves are fixed in the pockets of a coat. The outer head is really two masks, one for the face and one for the back of the head; they close over the skeleton's skull and are held in place by a hat that is attached loosely to the skull. The costume, which is open at the top to insert the skeleton, is gathered and held together by the collar, which is split at the back of the neck. The collar is fastened by a small galvanized wire pin through a small loop of wire: a pull-string from this pin opens the costume, allowing it to fall to the ground, causing the mask to open as it does so.

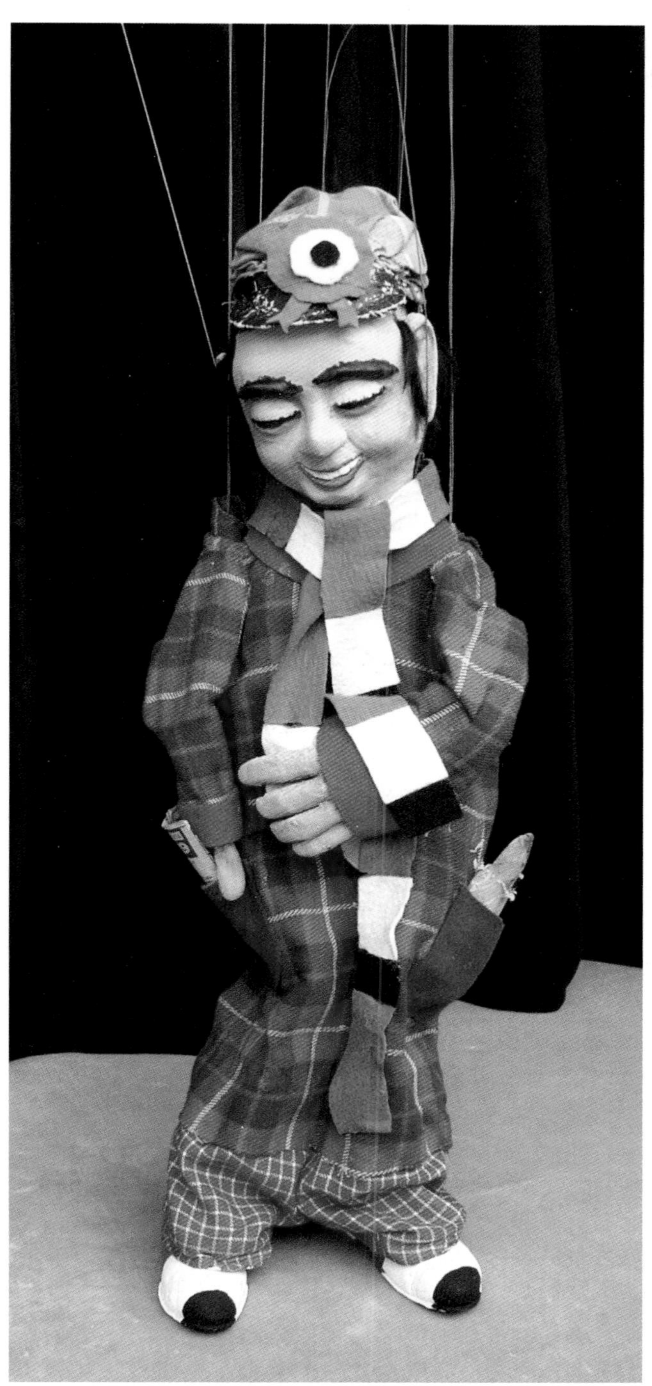

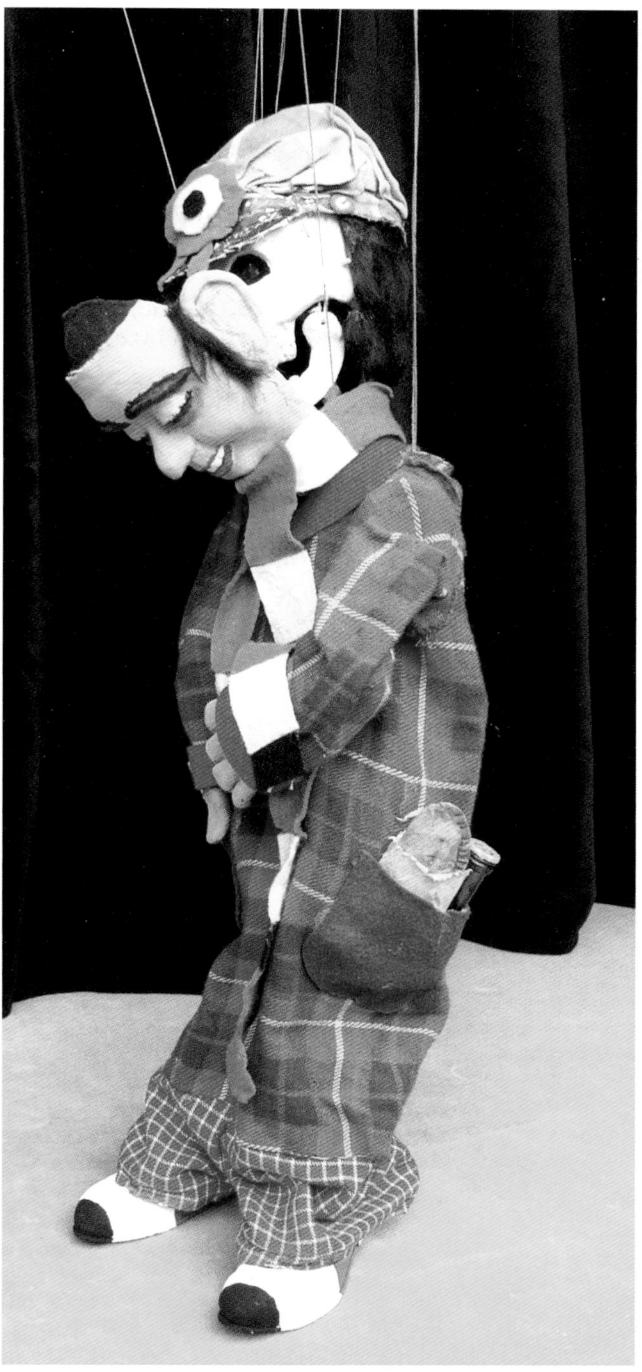

ABOVE AND PAGES 176–7: Janner Oggie, a football supporter, by Gordon Staight. The puppet jumps out of his skin when he hears that Plymouth Argyle have won the cup. A mask attached to the costume conceals the dissecting skeleton. My version omits the horizontal thread joining the tops of the legs so they can spread further apart.

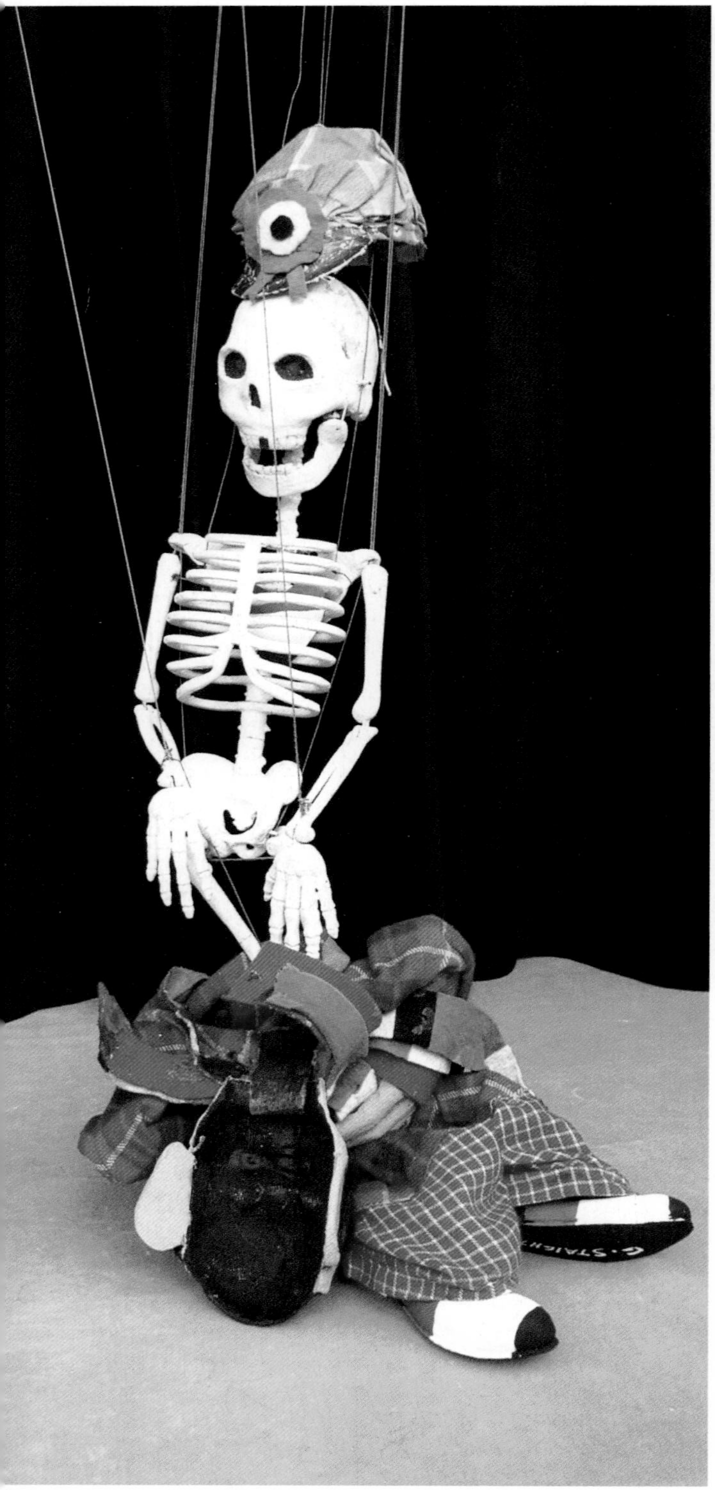

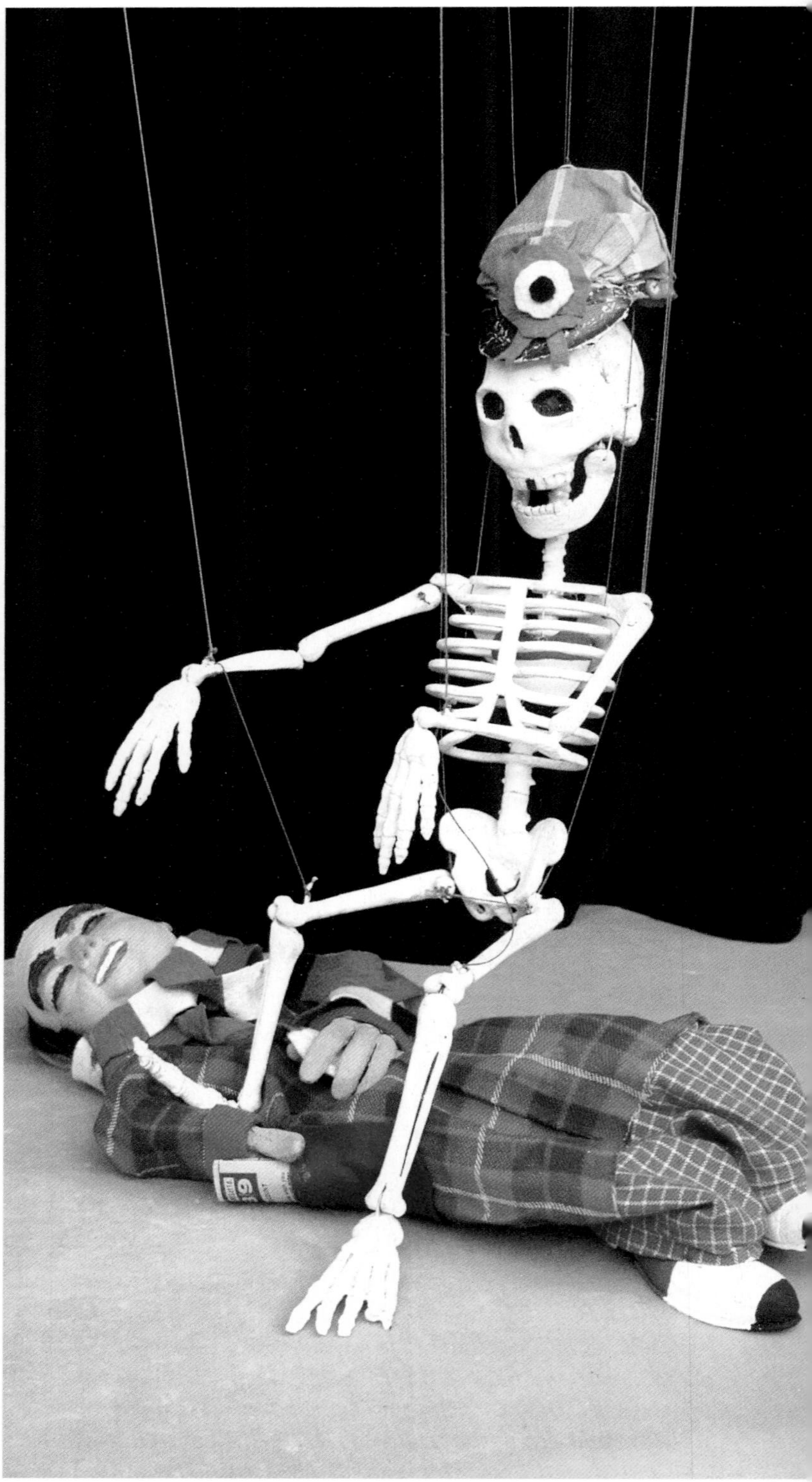

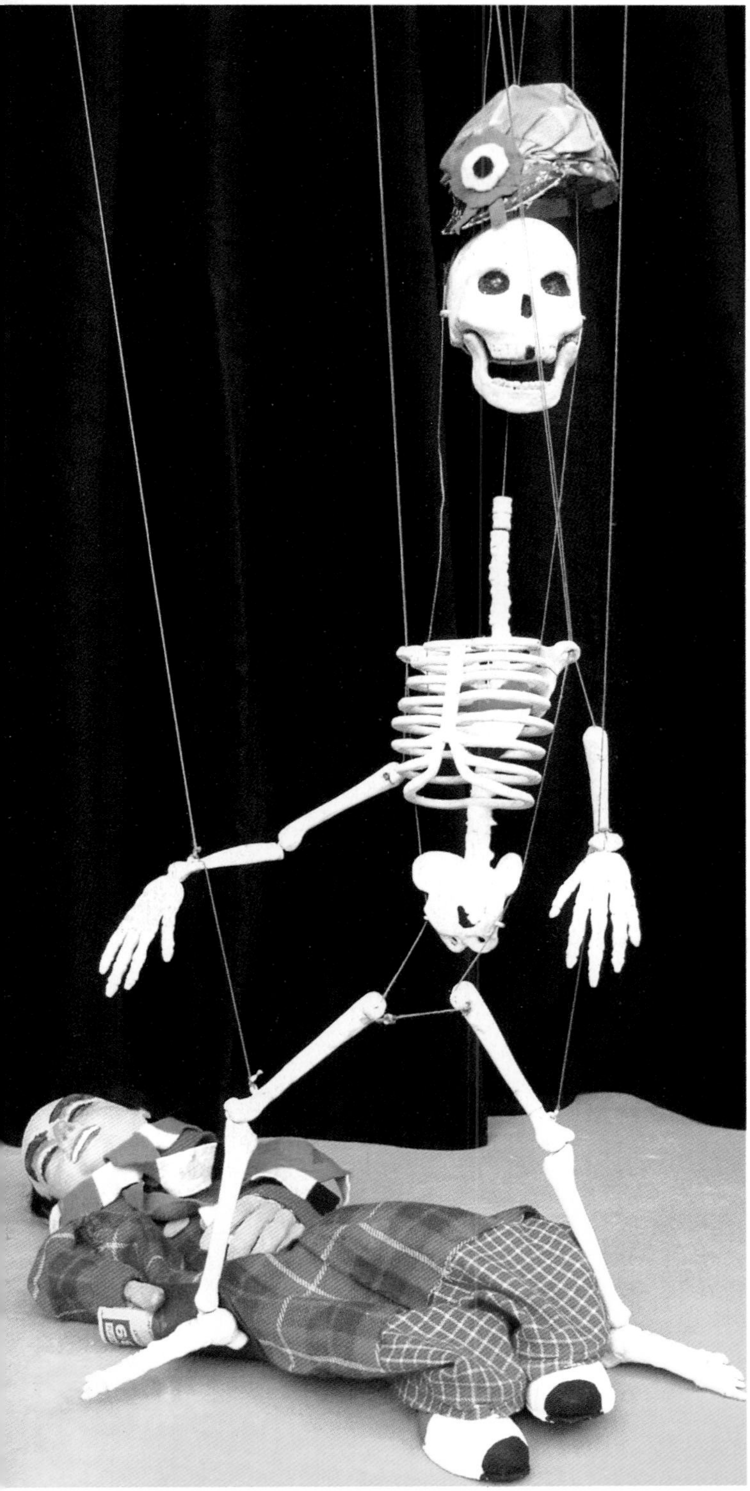

Native American Puppet

This is another version of the dissecting puppet. The puppet (illustrated on pages 178–9) does a rain dance but causes snow to fall (a shower of polystyrene chippings or theatrical snow). The entire body and neck are modelled in one piece without any joints. The elbow, knee and ankle joints are made with aluminium, like the skeleton, but the puppet has no wrist joints.

Rod-Marionettes

A Body Puppet

A body puppet is made in the same way as other marionettes. It is suspended on strings that are attached to a cloth-bound ring that fits on to the puppeteer's head. Shoulder strings are attached to a strap that hangs around the puppeteer's neck. Movement of the puppeteer's head brings about movement of the puppet. Strong rods are used to operate the hands; for ease of manipulation, the ends of the rods are glued into short dowel handles. Some figures have flowing robes but no

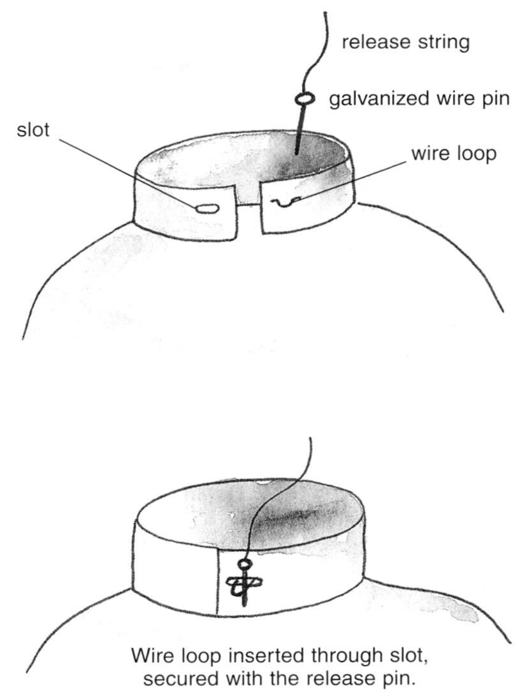

The securing and release mechanism for Janner Oggie's costume.

Twonky Feathers, by Gordon Staight, is a variation on the dissecting puppet. His rain dance only succeeds in producing snow.

legs or feet; others have legs and feet that move freely, while some feet are attached to the puppeteer's shoes. There are a number of ways of doing this: one of the most satisfactory is to have long, shaped, plywood strips to which are attached the puppet's feet and the soles of slippers for the puppeteer.

Sicilian-Style Rod-Marionettes

The basic wooden construction is very much like other marionettes. The head and neck are carved in one piece and the body often has no waist joint, though some figures have a separate pelvis held in place by strong cords that are released when the puppet is cut in half in battle. Wooden legs are suspended from the pelvis on strong wires. There are no wrist or ankle joints.

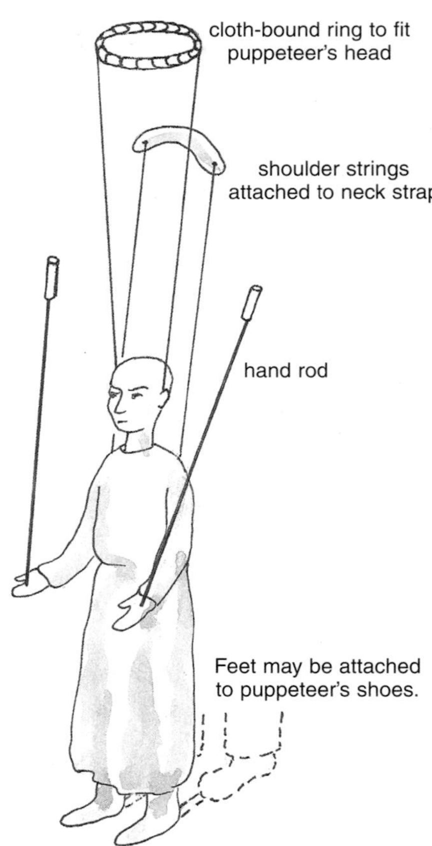

Controlling a body puppet style of rod-marionette. If necessary, the feet may be attached to the puppeteer's shoes.

There are two main traditions of these figures that differ in certain respects. One has wooden upper arms and forearms and unjointed legs. The other has knee joints and wooden forearms but tubes of fabric for the upper arms.

These marionettes differ most significantly from others in their means of control. There are many styles of

The Sicilian rod-marionette Orlando Furioso has a main control rod with a looped top, a rod to the sword hand and a string to the shield arm.

control for rod-marionettes in different countries, a selection of which is illustrated (*see* pages 181–2). The Sicilian figures have strong metal rods to both the head and sword arm, the shield arm is controlled by a cord, and a further cord lifts or lowers the visor. Some have a cord to a sword that is not permanently attached to the hand. The rods vary in thickness from 4–6mm depending on the tradition.

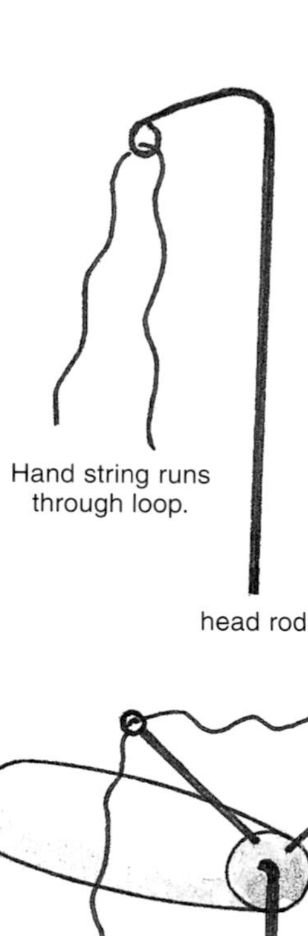

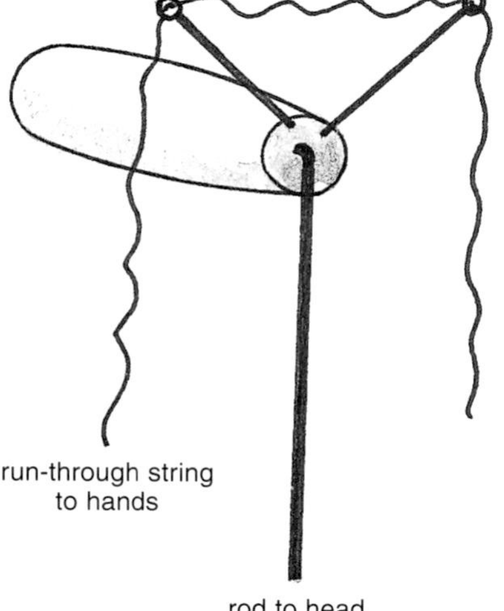

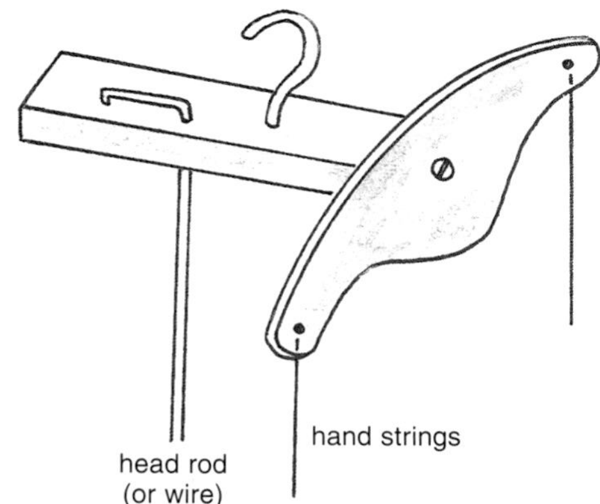

THIS PAGE AND PAGE ***182:***
A variety of traditional controls for rod-marionettes.

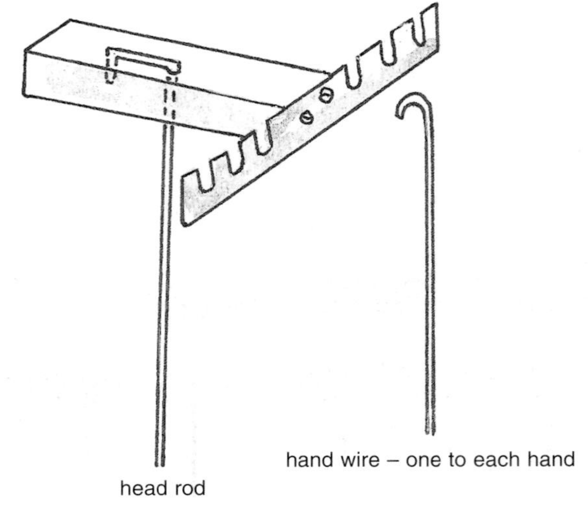

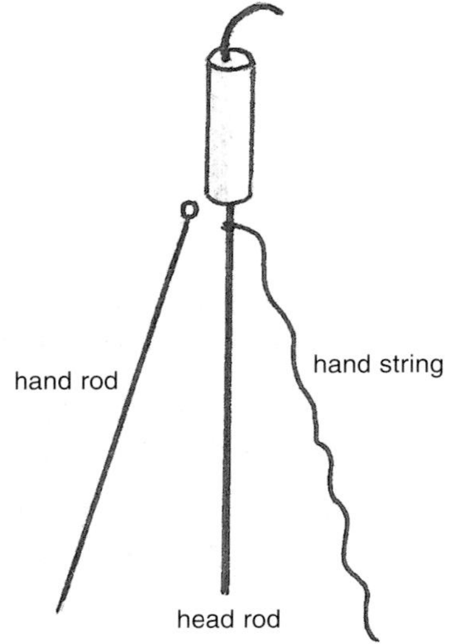

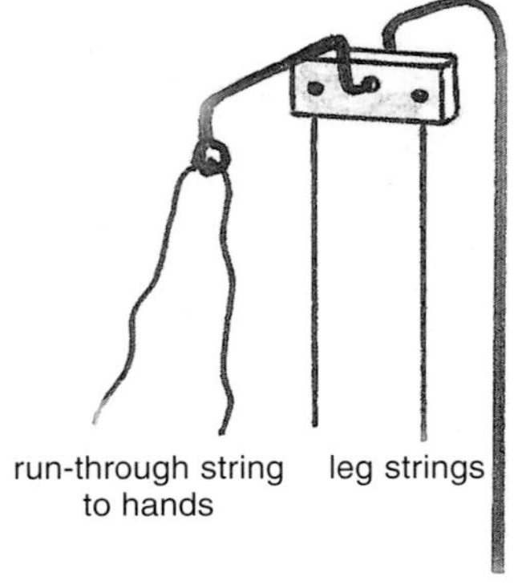

ABOVE, LEFT, BELOW AND TOP RIGHT: *More traditional controls for rod-marinettes.*

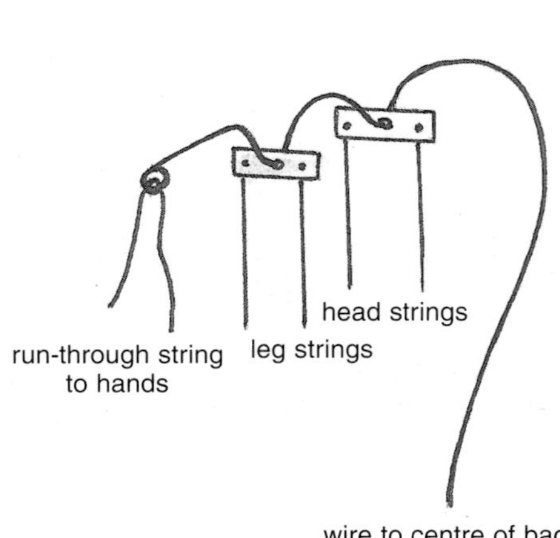

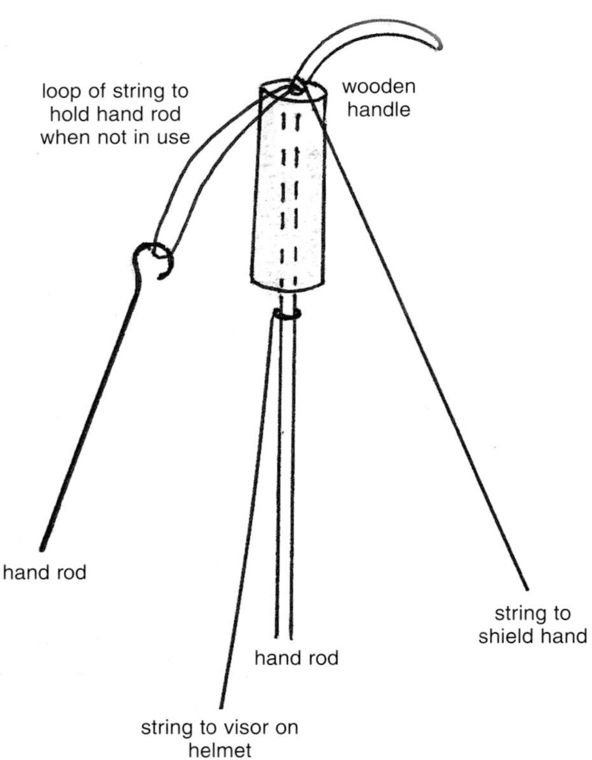

A Sicilian control in the Palermo tradition.

Operating a Sicilian knight: a wooden handle assists control and the hand rod hooks into the dangling loop of string when not in use.

A run-through string passes through the right hand to the handle of the sword.

Pulling the string taut enables the puppet to draw the sword and do battle.

The main rod passes down through the head and neck and a looped end hooks into a strong piece of wire fastened securely in the body, bridging the neck groove. During a performance the puppet may be beheaded by firm downward pressure and a quick twist of the rod to uncouple the head rod from the body.

The figures that do not have a sword fixed permanently in the right hand carry the sword in a metal sheath on the left hip. A cord attached to the top of the hand rod runs through a hole in the clenched right hand to the hilt of the sword. The rod is used to place the hand on the sword and the run-through string is pulled taut for the puppet to grasp the hilt and draw the sword from its sheath. With practice it is possible to replace the sword in the sheath and free the hand.

Some rod-marionettes have leg strings but this style has none. Very slight sideways movement of the control, while twisting the head rod, transfers weight to one leg and creates a momentum that causes the other leg to swing. Despite the apparently limited means of control and the weight of the Sicilian figures (approximately 4kg/9lb), the performances are exciting affairs, full of vitality. The puppets battle each other, slay witches and dragons, and many scenes end with the stage piled high with puppet bodies – a grand puppet tradition built upon stories that are great puppet fare.

USEFUL ADDRESSES

ORGANIZATIONS AND CENTRES

There are national and regional groups throughout the world, and also UNIMA (L'Union Internationale de la Marionnette), the international puppetry organization. Some are membership organizations which have events for their members but have no permanent base you can visit; others have centres with libraries, workshops, exhibits and performances. Some of the centres will have restricted opening times, so always make contact before visiting. Many now have websites and the following organizations will have contact information about other organizations nationally and internationally.

British Puppet and Model Theatre Guild
www.puppetguild.org.uk
Membership Secretary: Judith Shutt
Little Holme
Church Lane
Thames Ditton
Surrey KT7 0NL
Membership organization, one of the oldest existing puppetry organizations in the world

Scottish Mask and Puppet Centre
8-10 Balcarres Avenue
Kelvindale
Glasgow G12 0QF
Tel: 0141 339 6185
e-mail: info@scottishmaskandpuppetcentre.co.uk
www.scottishmaskandpuppetcentre.co.uk
Contact: Malcolm Knight
Thriving centre with a full programme of events

UNIMA British Centre
www.unima.org
Membership Secretary: Martin MacGilp
10 Cullernie Gardens
Balloch
Inverness IV2 7JP
International, non-governmental, membership organization

The Puppet Centre Ltd
(formerly the Puppet Centre Trust)
Battersea Arts Centre (BAC)
Lavender Hill
London SW11 5TN
Tel: 020 7228 5335
Fax: 020 7228 8863
e-mail: pct@puppetcentre.demon.co.uk
www.puppetcentre.com
National charitable trust, reference centre for all aspects of puppet theatre; open to all

WEBSITES

PuppeteersUK: Puppets Online
www.PuppeteersUK.com
A one-stop source of information about many aspects of puppet theatre, events and performers

Puppetry Home Page
www.sagecraft.com/puppetry/organizations/index.html
Contains lists of organizations worldwide (not comprehensive)

PUBLICATIONS

Ray DaSilva, Puppetry Bookseller
63 Kennedy Road
Bicester
Oxfordshire OX26 2BE
Tel/Fax: 01869 245793
e-mail: dasilva@puppetbooks.co.uk

Professional Contributors

The following are contributors to this book who have permanent or touring companies.

MovingStage Marionettes
Gren and Juliet Middleton
78 Middleton Road
London E8 4BP
MovingStage Marionettes is not a theatre but a major puppet company that creates the shows. Its performance venue is:
The Puppet Theatre Barge
Blomfield Road
Little Venice
London W9
Nearest underground station: Warwick Avenue
Box office: 020 7249 6876
e-mail: puppet@movingstage.co.uk
www.puppetbarge.com
www.movingstage.co.uk
Moors at Little Venice from autumn through spring; tours the River Thames in the summer season. Specializes in marionettes.

PuppetCraft
John Roberts, Artistic Director
1 Venton Oak Cottages
Dartington
Totnes
Devon TQ9 6DW
Tel/Fax: 01803 867778
e-mail: john@puppetcraft.co.uk
www.puppetcraft.co.uk
Major touring puppet company

Shadowstring Theatre
Contact: Paul Doran, resident solo puppeteer, specialising in marionettes, with permanent theatre and touring show based at:
Tropiquaria Wildlife Park
Washford Cross
Watchet
Somerset
(On the A39 between Williton and Minehead)
Tel: 01984 640688
e-mail: shadowstring@freenet.co.uk
www.geocities.com/puppetville/shadowstring.html
www.tropiquaria.co.uk

Lyndie Wright
Puppeteer, designer and maker: contributed photographs of the late John Wright's work. John and Lyndie Wright founded the Little Angel Theatre listed below. Enquiries about John's work should be addressed to Lyndie (not the theatre) at:
10 Dagmar Passage
Cross Street
London
N1 2DN
Tel: 020 7226 9612

Little Angel Theatre
14 Dagmar Passage
Cross Street
London
N1 2DN
Nearest underground station: Angel
Tel: 020 7226 1787
Fax: 020 7359 7565
e-mail: info@littleangeltheatre.com
www.littleangeltheatre.com
Major British company with permanent theatre; resident company also tours.

Amateur Contributor

Gordon Straight
Now retired, Gordon Straight is an excellent example of the long tradition of skilful and inventive amateur puppeteers, performing largely for pleasure and for charity. A long-time mentor to the author, who maintains his collection. Enquiries about his work should be addressed to:
David Currell
University Academic Advisor
Roehampton University
Grove House
Roehampton Lane
London SW15 5PJ
Tel: 020 8392 3385
e-mail: d.currell@roehampton.ac.uk

INDEX

INDEX

1	2	3	4	5	6	7	8	9	10
11	12	13	14	15	16	17	18	19	20
21	22	23	24	25	26	27	28	29	30
31	32	33	34	35	36	37	38	39	40
41	42	43	44	45	46	47	48	49	50
51	52	53	54	55	56	57	58	59	60
61	62	63	64	65	66	67	68	69	70
71	72	73	74	75	76	77	78	79	80
81	82	83	84	85	86	87	88	89	90
91	92	93	94	95	96	97	98	99	100
101	102	103	104	105	106	107	108	109	110
111	112	113	114	115	116	117	118	119	120
121	122	123	124	125	126	127	128	129	130
131	132	133	134	135	136	137	138	139	140
141	142	143	144	145	146	147	148	149	150
151	152	153	154	155	156	157	158	159	160
161	162	163	164	165	166	167	168	169	170
171	172	173	174	175	176	177	178	179	180
181	182	183	184	185	186	187	188	189	190
191	192	193	194	195	196	197	198	199	200
201	202	203	204	205	206	207	208	209	210
211	212	213	214	215	216	217	218	219	220
221	222	223	224	225	226	227	228	229	230
231	232	233	234	235	236	237	238	239	240
241	242	243	244	245	246	247	248	249	250
251	252	253	254	255	256	257	258	259	260
261	262	263	264	265	266	267	268	269	270
271	272	273	274	275	276	277	278	279	280
281	282	283	284	285	286	287	288	289	290
291	292	293	294	295	296	297	298	299	300
301	302	303	304	305	306	307	308	309	310
311	312	313	314	315	316	317	318	319	320
321	322	323	324	325	326	327	328	329	330
331	332	333	334	335	336	337	338	339	340
341	342	343	344	345	346	347	348	349	350
351	352	353	354	355	356	357	358	359	360
361	362	363	364	365	366	367	368	369	370
371	372	373	374	375	376	377	378	379	380
381	382	383	384	385	386	387	388	389	390
391	392	393	394	395	396	397	398	399	400